History of the
UNITED STATES OF AMERICA

From Reconstruction to a
New World Order

History of the
UNITED STATES OF AMERICA

From Reconstruction to a New World Order

ARCHANA OJHA

Orient BlackSwan

All rights reserved. No part of this book may be (i) modified, reproduced or utilised in any form, or by any means, electronic or mechanical, including photocopying, recording or by any information storage and retrieval system, in any form of binding or cover other than in which it is published, without permission in writing from the publisher; or (ii) used or reproduced in any manner for the purpose of training, development or operation of artificial intelligence (AI) technologies and systems, including generative AI technologies, without permission in writing from the copyright holder.

HISTORY OF THE UNITED STATES OF AMERICA:
FROM RECONSTRUCTION TO A NEW WORLD ORDER

ORIENT BLACKSWAN PRIVATE LIMITED

Registered Office
3-6-752 Himayatnagar, Hyderabad 500 029, Telangana, India
e-mail: centraloffice@orientblackswan.com

Other Offices
Bengaluru, Chennai, Guwahati, Hyderabad, Kolkata,
Mumbai, New Delhi, Noida, Patna

© Orient Blackswan Private Limited 2026
First published 2026

ISBN 978-93-6973-247-0

Typeset in
Adobe Garamond Pro 11/13
by Le Studio Graphique, Gurgaon 122 007

Printed in India at
B B Press, Tronica City, Ghaziabad, U. P. 201 103

Published by
Orient Blackswan Private Limited
3-6-752 Himayatnagar, Hyderabad 500 029, Telangana, India
e-mail: info@orientblackswan.com

Contents vii

• The Emergence of NAACP *173* • Understanding Southern Black Activism: The Context of Racial Segregation *174* • Booker T. Washington, Educationist and Accommodationist *176* • Race Relations in Urban USA *183* • W. E. B. Du Bois: Intellectualism and Pragmatism *184* • Marcus Garvey: Building a Mass Movement *192*

8. **The Civil Rights and Black Power Movements: Martin Luther King, Jr., and Malcolm X**   **201**

Introduction *201* • Emergence of Major Civil Rights Organisations *203* • Life History of Martin Luther King, Jr. *204* • Beginning of the Freedom Struggle: Direct-Action Sit-in Protests *207* • Introduction of Confrontational Policy Based on a Radical Approach *211* • Legacy of a Great Leader *214* • Emergence of Black Organisations *216* • The Multiple Lives of Malcolm X *216* • An Independent Black Leader *219* • Conclusion *221*

9. **Women in American History**   **223**

Introduction *223* • Women's Changing Role in the Nineteenth-Century American Economy *225* • The Impact of White Settlements on Indigenous Women *227* • The Enslavement of Black Women *228* • Women's Activism in the Early Nineteenth Century *233* • Views on the Temperance Movement *235* • Women's Entry in Public Spaces *236* • Women and Abolitionism *239* • The Suffrage Movement *241* • 'Feminine Mystique' *244*

10. **The Spanish-American War of 1898: The Onset of American Imperialism**   **251**

Introduction *251* • The Rise of US Imperialism *251* • Expansionism in the Early Years *253* • The Rise of Big Business Organisations *254* • The Rise of New Frontiers *255* • The Beginning of American Expansionism in Latin America *255* • The Importance of the War *260* • Conclusion *262*

11. A History of US Intervention in
    World Wars I and II   264
    Introduction: The Emergence of American Exceptionalism *264*
    • Woodrow Wilson's New World Order *267* • World
    War II and the United States *273* • The Pre-World War II
    Context *274* • Japanese Aggression *277* • America in
    Africa and Europe *280* • Shift in US Foreign Policy *281*
    • Conclusion *282*

References   287
Index   302

Figures and Tables

FIGURES

1.1	Campaign button used in republican party canvassing (1864)	23
1.2	'The Union As It Was', wood engraving by Thomas Nast published in *Harper's Weekly* (1874)	32
1.3	First senators and representatives of colour, 41st and 42nd Congress of the USA (1872)	40
2.1	The cover of a train timetable advertising the Union and Central Pacific Railroad Line (1881)	55
2.2	Barriers in the path of the 'revenue reform' train, cartoon, by George Yost Coffin (c. 1880–1890)	65
3.1	Two girls don banners calling to 'Abolish Child Slavery' in English and Yiddish, most likely at a Labour Day Parade in New York City (c. 1909)	85
3.2	A promotional 'stickerette' of the IWW	97
4.1	Two young women of the Lowell Mill, tintype (c. 1870)	105
5.1	US Post stamp commemorating the National Grange (1967)	118
5.2	Woodrow Wilson priming the pump of prosperity, cartoon by Clifford Berryman (1914)	133
6.1	'Migrant Mother, Nipomo, California', one of the most famous portraits of the Great Depression era, by Dorothea Lange (6 March 1936)	140

6.2	'New Deal' WPA art, mural in New Jersey by Charles Ward (c. 1932), photographed by Carol M. Highsmith in 2010	150
7.1	Booker T. Washington on his education tours, photo collage by Emmett J. Scott (1916)	178
7.2	A portrait of W. E. B. Du Bois, by James E. Purdy (1907)	185
7.3	UNIA march, Harlem, New York City, by James Van Der Zee (2 August 1920)	195
8.1	US Marshals with young Ruby Bridges on school steps, New Orleans (1960)	208
8.2	Civil rights march on Washington, DC (28 August 1963)	212
8.3	Civil rights march on Washington, DC (28 August 1963)	215
9.1	Signatories of the Declaration of Rights and Sentiments (19–20 July 1848)	237
9.2	Poster of the NAWSA showing states where suffrage had been granted (1912)	243
9.3	'War Mother', an example of propaganda pins given to women during the war (1916–1918)	247
10.1	'The Great Rapprochement', poster used to promote the United States and Great Britain Industrial Exposition (1898)	257
11.1	A cartoon praising Theodore Roosevelt's move to build the Panama Canal (1904)	266
11.2	President Woodrow Wilson asking Congress to declare war on Germany (2 April 1917)	270
11.3	The USS *Shaw* explodes as Japan attacks Pearl Harbour (1 December 1941)	279

Tables

1.1	Timeline of the Reconstruction Period (1865–1877)	19
6.1	The New Deal	142

Abbreviations

AAA	Agricultural Adjustment Administration
AAVE	African American Vernacular English
ACS	American Colonization Society
AOH	Ancient Order of Hibernians
AFL	American Federation of Labour
AME	African Methodist Episcopal Church
CCC	Civilian Conservation Corps
CORE	Congress of Racial Equality
FCA	Farm Credit Administration
FCC	Federal Communications Commission
FCIC	Federal Crop Insurance Corporation
FHA	Federal Housing Administration
FLRA	Female Labour Reform Association
FSA	Farm Security Administration
ICC	Interstate Commerce Commission
IWW	Industrial Workers of the World
KKK	Ku Klux Klan
NAACP	National Association for the Advancement of Colored People
NEWA	New England Workingmen Association
NLU	National Labour Union
NRA	National Recovery Administration
PWA	Public Works Administration
REA	Rural Electrification Administration
SCLC	Southern Christian Leadership Conference

SNCC	Student Non-Violent Coordinating Committee
SPA	Socialist Party of America
SSB	Social Security Board
TVA	Tennessee Valley Authority
UNIA	Universal Negro Improvement Association and African Communities League
WBA	Workingmen's Benevolent Association
WPA	Works Progress Administration

Preface

The rise of the United States of America as a nation (1776) was unique because it was a settler society and economy. In the period from the eighteenth to the nineteenth century, the country expanded by marginalising Indigenous nations through the appropriation of their sacred lands and natural resources, which pushed them to near extinction.[1] This modern and model continental nation, situated between the Atlantic Ocean in the east, and the Pacific Ocean in the west, with its distinct brand of capitalism, developed in the vast geographical space that had once been the ancestral sacred lands of Indigenous nations.

The factors that assisted in the rise and expansion of the US as a nation-state—geography, economy, politics, and culture—continue to play a dominant role even in the twenty-first century. The idea that later came to be termed American exceptionalism initially emerged during the period of colonisation. Puritan settlers developed a notion of 'divine favour' and believed that they had a sacred calling to occupy and settle America, which, many believe, assisted the settlers during the War of Independence. This was the context to the emergence of the world's 'first modern nation', imbued with a constitution that promised liberty.

The US used its geographical assertiveness to dominate the Western hemisphere. This played out in stages. According to US President Thomas Jefferson, virtuous Americans had established a federal republic (an 'empire of liberty') built on moral and political foundations that would ensure its survival in perpetuity as a 'beacon to the world'. This nation would rule the entire Western hemisphere (as envisioned by another American president, Andrew Jackson, through his notion of the expansion of liberated capitalism) and eventually the world (as inherent in the Puritan perspective, and later articulated by Woodrow Wilson). The USA, as the predominant polity in the world, would introduce the ideal of human perfection.[2] The global expansion of American liberty and democracy was formalised in the Monroe Doctrine. The promulgation of an Open Door policy after the War of 1812 (accompanied by the spread of Christianity in South America) eventually led to the Spanish-American War of 1898, which allowed the US to make a grand entry into the ranks of the great world powers. Theodore Roosevelt envisioned a US-controlled Panama Canal, carved out of the South American state of Colombia, to link the two seas and races—Anglo-Saxon—thereby integrating religion, democracy, and trade into the greater American empire. These factors combined to produce the American brand of nationalism, which eventually gave rise to American imperialism. This imperial project was justified through the twin discourses of exceptionalism and universalism, wherein the US was projected as an exemplar for the rest of the world. Thus, American exceptionalism and universalism, along with an ideology of moral 'obligation' (drawing from the 'White man's burden'), can explain the USA's rise to power and its ability to bring the rest of the world into its orbit.

By 1910, American capitalism had taken root on the back of rapid industrial expansion, greater in scale than the combined industrial bases of Britain and Germany. This growth coincided with the influential theory of Social Darwinism,[3] which popularised the belief that a new power had risen on the horizon. It was President Woodrow Wilson who integrated American imperialism by dispatching troops to Mexico, Cuba, Haiti, the Dominican Republic, Nicaragua, and, in 1917, pushing the US into World War I. He believed that the US had the privilege of 'fulfilling' her destiny and 'saving' the world,[4] and thus placed his own ideological imprint on the American brand of religion, capitalism, liberal democracy, peace, and power, all rolled into one.

The Great Depression of 1929, which ended the credit bubble and resulted in failures of American banking institutions, led policy framers to realise for the first time that US industries, agriculture, and currency could not remain unaffected by international financial markets. For the first time, American capitalism was at risk due to the absence of a federal policy to deal with such an eventuality. The period marked the end of the accumulative phase based on the gold standard, high tariffs imposed since the end of the Civil War, low taxation, and unregulated mass production. To some extent, this was also the fallout of massive labour strikes and social strife, which forced the Democratic Party under Franklin D. Roosevelt to implement measures of financial stabilisation, emergency relief, social reform, and infrastructural development, collectively known as the New Deal. Although the recession of 1937 threatened to undermine the New Deal, with war clouds looming and a demand for rearmament, the government policy emerged as a watershed for the US. It ushered in technological innovation, reduced unemployment, and set the stage for the global dominance of American capitalist economy. Roosevelt's first term emphasised domestic measures to overcome the crisis. In his second term, when wars in East Asia were threatening to impact Europe, pressure began to build in the US to strengthen its military forces, which gave the New Deal a second wind. For the first time in US history, the internal economy was recognised to be dependent on external factors. Under Franklin D. Roosevelt, US developed a policy that juggled isolation and intervention, nationalist pride and global ambition, seeking to reorganise the world to its own advantage. The rationale for this was what was good for the US was good for the world, since the universal and the particular were intertwined.

This volume studies the emergence of the American brand of liberal-capitalist world order premised on 'free trade', which, the US believed, would remain bound to its economic power. However, American hegemony faced pressures and resistance both internally and externally. Domestically, it had to contend with the fallout of deeply unequal and violent race relations, growing mobilisation among American women for their rights, and a clamour for governmental reform and welfare measures. The last factor was reflective of the rising power base of the working class. Externally, the onset of the Cold War at the end of World War II halted the progression of US dominance in the world.

Notes

1. Interestingly, Thomas Jefferson was a staunch advocate of democracy and the natural rights of men, as proposed by John Locke. Louis Hartz, in his book *The Liberal Tradition in America*, brought Jeffersonian and Lockean ideas in conversation with the theory of justice articulated by the twentieth-century political philosopher John Rawls. The absence of a feudal tradition in colonial America, according to Hartz, created a political culture based on Lockean liberalism, with an emphasis on self-help, economic individualism, and competition as the centrepiece of American political thought.

2. One of the founding figures of the USA, Benjamin Franklin presented a model of 13 virtues to achieve personal growth and perfection. These virtues are centred on self-discipline—a continuous growth process based on an individual's effort to pursue their own destiny. This is achieved through hard work, consistent self-improvement, and a progressive thought process that makes an individual self-virtuous. Together, these individuals establish an equitable and harmonious society and state.

3. The theory promoted the growth and expansion of a free-market, capitalist economy. Its main proponents, owners of big business corporations and individuals with vast accumulated wealthholdings, had to set in place a system to justify why the working classes remained at the bottom of the socio-economic system and continued to suffer in poverty. The system, where only a privileged minority held the majority of wealth, necessitated an ideology that would mark out these privileged few as superior and hence deserving of their privileges. This logic of exclusivity reinforced other kinds of social hierarchy, thus promoting racism, eugenics, and discrimination. The economic system thus served to affirm the ethnic and racial superiority of the White population over their Black and Indigenous counterparts.

4. See Woodrow Wilson, 'Address in the Princess Theatre in Cheyenne, 24 September 1919', in *Papers of Woodrow Wilson* 63 (New Jersey, 1990), p. 469.

Acknowledgments

To write and complete a book takes time, immense effort, determination, and single-minded devotion, which can become difficult to balance due to the uncertainties of life and circumstances that often derail the best of intentions. However, the support and assistance that one receives make the journey easier to navigate. My thanks go first to Kamala Nehru College, University of Delhi, for granting me sabbatical leave, which provided an uninterrupted year during which I could devote time and energy to giving final shape to both volumes. The idea for this book emerged during my doctoral work at Jawaharlal Nehru University in Delhi, and I became more determined to work on it when I had the opportunity to teach postgraduate classes at the University of Delhi, where the history of the USA was a very popular optional paper among students.

At a personal level, this book on American history would not have seen the light of day without the efforts put in by the doctors who worked tirelessly to bring me out of my near-terminal illness. I sincerely appreciate the efforts of my chief surgeon, Dr Praveen Kumar Garg, and all the specialists at AIIMS, Delhi, in particular Dr Vinod Raina, Dr G. K. Rath, Dr Ajay Gogia, and their respective teams of doctors, nurses, and administrative staff. My doctor friends, Dr Dhananjay Gupta and Dr Ajay Dave, have both helped me develop a deeper appreciation for the spirit of humanity, empathy, and kindness. I thank my homoeopathic doctor, Poonam Jain, whose support and advice I cherish till this day. I also wish to appreciate my older brother's doctors at AIIMS and the Army Hospital, Delhi, with special thanks to Dr Vinay Goyal, Dr S. S. Kala, Dr Manmohan Singh, Dr Roopa Rajan, Dr Kanwaljeet Garg (all at AIIMS, Delhi), and Dr K. K. Brar (Army Hospital, Delhi). Their tireless efforts in caring for my brother, and my years of interactions with them (which allowed me to witness firsthand their dedication to the medical profession), inspired me to devote my energies and time to complete this book and dedicate it to my brother Rajiv Ojha, who, despite the tremendously difficult circumstances, gave me the space and time I needed to complete this voluminous task, with a steadfast belief in my abilities.

I also wish to express my appreciation for the long-standing friendship and support spanning decades of Tashi Motup Kau, Abhilash Kaul, Virendra Sahni, Phunchok Stobdan (former Indian ambassador to Kyrgyzstan), Radha Kant Purohit, Ashok Dutta, G. S. Khurana, Rakesh Awesthi, Rajiv Lochan, B. S. Katiyar, and also Nanik Pardasani, Jaspal, Piyush Goyal, Harshvardhan, Usha Kala, Savitri, and V. K. Sahni. Without their support, I would not have been able to navigate the unsurmountable hurdles in my life. I extend my gratitude to Nilanjana Majumdar, Sanna Jain, and the entire team at Orient BlackSwan for their support and encouragement, as well as to the reviewers for their valuable comments, observations, and suggestions that have contributed to the fruition of this work.

The reason behind writing these two volumes is both personal and professional. Once I secured permanent employment after years of struggle, I began to read extensively about North American history, and these readings led me to research Indigenous societies and how they were colonised, and to learn that they continue to be marginalised in their own land even today. This research also led me to secure three fellowships, providing me with the opportunity to travel, undertake study, and live within some of the Indigenous nations in both Canada and America. My decision to move away from Indian history and study Indigenous societies of North America occurred at a time when the study of history was beginning to broaden, becoming interconnected and global in nature. These field trips allowed me to establish a deep-rooted connection with these Indigenous nations, a connection not borne out of any imperialist or exploitative intent, but a genuine desire to study Indigenous nations and their current status. This study aimed to provide a perspective on how colonised nations (such as India and Indigenous nations) can establish common threads of deep understanding and evaluate the governance policies of the modern nation-state that once ruled, or continues to rule, over them. The history of modernity, technocracy, and military power obscures many histories of cultures, communities, and nations that were deliberately marginalised and pushed towards near-extinction. History is witness to the fact that the greatness of some nations has come at the cost of the destruction of their original societies. This phenomenon validates the need for study, research, and analysis to determine whether modernity will continue to overwhelm and weaken Indigenous peoples or provide equal space for them to grow and nurture their distinct cultures.

The current volume covers the period from 1865 to the 1960s, a unique era in US history, marked by the complex interplay of change and violence. The generation that suffered through the Civil War and witnessed the violent era of Reconstruction saw the nation-state emerge to become an economic powerhouse, marked by the unprecedented growth and development of American capitalism, both within and beyond the geographical boundaries of the transcontinental nation. It seemed that the US would march onto the world stage with a momentum never before seen in history. However, this march faced its most challenging hurdle in subsequent decades, with the Great Depression, the New Deal, and the two World Wars, which brought about even more bewildering changes. At the end of World War II America emerged as a superpower, but also as a nation-state with a fractured society and a sense of alienation. This was despite revolutionary changes in communication, transportation, and economic systems that connected Americans as never before. At this juncture, it was the civil rights activists who utilised the power of demonstrations, marches, petitions, and the right to vote to abolish racial discrimination, securing the support of the federal government, businesses, organisations, and individuals to establish a new foundation for economic, political, and social life. This volume opens a window into this transformative phase of US history, evident in the significant shifts characterised by the emergence of a more democratic American society and greater American involvement in global affairs.

I hope this book on American history will be of immense benefit to educators, students, and those interested in understanding how the United States acts, thinks, and expands its power. The book also reflects the growing intellectual aspirations of India, in seeking to show that we too can write, reflect, and analyse the history of others.

Archana Ojha
November 2025

Introduction

The American Civil War (1861–1865) was marked by immense loss of human life and widespread destruction in the country, far exceeding the toll borne by the USA even in later conflicts like the two World Wars. At the end of the Civil War, the Confederacy lost and the institution of enslavement was abolished. While this was an important victory in the struggle for racial equality and the opening up of new opportunities, the planter-enslaver class that had dominated the South resented the loss of their 'property' and the southern economy remained backward. The North, on the other hand, experienced economic growth driven by westward expansion, marked by the Homestead Act in 1862[1] and the Pacific Railroad Act.[2] This marked a new phase in economic growth and development through legislative measures. Federal grants were disbursed to establish new universities[3] and to secure an educated workforce for the emerging industries. The wartime necessity to manufacture arms, ammunition, clothing, and associated war materials led to phenomenal industrial expansion. Political leaders from the North and the West, particularly members of the Republican Party, dominated national politics for over 50 years, from the 1860s to 1929.

This volume concentrates on the period after the Civil War and covers up to the USA's participation in the two World Wars, at the end of which the nation emerged as a global superpower. By the late 1890s, the USA, spanning the eastern to the western coast of North America, began to pursue imperialistic ambitions based on its economic wealth, military industries, and new urban centres, which grew to be much larger than those in Europe. By the beginning of 1900, American society had witnessed multiple transformations and wealth inequality had risen significantly, leading to new forms of class and social conflict. New fault lines emerged as fresh waves of immigration took place, and these social reconfigurations also increasingly intensified racial conflicts in the country. More powers were given to the federal government in an effort to mitigate these problems, further altering the political landscape of the US. These changes eventually affected how the nation-state dealt with labour issues and crises such as the Great Depression of 1929. By the mid-twentieth century, the 'New Deal' policy allowed the US to cement its position as a technocratic nation, and its interventions in the two World Wars enabled it to emerge as a superpower in their aftermath.

The USA after the Civil War

Chapter 1, 'Reconstruction: Black Freedom, Won and Lost', outlines the dilemma faced by the country in tackling the seceded southern states. It analyses the moderate path undertaken by President Abraham Lincoln and his successor Andrew Johnson, both Republicans, through the presidential Reconstruction Plans that sought to restore political stability by creating a roadmap for reunification. This approach was opposed by a radical faction of Republicans, who eventually succeeded in steering the Congress towards a more radical Reconstruction programme (1866–1868). This programme aimed to limit the politico-economic dominance of the planter class and prevent former Confederate officials and leaders from returning to positions of power and authority. Its advocates emphasised that an end to slavery could only be achieved by constitutionally bestowing newly emancipated Black citizens with full civil rights, including the right to vote. The chapter examines this period with an emphasis on transformations that reshaped the South's social structure—previously characterised by enslavers, enslaved people, and yeomen farmers—into a 'New World' of landlords, merchants, sharecroppers and tenant farmers.

Introduction 3

This shift placed formerly enslaved people in a no-man's-land: they were no longer enslaved, but remained marginalised due to economic and material impoverishment as well as persistent racism. The planter class retained their landholdings and thus remained powerful, which enabled the creation of a new sharecropping system. The purpose was to keep the freedmen deprived of the power to independently purchase seeds, tools, and livestock. Additionally, yeomen farmers were pushed into poverty and forced to become tenants due to the consequences of the Civil War, as successive crop failures and fluctuating crop prices forced them into debt.

The Reconstruction period marked the end of 'Lincoln's America' and saw the consolidation of conservative racial politics in the South, which gradually extended its tentacles into the North. This politics emerged in response to a spate of legislative and federal measures aiming to provide greater rights, entitlements, and support to Black citizens in the aftermath of enslavement. Radical Republicans passed the Reconstruction Act in 1867, which led to the rise of new state governments across the South. Such legislation reflects a long history of political struggle by Black people, both free and enslaved, and organised abolitionist or antislavery movements that demanded racial equality. The radical programme was also supported by White immigrants from the North and sympathisers in the South (termed 'carpetbaggers' and 'scalawags', respectively, by their detractors). This was followed by the 14th Constitutional Amendment (1868), which granted citizenship rights without racial or religious bias, and the 15th Constitutional Amendment (1870), which prohibited any curtailment of the right to vote on account of race, colour, or previous condition of servitude, whether at the state or federal level. These moves did not go unchallenged, as the former planter class managed to retain power in local and state government bodies, and these representatives implemented the 'Black Codes' to curtail the newfound freedoms enshrined in federal law. Secret racist and White supremacist organisations began to emerge in all the former Confederate states. They unleashed violent racial attacks on Black citizens in New Orleans, Arkansas, South Carolina, Mississippi, Louisiana, and Texas in particular. The Ku Klux Klan (KKK), which comprised Confederate veterans and had emerged in the state of

Tennessee before quickly spreading throughout the South, heralded an unprecedented wave of racial violence in the US. The Republican Party ostensibly offered Black Americans, who largely supported the party, opportunities to economically uplift themselves with federal land grants given for educational institutions and the development of railroads. However, many Republican policies backfired due to an increase in taxes, persistent accusations of corruption, and aggravated racial tension and divisions in the South. The chapter also examines this period from the perspective of:

(i) The changing nature of federal–state relations as the former, for the first time, assumed authority to enforce the civil rights of citizens against state violations.
(ii) The Civil Rights Act of 1866, which gave the principle of equality before the law.

This transformative phase marked the beginning of significant changes that were not enough to bring racial equality and dignity to Black citizens, yet marked a watershed in American history.

Industrialisation, Economic Transformations, and the Question of Labour

Chapter 2, 'The Rise of Big Business Corporations', concentrates on the period after Reconstruction. The US underwent rapid industrialisation and quickly became a leading economic and military power. During the Civil War, industrial production increased and wartime contracts led to the rise of influential businesspeople; these industrialists later began to invest their newfound wealth in other fields. The destruction of the southern economy propelled an increase in American tariffs to protect nascent American industries, a policy that continued from the 1860s to the 1930s. The rise of big business corporations, along with giant strides towards instituting a technocracy, sparked economic, political and social transformation associated with the onset of the Gilded Age.[4] Three factors accelerated this transformative process: (i) the expansion of railways, which provided the connectivity needed for industries and new markets;

(*ii*) advancements in steel production, where the application of the Bessemer technique enabled the production of new types of rails, bridges, factories and high-rise buildings; and (*iii*) the increasing use of electricity, which completely transformed the social and economic landscape of the nation. Taken together, this period marked the beginning of mass production based on business management systems that increasingly moved towards consolidation and monopolisation, and which saw immense expansion in production, marketing and the availability of credit.

Chapter 3, 'History of the US Labour Movement', delves into the rise of trade unions and massive labour unrest in the US. The working classes (which were stratified by race, ethnicity, and immigration history) converged in new economic hubs in growing numbers, creating a 'melting pot' or a 'salad bowl' with its inherent contradictions and complexities. Their growing political participation eventually led not only to the rise of new and more efficiently managed labour unions, but also to the emergence of new social and cultural dynamics. The chapter analyses labour history 'from the bottom up', based on the premise that in any society, diverse social classes (and not just ruling or elite classes) operate to establish society and bring about changes. It also focuses on the positioning of the working class within the economic marketplace, their living standards and organisational power. The chapter dwells on the rise of trade unions as economic institutions with intense political activities, as well as the study of competing labour organisational structures and their labour leaders. The increase in new labour historians in America owed much to the influence of E. P. Thompson's *Making of the English Working Class* (1963). The pioneer of labour history in the US was Herbert Gutman,[5] who focused on how the labour force responded to situations and circumstances they themselves did not choose, right from the colonial period. In this context, Gutman delineated the patterns of growth and development of contending labour systems based on three types of economic activities:

(*i*) plantation production of commercial crops like tobacco, rice, indigo, sugar and, later, cotton, all based on chattel slavery;

(*ii*) family-based agricultural production; and

(iii) artisanal production that was connected to mercantile port centres.

In tracing the colonial antecedents of the working classes in the US, the chapter also highlights the evolution of a system of indentured labour due to the disproportionate land–man ratio: The easy availability of land, contrasted with acute shortages of labour, pushed the colonists to devise this system. Gradually, the shortage of labour fostered a sense of independence and personal liberty, particularly in the northern colonies. This sentiment came into play after 1760, when Britain sought to impose its colonial authority and sovereign powers through taxation and mercantile control, which was opposed by the labouring classes. The same courses later played a significant role in the post-revolutionary period. The boot and shoe trade that developed in 1800 was organised in terms of household units, with each household operating on the basis of internal hierarchy, interdependence, and egalitarianism among different kinds of workers. This formed a relationship between shoe-working households and other households, like farmers and craftsmen, who together established a 'republican community'. By 1830, this led to the establishment of a centralised shop focused on credit and protecting the national market, transforming it into the centre of a vast 'putting-out' or workshop system. The system of merchant manufacturing expanded the scale of this enterprise. It lowered the cost of shoe production, but in the process, the shoemaker became a wage labourer. By the 1860s, sewing machines and mechanical stitching gave way to factory production.

Labour historians also analysed changes associated with the Gilded Age, and this scholarship addresses three broad sub-themes:

(i) The rise of new industrial towns like Chicago, New York, San Francisco, and Philadelphia, which became a magnet for immigrant workers.
(ii) Development of a distinct set of beliefs, values, norms, and class consciousness shared by the working classes, based on their work experience, knowledge and shared identity.
(iii) Patterns of collective action, power dynamics and political influence of the working classes and their trade unions. (In

particular, this involves the study of the Irish-American working class, and of organisations like the National Labour Union, The Noble and Holy Order of the Knights of Labour, the American Federation of Labour, the Socialist Labour Party and Socialist Party of America, along with the Industrial Workers of the World.)

Interestingly, Thomas Dublin focused on collective action among the young women workers of the Lowell Mill in Massachusetts,[6] an early example of women's collectivisation. This aspect has been addressed in Chapter 4, 'The Lowell Textile Mill Girls: Emergence of Women's Unions and Labour Strikes'. Dublin concluded that these women workers had secured unprecedented economic independence, and for a significant number, this translated into a set of personal freedoms. The women workers at Lowell Mill became the first industrial proletariat. Initially residing with their families, they later moved to boarding houses, under the supervision of more experienced women workers. The Lowell Mill owners devised a planned, protective, and educational environment for female workers coming from farms and villages. The supervised boarding houses evolved into a community centred around sewing, reading, and the affordances of urban life, fostering a newfound sense of freedom and the opportunity to enter public spaces. However, the workers also had to contend with the monotony of work, low wages, and unhealthy working conditions, which fostered discontent. Driven by republican values and an awareness of their rights as enshrined in the Declaration of Independence—that 'All Men are Created Equal'—and spurred on by the knowledge that wage cuts and market compression were passed on to the workers rather than being absorbed by the mill owners, women workers began to demand reforms. This led to a strike, with persistent demands for shorter working hours and better working conditions. While these strikes were a landmark event in labour history, women workers found themselves sidelined in the industry. As a result, by the late 1840s and 1850s, Irish labourers began to be preferred over other groups.

Chapter 5 is titled 'The Populist Movement and the Progressive Era'. In the period from 1893 to 1897, repeated cycles of depression impacted America. These significantly affected American farmers, who experienced a continuous fall in crop prices as railroad transportation rates continued to rise and many banks closed down. The chapter analyses the Populist Movement as a form of radical opposition by American farmers to the development of capitalist institutions and corporate capitalism, and it looks at how they challenged prevalent economic and political ideas in the country. The Progressive Movement, on the other hand, evolved from the urban and service class professionals, along with women's groups and with support within the business and political class. US presidents Theodore Roosevelt and Woodrow Wilson emerged from Progressive Movement politics. Scholarship has shown that the movement was rooted in the moral and ethical frameworks of evangelical Protestantism. It was committed to removing social conflict and the adverse impact of industrialisation through the application of new 'scientific' frameworks of social science methods within the broader framework of American capitalism.

Between the two World Wars, the US underwent phenomenal economic expansion. This was followed by the period of the Great Depression, which necessitated a set of transformative policies to lift Americans out of economic hardship. As detailed in Chapter 6, 'The New Deal',[7] this was an innovative experiment in political, economic, and financial reform. While historians no longer accept this period as the 'age of Roosevelt',[8] there remains a consensus that this was a historically significant period. The New Deal has been examined from the perspective of the limitations imposed on the US government by America's political and economic institutions. These limitations led to unprecedented change within the nation, as explored in William Leuchtenburg's *Franklin Roosevelt and the New Deal* (1963), an extremely influential study of the reforms.[9]

Struggles for Equality: The Anti-Racist and Women's Movements

In the postbellum[10] period, in particular the period from the 1870s onwards, was marked by mob violence and political assassinations in the South that assisted in the collapse of the radical southern

Republican governments, except in Florida, South Carolina, and Louisiana. With the implementation of the Posse Comitatus Act of 1878, Black Americans lost the protection of federal military force, since the Act prohibited the use of military forces in law enforcement. This was followed by the Supreme Court's 1883 verdict that struck down the Civil Rights Act of 1875. The Act had guaranteed free access to public spaces, including restaurants, inns, transportation, parks, and amusement places, for African Americans. By the 1880s, more discriminatory measures, like poll taxes and literacy tests, emerged to exclude Black citizens from voting. These went hand-in-hand with the formulation of segregation policy through 'Jim Crow' laws. In the *Plessy v. Ferguson* case (1896), the Supreme Court legitimised racial segregation by instituting the norm of 'separate but equal' provisions according to race.

The Jim Crow laws institutionalised racial division and reinforced the social inferiority of Black people, and also marked the rise of 'convict labour', a growing form of corporate public slavery whereby Black prisoners were given over to private contractors to work as labourers without pay. The period from 1890 to 1925 has been characterised as one ruled by 'lynch law', with several cases of White mobs persecuting and murdering Black people, and also participating in racialised humiliationand torture (including particularly egregious cases of immolation and sexual violence). In a film produced by D. W. Griffith titled *Birth of a Nation*, mass media was for the first time harnessed to establish the myth of the supremacy of the White race, which helped in the revival of the Ku Klux Klan and other White racist groups. These groups continued to flourish till the late 1940s.

Chapter 7, 'The Struggle for Equality: The African American Movement', evaluates these racial conflicts. The chapter focuses on prominent African American leaders and highlights their influential role in shaping American society and polity. It also explores their commitment to construct an independent Black identity through the African American movement, and how these Black communities became important socio-political stakeholders during the Reconstruction era and after. The chapter assesses the leadership of Booker T. Washington, a Black leader and educator who advocated a gospel of self-improvement and hard work to bring about gradual change. His conciliatory approach brought him the support of many White, conservative business magnates who had their own agenda in terms of the Black labouring classes. Despite his stature and contributions, to many radical and educated Black people, Washington's approach was too conservative and accommodationist. This led to the emergence of W. E. B. Du Bois, the first Black person to hold a doctorate from Harvard University. In 1910, he founded the National Association for the Advancement of Colored People (NAACP). In the 1920s, Jamaican-born activist Marcus Garvey rose to prominence and assumed the role of an almost messianic prophet who would lead all exiled Africans back to their 'motherland'.

Persistent racial violence triggered the Great Migration from the South, particularly following the end of World War I, when a labour shortage in northern industries led to a large-scale migration of Black people to New York, Chicago, Detroit, and Philadelphia. The *Brown v. Board of Education*[11] decision in 1954 contributed to the spread of the Civil Rights Movement, which had developed in response to large-scale repression by the White establishment against Black people and people of colour in general. One of the inception points of the organised Civil Rights Movement was in 1955, when worker and NAACP activist Rosa Parks refused to give up her bus seat for a White passenger in Montgomery, Alabama. The outrage in response to racial segregation brought Martin Luther King, Jr. into a leadership role and he worked with other activists to develop a political movement through bus boycotts, marches, and sit-ins. Chapter 8, 'The Civil Rights and Black Power Movements: Martin Luther King, Jr. and Malcolm X', concentrates on the period from 1954 to 1965 that saw the rise of the Civil Rights Movement, built on Black activism, and the support it received from the federal government, the judiciary, and large sections of the public. Among the political establishment, liberals and enlightened conservatives alike understood that desegregation would also allow them to better project the USA as a land of freedom and equality, and as a crusader of the anti-communist movement. Television also played a significant role through live broadcasts of racial conflicts as well as anti-racist protests, which proved powerful in shaping public sentiment, launching the issue of Black rights onto the national stage. Black leaders used protests and boycotts to challenge legal segregation and exposed such practices as a source of a national and international embarrassment. The movement saw the emergence of new groups and coalitions, including the Southern Christian Leadership Conference (SCLC), the Student Non-Violent Coordinating Committee (SNCC), the Congress of Racial Equality (CORE), working along with the older NAACP to secure equality through non-violence and a Gandhian civil disobedience movement. The use of such tactics proved politically necessary, enabling them to maintain a moral high ground as they turned public opinion in their support.[12]

By the mid-1960s, the Civil Rights Movement had achieved many of its goals and effected widespread social change. However, racial tensions and violence began to reappear in the northern cities due to unemployment, insufficient housing, and biased policing. Despite an increase in social welfare expenditure by the federal government, aiming to build a 'great society', many Black people found these measures to be inadequate and exclusionary. Continued racism and disillusionment led to the rise of Black nationalist aspirations that supported separatism instead of integration and advocated for the right of self-determination and armed self-defence of Black communities. This crystallised in the notion of Black Power, a term coined by Stokely Carmichael. The emergence of the Nation of Islam, also known as the Black Muslim Movement, gained support in urban areas with a large Black population. Malcolm X, the charismatic leader of the movement, initially advocated for a radical approach by establishing the Black Muslim and pan-African organisation. However, he eventually adopted a revolutionary socialist approach and aligned himself with emerging socialist movements of the 'Third World' or the Global South.

Chapter 9, 'Women in American History', highlights the critical role of nearly all American woman—especially Indigenous women, enslaved and later free Black women, as well as immigrant, working class, and rural women across racial and ethnic lines—in shaping American society and politics. The chapter examines how women resisted physical and mental exploitation and marginalisation from the colonial period to the twentieth century, and how diverse histories of women shaped the nation. This is a significant intervention based on research by American scholars who re-examined developments such as the Temperance movement through a new lens.[13] Women scholars began to approach research from feminist perspectives, refusing to normalise women's subordination and defying the long-held notion of women's 'passivity' in larger social and political arenas. Feminist scholarship thus exposed conventional history as male-dominated, male-sourced, and male-centred. New scholarship on the historical experiences of Black women offer insights into how the experience of enslavement, racial discrimination, and poverty shaped their distinct identity. Much of this was based on archival material that captured Black women's voices, highlighting their forms of resistance, activism, and instrumental roles in public health, social welfare, religious congregations, education, and the struggle for civil rights. The chapter also highlights how women were excluded from the corridors of political and economic power and kept at the fringes of society due to patriarchal dominance.

The USA on the World Stage

The sheer size of the nation and diversity of its population, along with persistent racial violence, prompted American political leaders to devise new styles of patriotism based on American militarism. This culminated in the Spanish-American War of 1898 and marked the emergence of the American brand of imperialism. The study of US foreign policy in Chapter 10, 'The Spanish-American War of 1898: The Onset of American Imperialism', focuses on a distinct brand of international politics guided by domestic issues. Its trajectory began with the War of 1812, which reflected the growing imperialist aspirations of the nation-state, expanding in scale over the next century as the US moved from a policy of isolationism to one of 'associationalism', to eventually become a global superpower by the end of World War II.

It was during the Civil War that the USA demonstrated its ability to integrate technological advancements in arms and ammunition, as well as the capacity to mobilise an army on short notice. In 1867, Russia sold the territory of Alaska to the United States for a price of

US $7.2 million, which, in the words of Secretary of State William H. Seward, was a 'magnificent bargain'. Soon, the US cast its gaze over the whole of North America. There was growing apprehension in Britain that the disagreements between the two nations could easily escalate into military conflict over British-controlled territories—an outcome narrowly averted during the 1895 dispute over Venezuela's boundary with British Guiana. This was precipitated by the Irish lobby in the US, known for its anti-Britain stance, which marked the growing influence of domestic politics over American foreign affairs. In 1895, Cubans launched a nationalist revolt against the Spanish Empire, which received widespread coverage in the American press, particularly in William Randolph Hearst's *New York Morning Journal* and Joseph Pulitzer's *New York World*. The press reported in detail about Spanish 'concentration camps'. Amid rising tensions in February 1898, a mysterious explosion led to the destruction of the American battleship USS *Maine* in Havana harbour, and the press blamed it on Spanish action. As a result, war was declared in April 1898 and Cuba came under the American sphere of influence. A naval victory in Manila Bay brought the Philippines under US control, which in turn contributed to the signing of the Treaty of Paris of 1898. The US thus took control of Puerto Rico, Guam, the Philippines, and Hawaii. This marked the beginning of America's rise as a global power.

Chapter 11, 'A History of US Intervention in World Wars I and II', shows how this idea was reinforced by Theodore Roosevelt (US president from 1901–1909), who became a peacemaker in the Russo-Japanese War of 1905 and, in 1907, sent a 'Great White Fleet' on a world cruise to demonstrate the growth of America as a naval power. In 1902, he invoked the Monroe Doctrine to prevent European powers from interfering in Venezuela. It was Roosevelt who formulated the policy of establishing American dominance in the Pacific and the Caribbean by building a canal between them. The Panama Canal was constructed between 1906 and 1914, facilitating the easy movement of American ships between the oceans and enabling its use in the event of a war with Britain or Japan. The rise of American imperialism, whereby the US began to treat small nations in the Caribbean as de facto colonies, marked a significant shift in global power dynamics. Cuba and Panama were considered to be American protectorates, and Puerto Rico was a colony. In 1905, America took over the finances of the Dominican Republic (1916–1920). The US army occupied Nicaragua in 1912 and again in 1926. The US came to control Haiti (1915–1934), and continued its interference in Mexico.

For a long time, scholars perceived the US as a 'reluctant power' that was drawn into global conflict by accident and forced to intervene in the Caribbean and elsewhere. Later scholars, however, began to point to the rise of new intellectual and social forces that facilitated American expansion. These forces were ideologically supported by new racial theories, intermixed with nationalism, a masculinist culture, and a perceived imperative to expand the USA's sphere of influence to encompass the entire Western hemisphere. Senator Albert Beveridge believed in the 'Teutonic germ' theory and used this as a justification for intervention in the Philippines.[14] Domestically, the US had for long grappled with similar racial hierarchies that dehumanised Black and Indigenous peoples, and the same ideology that propped up White supremacy at home guided it to consider the people of these nations as lawless 'lesser beings' who needed to be suppressed and controlled. Allied with this were popular notions of 'Anglo-Saxon superiority' and the theory of eugenics—another pseudoscientific doctrine based on the belief that social problems could be eliminated by promoting the 'breeding' of the 'fittest' and limiting the number of so-called inferior races.

The period from 1917 to the 1940s was a time when its involvement in global affairs gradually transformed the US into a global power, in turn shaping domestic American politics. During this period, foreign affairs became increasingly interlinked with internal matters, granting the federal executive unprecedented powers and facilitating American military expansion as well as the growth of the federal government. During this period of growing foreign aggression, the state worked to limit 'radical' elements within the US, especially the Germans (who did not want the USA to involve itself in European affairs or war), and the increasingly influential communists. Over 16 million Americans were drafted and served in the armed forces between 1941 and 1945,[15] and the absence of this huge workforce meant employment opportunities for women, who were given jobs in war production along with Black workers. This led to the massive wave of migration from the South to the North and West, and from rural to urban areas. This progression led to increased movement for social justice and bolstered the political aspirations of marginalised groups, especially women and African Americans.

This volume concentrates on the shifting relationships between constitutionally guaranteed rights, privileges, and freedom, and the fault lines and conflicts within the US as it rose to a position of global prominence. The USA, established in 1776 as the world's 'first modern nation', had become so powerful by 1945 that it began to play a prominent role in shaping the international order. This made the US a global empire or superpower whose foundation was based on the growth and development of a phenomenal political economy and the American brand of capitalism.

Notes

1. The Homestead Act of 1862 was an attempt by the federal government under President Abraham Lincoln to initiate rapid westward expansion for faster economic growth and territorial expansion. The Act enabled citizens to claim ownership of 160 acres of public land, which would be made private in exchange for a small fee, provided the land was farmed for at least five years.

2. The two Pacific Railroad Acts passed in 1862 and 1864, respectively, made federal loans and land grants available to the Union Pacific and Central Pacific Railroad Companies. This enabled the construction of a transcontinental railroad for the economic unification of the nation and facilitated economic growth and expansion of the western region.

3. Federal grants in the form of the Morrill Acts of 1862 and 1890 established the land grant system to provide an educated workforce. The act of 1862 assisted in the rise of Kansas State University, Iowa State University, Cornell University, Massachusetts Institute of Technology, Rutgers University, and the University of Missouri, among others. In 1890, the focus was on the southern states, which led to the rise of universities and colleges that prioritised higher education for Black students, such as Kentucky State University, Virginia State University, and many others.

4. Mark Twain coined the term in reference to the period that extended from the 1870s to the 1890s, marked by industrialisation and urbanisation that ushered in unprecedented economic progress, but also sparked rapid social changes, creating grounds for increased conflict and tensions. Hidden beneath

the picture of 'glittering prosperity' was rising social disparity, racial violence, and staggering levels of political corruption.

5. Herbert G. Gutman, *Culture, and Society in Industrialising America: Essays in American Working-Class History* (New York, 1977).

6. Thomas Dublin, *Women at Work: The Transformation of Work and Community in Lowell, Massachusetts, 1826–1860* (New York, 1979).

7. The term was used for the first time by President Franklin D. Roosevelt in 1932 to provide immediate relief from the economic crisis, recovery of the American economy and reform to prevent this type of crisis from emerging in the future. The programme was carried out under the direct supervision of the federal government.

8. Arthur M. Schlesinger, Jr. *The Age of Roosevelt*, 3 vols (Boston, 1957–1960).

9. William E. Leuchtenburg, *Franklin D. Roosevelt and the New Deal, 1932–1940* (New York, 1963).

10. Postbellum is a Latin term that combines 'after' (post) and 'bellum' (war).

11. This 1954 verdict ruled that racial segregation in public schools was unconstitutional. This decision overturned the 'separate but equal' doctrine established in *Plessy v. Ferguson* and marked a major triumph of the Civil Rights Movement.

12. In 1957, the governor of Arkansas deployed the National Guard to prevent the court-ordered desegregation of the Little Rock public school system, which forced President Eisenhower to use federal troops to enforce the law. By 1961, the process of integrating Black students into southern universities began in earnest with the support of the federal government, and in 1962, this sparked campus riots at the University of Mississippi that were brought down by the federal troops. The backlash to civil rights activism resulted in the resurgence of the KKK, which aimed precisely to suppress the growing clout of the protestors. By the time of President John F. Kennedy, racial violence had become a national issue, especially as Black people began to be seen as communist sympathisers and began to connect their struggle with the 'Third World'. The power of the movement forced President Lyndon B. Johnson to sign the Civil Rights Act of 1964, which forbade discrimination in public facilities and employment. When another incident of brutal violence was unleashed on a protest march in Selma, Alabama, in 1965, the President passed the federal Voting Rights Act.

13. For the meaning of Temperance, see Archana Ojha, *History of the United States of America: From Independence to the Civil War* (New Delhi, 2025), pp. 102 and 242.

14. Daniel Levine, 'The Social Philosophy of Albert J. Beveridge', *Indiana Magazine of History* 58 (2), pp. 101–116. The Teutonic theory was a pseudoscientific race theory that claimed that only 'teutonic races' (Anglo-Saxon peoples) were capable of forming independent nations and governing themselves.

15. See the World War II army enlistment records, available at https://www.archives.gov (accessed October 2025).

CHAPTER 1

Reconstruction
Black Freedom, Won and Lost

Introduction

The intervening period between the end of the **Civil War (1861–1865)**, which resulted in the abolition of slavery with the **Emancipation Proclamation (the 13th Constitutional Amendment)**, and the beginning of the **Reconstruction era (1865–1877)**, brought for Black people 'freedom', although this freedom was circumscribed by White-dominated legislation, court decisions, and societal norms. The period represented an unprecedented storm of dislocation, distress, and utter chaos for African Americans on the one hand, and former enslavers and pro-slavery European Americans on the other. The latter evolved new strategies of segregation to retain their control over Black labour. The Reconstruction period marked the beginnings of a formal end to class-based and racial divisions associated with enslavement, but this remained incomplete in the face of immense social upheaval. Prior to the War, in the period between the victory of the Republican Party and John Brown's raid on Harper's Ferry, the South had been consumed with rumours of slave plots, rebellions, arson, and violence. The Civil War that followed eroded the political, economic, and social institutions of the South that were powered by the slave economy, and the loss brought to the surface a host of hidden systemic issues. Another outcome of the War was that more powers were transferred to the federal government, further reducing the states' strength and rights.[1]

INTERNAL TURMOIL DURING THE CIVIL WAR

During the Civil War, southern enslavers moved their enslaved 'property'[2] into the 'safer' interior (the Deep South). Enslaved people thus became 'refugees'. This hurried movement had multiple consequences: it loosened enslavers' control and capacity to enforce discipline over the enslaved, and it also led to the breaking up of enslaved peoples' families. Enslaved people were also mobilised for the War and brought into urban areas as labourers for the manufacture of arms and ammunition, mining, ironworks, textile mills, and food processing units, as well as the construction of roads, railroads, and hospitals. This further weakened the enslaver's control. Enslaved people were made to build military fortifications and perform other kinds of military labour, which brought them close to the borderlands and made it easier for them to escape to freedom.[3] As more White men were forced to join the army, the slave patrol force began to thin out, and this also increased the chances of being able to successfully flee to freedom. According to Clarence L. Mohr, writing in the context of Georgia, and C. Peter Ripley, in the context of Louisiana, the pressures of the Civil War resulted in the loosening of paternal and slave control mechanisms.[4] At one point, the Confederacy also flirted with the idea of recruiting enslaved people into its army, highlighting the inner contradictions of the South.

The situation in the North was similarly vague, particularly from the perspective of Abraham Lincoln. He did not fully believe in racial equality, as evidenced by the first Emancipation Proclamation, which stated that only enslaved individuals in certain areas would be freed, and they would be required to work on the same lands where they had previously been enslaved. The aim was to limit their freedom of movement and economic independence, preventing an influx of Black individuals into the North. However, as the Civil War dragged on, the need for a new labour force increased, and free Black individuals were employed as labourers and eventually recruited as soldiers in the Union Army.

The Reconstruction Era

The period from 1865 to 1877 has been termed the Reconstruction (a term borrowed from the **Military Reconstruction Acts of 1867**), when the victorious North worked to reconstruct the southern states and bring them back into the Union. The Reconstruction can be categorised in three broad phases: (*i*) Abraham Lincoln's Ten Percent Plan; (*ii*) Andrew Johnson's Reconstruction plans; and (*iii*) Radical Reconstruction. The first phase dates back to the Civil War, under Union President Lincoln, who had the singular aim of saving the Union and bringing the War to an early end to secure a peaceful reunification. He was opposed to slavery, but as a moderate in the Republican Party, Lincoln had initially set out only to stop its expansion into new territories of the USA, believing that this would eventually lead to its quiet extinction. According to Eric Foner, freedom became an 'arena of conflict' between the free Black population and the dominant White population during this period. Attempts were made to give new shape and structure to the southern political system, and to bring the newly emancipated Black population into the fold, which was met with multiple hurdles.[5]

Table 1.1: Timeline of the Reconstruction Period (1865–1877)

Year	Major Events
1865	End of the Civil War. Assassination of Abraham Lincoln. Andrew Johnson elevated to the Presidency—implementation of Black Codes in the southern states. Establishment of the Freedmen's Bureau to assist emancipated Black and poor White populations.
1866	The Congress passes the Civil Rights Act of 1866. Establishment of the Ku Klux Klan in Tennessee. Beginning of racial violence against freedmen and their supporters and sympathisers.

(Contd)

Table 1.1: *(Contd)*

Year	Major Events
1867	Radical Congressmen take over the Reconstruction process and divide the South into five military districts. This marks the beginning of the radical Reconstruction process.
1868	The 14th Constitutional Amendment passed, granting citizenship rights and protection under law to all born and naturalised American citizens. The Impeachment motion initiated against President Johnson.
1870	The 15th Constitutional Amendment passed, which denied discrimination based on race, colour, and previous conditions of servitude. All southern states brought back into the Union.
1871	The Enforcement Act passed to disband and destroy the Ku Klux Klan.
1874	The beginning of the Democratic Party's dominance in the House of Representatives and its thwarting of radical Reconstruction efforts.
1877	Following a disputed result in the presidential elections of 1876, the 'Compromise of 1877' paves the way for the Republican Party's candidate, Rutherford B. Hayes, to become president. Withdrawal of federal troops from the southern states. Beginning of the disenfranchisement of Black voters and the implementation of discriminatory Jim Crow Laws.

GRADED EMANCIPATION

The declaration of war and Lincoln's moves to restrict and later ban slavery sparked intense opposition among Democrats and radical Republicans, who were concerned about expansions to executive power under the pretext of fighting the Civil War. They therefore termed it a 'needless conflict'. Northerners also opposed the terms of compulsory conscription, which exempted those who could afford to pay US $300. Within his own party, the Republicans, radical members aggressively advocated for an anti-slavery crusade. The President instead pursued a policy of 'protectionism'. He first increased tariff duties to apply pressure on the South to end the War, followed by the **Homestead Act passed in 1862**, which allowed for any adult citizen to claim 160 acres of surveyed government land in the West, provided they lived on and cultivated the land. Soon after this, the **Morrill Land-Grant Act of 1862** provided grants of land to the states for setting up agricultural and mechanical colleges. To win the War, Congress passed many Acts that granted more powers to the President, making the federal government's executive branch extremely powerful. Still the War continued, forcing the President to pass the **Compensated Emancipation Act of 1862**, under which slavery would be gradually abolished in the district of Columbia. In his next step, also in 1862, Lincoln ordered the confiscation of all property of those who supported the secession of the South from the Union. When the Civil War did not end in 1863, the National Banking System was implemented to stabilise the American dollar and issue federal bonds to secure funds to continue the War. However, the continued resilience of the South forced Lincoln to reconsider his views against abolition. In the Emancipation Proclamation of 1863, he declared enslaved people 'free'—however, this was meant to be implemented only in the seceded southern states.

According to W. E. B. Du Bois, in his book, *Black Reconstruction* (1935), enslaved people had staged a 'general strike' that forced Lincoln to announce emancipation. Many scholars have concurred with this reasoning and emphasise the role played by Black people in their own emancipation. Along with military and diplomatic pressures, the arrival of a large number of Black refugees put pressure on Lincoln to announce their freedom. Other historians view Black engagement with the War as preparatory grounds for future political struggles for equality, civil rights, and substantive freedoms. The Emancipation Proclamation and the end of the Civil War meant for the southern White elites a sudden end and abrupt transformation of their 'personal property'. Formerly enslaved people now exhibited a more 'liberated' personality and evolved new strategies of survival to cope with a society that remained deeply racist even after abolition. Rayford Logan has termed this period a 'nadir' of African American history due to the systematic and often violent pushback against any movement for racial equality and civil rights.[6] It was also becoming clear to the White population that they understood Black people far less than they had assumed. Herbert Gutman has shown that after the War, many formerly enslaved people travelled great distances in search of lost family members—wartime uncertainty had only sharpened their understanding of the importance of their families, and they were further motivated by the desire for land, mobility, education, and religiosity.[7] Amidst this atmosphere of complete turmoil, America prepared to reconstruct itself from the ashes of the Civil War.

ABRAHAM LINCOLN'S PRESIDENTIAL RECONSTRUCTION PLAN

The decision to allow '**contrabands**', or runaway slaves, to join the Union Army was a key turning point in the course of the Civil War. The Union Army was soon able to secure a victory. Hoping to facilitate a painless and quick process of reunification of the USA, Lincoln passed the **Ten Percent Plan in 1863**. All ex-Confederate officials were required to take an oath of loyalty to the Union before their confiscated property was restored to them. However, all the high-ranking civil and Confederate military officials who had resigned from Congress to join the Confederate States of America were required to apply for a presidential pardon. After 10 per cent of the White male population of each state took the oath of loyalty to the Union, the state would be permitted to form a new constitution with the inclusion of the 13th Amendment, and the state could then rejoin the Union. Abraham Lincoln's plan primarily aimed to garner continued support among the southern Unionists (who had opposed secession from the very start), especially the former Whigs, and thereby to expand the political base of the Republican Party in the southern states.

However, the Ten Percent Plan faced severe opposition from radical members of the Republican Party, who feared that this plan would restore the political power of the enslaver class. Most importantly, they pointed out that Lincoln's plan made no provision to provide federal support to free Black people. In 1864, the radical Republicans in Congress pushed through the **Wade-Davis Bill**, which dealt with the Confederates much more stringently. The Bill brought all seceded southern states under the rule of a military governor; unlike the Ten Percent Plan, here, at least 51 per cent of the White male population of each state would have to take the oath of loyalty to the Union. They would then select non-Confederate delegates to the state convention, which would repeal the Act of Secession and ratify the abolition of slavery. Further, each southerner was required to take an oath that he had never voluntarily supported the Confederacy. The plan, interestingly, had no provision for Black suffrage. Although the Bill was passed by both Houses, Lincoln used the presidential pocket veto to prevent its enactment into law. In the meantime, the states of Arkansas, Louisiana, Tennessee, and parts of Virginia moved for readmission into the Union under the Presidential Plan, a move that the Congress blocked.

FIG. 1.1: Campaign button used in republican party canvassing (1864)

Source: Wikimedia Commons.

The war efforts and attempts to re-unify the nation enhanced Lincoln's popularity, leading to his victory in the 1864 presidential elections, with Andrew Johnson as the Vice President. However, on 14 April 1865, as the Civil War was coming to a close, Lincoln was fatally shot by John Wilkes Booth as part of a failed pro-Confederate conspiracy.

Reconstruction Under Andrew Johnson

In 1865, following **Lincoln's assassination**, Andrew Johnson became the next president. This marked the beginning of the second phase of the Reconstruction, as he unveiled his own **Presidential Plan**. Johnson had begun his political career as a Democrat and had later made a politically opportune shift to the Republican Party, and his hidden sympathies to the southern White cause were reflected in his actions. In Johnson's plan, the states were required to take an oath of allegiance and secure a Presidential pardon, after which they would receive general amnesty; the confiscated property of Confederate enslavers would be restored to them, except for the formerly enslaved people who were no longer to be considered private property. The oath-takers were required to elect delegates to state conventions, and each state convention would have to proclaim the illegality of secession, repudiate state war debts as they belonged to the Confederacy, ratify the 13th Amendment, and bar all Confederate officials whose income was more than US $20,000 from participating in state politics.

Johnson permitted the implementation of **Black Codes** in the southern states—these replaced the earlier slave codes and their singular purpose was to maintain a White supremacist social order. The codes, enacted by state and local legislatures, instituted racial segregation in public places; prevented inter-racial marriage; instituted legal provisions that effectively prevented African Americans from testifying against White people or serving on juries; and, most importantly, controlled Black labour. Newly freed Black individuals were prevented from leaving the plantation in South Carolina. Black people were now required to obtain special licences to enter non-agricultural employment, effectively forcing them to work as field hands or labourers at the very plantations where they had once been enslaved. Mississippi prohibited Black persons from buying and selling farmland. In other southern states, any Black individual who was found without a lawful job was arrested on the charge of being a 'drifter', under new vagrancy laws, and auctioned off to employers who would pay their fines. The result was that Black people were neither enslaved, nor free; the Black Codes became another politico-legal structure to control Black labour. Further, the period from 1865 to 1866 saw the beginning of a new pattern of racial violence in the southern states.

The Radical Reconstruction Phase

To prevent the President from implementing a conservative reconstruction plan, and alarmed by the explicit racism of the Black Codes, radical Republicans in Congress renewed their efforts. This marked the third phase of the Reconstruction period. The tenure of the Freedmen's Bureau was extended, and Congress passed the **Civil Rights Act of 1866**, which legally prevented state governments from implementing any discriminatory legislation on the grounds of race. Congress also barred all the former Confederate officials from the state constitutional conventions. However, the use of veto power to block the enactment of radical policies forced the radical members of Congress to initiate the process of impeachment against President Johnson.

By law, Black populations were now to be protected by their respective state governments, but with no economic support from government agencies, economic independence remained a utopian wish. The **Bureau of Refugees, Freedmen and Abandoned Lands**, also known as the **Freedmen's Bureau**, set up in 1865, was meant to offer important safeguards. It provided relief, rations, and medical care; built schools and employment opportunities; and protected the rights of Black workers, including running special military courts to settle labour disputes, and invalidating labour contracts forced upon freedmen by the Black Codes. The Bureau was empowered by the Civil Rights Act, which strengthened the 13th Amendment by providing legislative meaning to the concept of freedom. The Act granted US citizenship to the Black population[8] and guaranteed equal protection under the law. A veritable masterstroke, the passage of this Act in Congress invalidated the Black Codes in the southern states and also introduced a transformational change in federal–state relations, taking away the citizens' rights from the states and making it a federal subject to apply the principle of equality before the law irrespective of the race for all naturalised American citizens. The Civil Rights Act became the first major legislation in the United States to become law despite being vetoed by the President.

In another significant step, the Congress passed the **14th Amendment Bill in 1866**, which prohibited states from infringing on citizens' rights, privileges, and immunities; in other words, from depriving them of life, liberty, and property without due process of the law. Although some of these provisions were included in the Civil Rights Act, it was thought that a constitutional amendment would be a better safeguard since it is harder to repeal. The amendment disqualified anyone who had previously taken the oath of loyalty but then participated in an insurrection or rebellion from holding state or federal office. Effectively, Confederates were barred from holding any government posts in 1867. Apart from Tennessee, which had ratified the 14th Amendment in July 1866, the southern states refused to ratify the Amendment.[9] The Congress then passed the **Reconstruction Act of 1867**.[10] As per the Act, the South was divided into five military districts till the time that each state held a constitutional convention (with delegates chosen by an electorate consisting of eligible White and Black voters). New state constitutions were framed, which then required approval of the new electorates and Congress.[11] In the meantime, the Radical plan to impeach President Johnson failed and the motion was defeated in 1867. However, Johnson's popularity had declined considerably and he had little choice but to give the Republicans a free hand. The Reconstruction Act was followed by the **15th Constitutional Amendment (1870)**, which prohibited any denial of voting rights based on race, colour, or 'previous condition of servitude' (thus explicitly barring disenfranchisement of the formerly enslaved).

The unrelenting efforts of radical Congressmen led to the readmission of all the southern states into the Union. Furthermore, the Republicans found significant political success in the South during this period, owing largely to the emergence of new social groups that facilitated the process of Reconstruction. Some prominent new groups were (*i*) free Black citizens, (*ii*) northerners who arrived in the South after the Civil War, derisively termed 'carpetbaggers', and (*iii*) White southerners who supported abolition and radical Reconstruction, termed 'scalawags' by their opponents. They supported various reforms, including the introduction of judicial and racial equality at the level of local governance, assistance to the poor, opening up of public schools funded by state governments, special measures to empower Black labourers, an equitable taxation system, and the construction of public infrastructure such as roads. Racial segregation in public transport and accommodation was outlawed through the **Civil Rights Act of 1875**. To create a New South by initiating programmes of economic development, the Union government began railroad expansion, for which new taxes were imposed.

All these measures were met with opposition as the South was still predominantly racist and unwilling to give space to free Black people, and this racist mentality assisted in the rise of White supremacist groups like the Ku Klux Klan. This racist paramilitary group has often been characterised as the first terror group in the US, and it unleashed a reign of terror against Black Americans as well as White supporters of radical efforts at Reconstruction. This forced the government to initiate both legal and military action against these White terror groups. However, in the meantime, most of the southern Republicans began to withdraw from anti-racist efforts, and the expansion of federal powers came under fire due to charges of large-scale corruption. With rising racial conflict and diminishing popularity of the Republican governments, Reconstruction began to be seen as a failed attempt. In 1873, once the economic depression set in, political reconstruction took a backseat and economic problems highlighted by the Democrats dealt another blow to the government, resulting in the resurgence of the Democrats, who regained control of the House of Representatives by 1874 amidst continued racial violence that raged in the southern states. In the presidential elections of 1876, the Republican presidential candidate

Rutherford B. Hayes negotiated with the Southern officials to come to power and promised to end the Reconstruction and recall federal troops from the South. The result was the near-disappearance of the Republican Party from the South, non-implementation of the 14th and 15th Amendments on the ground, continued racial violence against Black people, and from 1870, the open implementation of the **Jim Crow laws**, a racist set of laws at the local and state levels that institutionalised racial segregation in the South.

Emergence of New Social Groups

Newcomers from the North

Carpetbaggers were the new social group that entered the South, allegedly to secure wealth and power. The pejorative term 'carpetbagger', which stuck in the South, comes from the idea that many of them arrived with all their possessions stuffed into travel bags made of cheap carpet material. These were Union soldiers, business people, and professionals who hoped to buy land, open factories, build railroads, and work as missionaries, teachers, and Freedmen's Bureau agents. They formed a society known as the **Union League** to get Black support, and eventually came to control at least one out of every three political offices in the South. Historians largely concur that most carpetbaggers were northerners or 'Yankees' who were educated enough to realise the potential for economic growth and who sought to invest their wealth in the South. According to Richard Nelson Current, most carpetbaggers were honest, romantic, imbued with the spirit of supporting Black people in their fight to secure liberty and due justice denied to them for centuries. This opinion is very similar to that of William C. Harris, who stated that they were mostly northerners who went to the South after the Civil War.

From 1865 to 1866, many carpetbaggers invested their wealth in commercial and planting enterprises. Still, many suffered reversals of fortune in their quest for money and philanthropy, and circumstances forced them to leave the South. This situation changed when the Congressional Reconstruction policies began to be implemented, sidestepping the Presidential Reconstruction Acts and providing an opportune time to those carpetbaggers who were still struggling to find their footing in the South. They gradually became involved in southern politics by joining the Republican Party, which had come into power in most southern states. Eventually, some of them became embroiled in corruption, but many remained involved in the cause of social justice and wanted to create conditions suitable for integrating the Black population into southern society. They were important proponents of republican idealism, particularly in popularising ideas of individualism, liberty, and democracy for all. They had fought and supported the cause to end slavery in the South, which they believed was the cause of the South's economic backwardness, inefficiency, ignorance and poor standard of education, racial intolerance, and acceptance of violence in their everyday existence. They believed that only the Republican Party could reform the South by ensuring loyalty to the Union, freedom for Black people, and tolerance for all ethnic communities.

The carpetbaggers were in power from 1870 to 1876, when they implemented the beginning of a racially integrated public school system. They made concerted efforts to implement and execute, on paper and in spirit, the 14th and 15th Amendments. However, many of them got involved in railroad and road construction activities, where maximum corruption took place, and fingers were pointed at them by their southern White opponents. Despite their best intentions and few incidents of anomalies, the efforts and actions of carpetbaggers were negated by the terror acts of the Ku Klux Klan, which used all possible avenues to prevent giving equal space to free Black people in America.

'Traitors' in the South

'Scalawags' were:

(i) White southern supporters of the Republican Party, former Whigs, and entrepreneurs;
(ii) supporters of the national banking system;

(iii) proponents of high protective tariffs, including small farmers from North Carolina, Georgia, Alabama, and Arkansas; and
(iv) former Unionists who wanted to improve their economic position.

Many of them held key positions in the local and state governments. They were branded as traitors, or 'scalawags', for their support of the Republican Party, as many in the South blamed Republicans for allegedly pushing the South into war and later placing the region under military rule. Scalawags included formerly enslaved people, yeoman farmers, and some planters. Most scalawags were of lower-class status when compared with the politically powerful enslaver planter class. They advocated for the modernisation in the South in the form of better education, infrastructure and transportation.

Scalawags took the political lead after the Civil War, particularly in establishing and administering Republican state governments. They propagated a policy of moderate reform and hoped to get the support of White southern Democrats. This included economic reform and a gradual increase in the political and civil status of the southern Black population. Their withdrawal began when the South began to be afflicted with the economic crisis, White hostility, internal factionalism and terror acts of the Ku Klux Klan. From the 1870s, the scalawags began to shift towards the Redeemers (a loosely structured coalition in the South, part of the Democratic Party, whose aim was to undermine radical Reconstruction and the Republican Party) and later began to support Jim Crow laws that instituted racial segregation.

The Ku Klux Klan

Race violence was embedded in institutions like chattel slavery, and became an entrenched feature of Southern life after 1865. Along with the infamous Ku Klux Klan (KKK) were similar organisations like the Knights of the White Camelia, Grand Cyclopes, Grand Wizards, Grand Dragons, Red Shirts, Knights of the Rising Sun, Order of the Pale Faces, Knights of the Black Crosses, the Southern Cross, White Liners, and the White Brotherhood League. The KKK was a paramilitary organisation whose purpose was to secure the political interests of the Democrats, the southern planter class, and to thereby secure the restoration of White supremacy. It sought to destroy the Republican Party, undermine the Reconstruction state governments, bring Black labour back under White control, and suppress civil rights with a broader aim to restore racial subordination. The organisation systematically focused on specific targets. Their main agenda was to maintain White terror, and according to historian David R. Roediger, the KKK was the 'military arm' of the Democratic Party.[12]

Members of the KKK were not only poor White people, but also young planters and lawyers. They wore a disguise—a long, flowing white robe and hood capped by horns, and sometimes claimed to be the ghosts of Confederate soldiers. This provided, in Du Bois's words, 'glamour to terror'.[13] Its leaders were planters, merchants, lawyers, and even Protestant church ministers.

The KKK destroyed the Republican Party organisation by assassinating leaders, especially politically active African Americans, and by forcing them out of the strife-torn South through violence. These tactics of violence, including shocking incidents of lynching Black people and open threats, were so effective that they led to the closure of public schools, Black churches, and associated institutions that worked for the cause of mitigating racial differences in the South. Between 1869 and 1871, the violence was so extreme that the Black community came together to demand government action to restore constitutional order. Black community members called into question the 'barbarity' that White supremacists—representatives of the so-called 'superior' race—had resorted to in their campaign against Black rights.

The violence unleashed by the KKK made it impossible for 'everyday politics' to function in the South. There was extreme political violence, and no political opposition and opponents were tolerated. Both carpetbaggers and scalawags pointed out that while in the North, politics was focused on finances and individual capacity, in the South, it was focused on life, earnings, livelihood, and questions of human dignity and acceptance in society. However, the terror unleashed by the KKK prevented the implementation of any serious reforms.

Fig. 1.2: 'The Union As It Was', wood engraving by Thomas Nast published in *Harper's Weekly* (1874)

Source: Wikimedia Commons.

When the KKK was dispersed, other violent groups emerged, and these White leagues, like in Louisiana, began to align with Democrats and received their support. Some of them were known as Rifle Clubs or Red Shirts. They unleashed violent race-based campaigns aimed at arousing a sense of 'race solidarity' among White voters and discouraging Black voters. Elections were carried out 'peacefully if we can, forcibly if we must'—a clear indication of the disruption of a fair voting process. In the face of such violence, the last remaining Republican governments were removed from Alabama, Mississippi, South Carolina, and Louisiana between 1874 and 1876.

The Freedmen

For emancipated Black people, the era of Reconstruction was a short and very brief respite from two centuries of oppression, exploitation, and the legacy of slavery that had left them economically impoverished, uneducated, and without any capital or resources. This created significant inequalities, and some argued that in material terms, the status of freedmen scarcely improved, with the exception that they could remove the markers of slavery and regain control over their personal appearance and conduct. Slavery had left behind persistent racism and prejudice against Black people, and White people continued to see them as racially unequal and, therefore, inferior. With Emancipation, a dramatic disparity began to emerge between the wealth holdings of Black and White Americans, ensuring continuing subjugation. Black individuals remained tied to the agricultural sector through a system of tenancy, resulting in the development of three distinct classes of dependency: cash tenants, sharecroppers, and those engaged in tenant farming. This situation arose because Black people lacked ownership of land, agricultural tools, seeds, and capital. Consequently, debt peonage developed, wherein sharecroppers borrowed everything they needed from the landlord and often found themselves unable to repay the debt. The interest rates charged were typically very high, and under the sharecropping system, indebted croppers were required to remain on the landlord's land until all their debts were settled. Many radicals had predicted that disparities would persist after Emancipation, arguing that historical injustices and racial discrimination that would continue to hinder economic independence (in particular housing, labour, and capital) in spite of newfound constitutional freedom.

The Sharecropping and Tenancy Systems

The development of sharecropping and tenancy can be termed a failure of Reconstruction. This system bound both Black and White people in an analogous position that ended only in the 1930s (the period of the **Great Depression** and its aftermath) and due to the impact of the two World Wars. The **crop-lien system** emerged after the Civil War, particularly in the context of cotton cultivation. In this system, rural merchants provided credit to tenants and sharecroppers before the planting season. In return, the creditor held the agricultural produce in lien, meaning that the eventual harvest was given to the lender to repay the debt, and the lender then sold the crop to wholesalers.

This system led to soil depletion, land erosion, and agricultural backwardness. Tenant farmers got trapped in the system of debt peonage. Since the landowner maintained the accounts, and as the sharecroppers were illiterate, the landowner would inflate indebtedness to keep Black workers tied down in this new form of labour control to work as agricultural labourers. Most Black women were employed as house servants. The planter paid the sharecropper only a portion of the crop, which typically accounted for half the total harvest at the end of the year. The distribution of profits depended on whether sharecroppers provided their own tools, livestock, and seeds, or if the landowners provided them. The system trapped sharecroppers in a vicious cycle of credit financing and debt burden. It was only marginally better than the gang-based enslavement system, as it did not force children or women to perform hard labour, and the landowner could not inflict harsh punishments or inhumane forms of supervision. However, this gave the White population a monopoly over better-paying jobs. Tenants typically had livestock and agricultural tools but no land, so they rented the land from the planter and gave him a share of the crop, usually a fourth of the total production.

In both systems, the planters provided food, clothing, and other essentials to sharecroppers and tenants until the crop was harvested. The system had inherent contradictions, as the planters sought to maintain continued control over formerly enslaved labourers. For the freedmen, the system was a continuation of slavery, with no avenue for economic freedom. White people were able to monopolise better-paying work through these systems. This period saw the beginning of the **Populist Movement** that attempted to unite White and Black people, but the White landowners' policy of divide and conquer worked to bring to an end the era of Reconstruction.

Joel Williamson, in his book *After Slavery*, showed how freedmen in South Carolina assisted in the development of the sharecropping system, and simultaneously created Black-led institutions.[14] Leon F. Litwack's *Been in the Storm for So Long* adds to this analysis, reflecting on modes of resistance against social inequality and attempts by the emancipated to define their freedom at the level of family, community, and later in the political arena.[15] In *Rehearsal for Reconstruction*, Willie Lee Rose demonstrated that free Black people were more interested in the development of independent family farms, so that they could reunite their family and community and secure dignity with better conditions for earning a living.[16] Lawrence Powell's *New Masters* emphasised that while northerners wanted Black people to become wage-earners, the freed people wanted to secure farmland to become economically independent. James Roark, in *Masters without Slaves*, presented the 'dilemma' of southern planters as they sought new ways to extract labour when the free Black people began to contest racial control and power.[17] Roger Ransom and Richard Sutch's *One Kind of Freedom* narrates how the withdrawal of Black labour, particularly that of women and children, created a labour and economic crisis.[18] The purported solution, for the White elite, was discovered in the sharecropping system.

In recent research that also takes new sources into account, historians now believe that before sharecropping, there was a period of experimentation with several payment and labour systems. For example, labour squads were created that consisted of 2–10 labourers, and each squad was given a specific task. The planter shared the proceeds of the harvests with the workers. In *Good and Faithful Labour*, Ronald Davis asserts that freedmen created sharecropping and were only reluctantly accepted by the planters as no alternative could be found.[19] In a different line of interpretation, economic historian Gerald Jayne, in *Branches without Roots*, argued that sharecropping was insisted on by the planters and eventually developed 10 years after the Civil War, while labourers preferred short-term wage contracts that were not acceptable to the planters.[20] According to Jayne, sharecropping evolved from the **squad system**, which later came to be organised in family-based units. This system worked as long as the Republican Party controlled the southern state legislatures, labour had control over the share, and cotton prices were high. It collapsed when its supporting factors began to decline. Therefore, sharecropping developed due to efforts made by the planters to share their economic losses with their tenants, especially when cotton prices began to fall in the world markets.

Transformations in the southern economy and labour relations continued into the twentieth century. The **Great Migration**, sometimes known as the **Great Northward Migration** or the **Black Migration**, saw approximately 6 million Black people migrate from the rural South between 1910 and 1970. This meant that agriculture eventually faced a shortage of labourers, which culminated in long work hours on the plantations, a decline in total agricultural production, and a decrease in US cotton prices, which plummeted as the global demand for Egyptian and Indian cotton increased. These factors made the southern economy backward in nature.

Impact of Freedom and Reconstruction on Black Americans: The Long View

Immediately after the Civil War, Black people began reconstructing their families. This process was mixed, involving both conflict and harmony, as many families had become too disjointed due to circumstances to be successfully reunited. However, freedom proved to be limited and sporadic. For this reason, after 1877, which marked the end of the Reconstruction era, Black communities began to educate themselves and build independent institutions and movements, which would eventually culminate in the beginning of the **Civil Rights Movement**.

Economically, African Americans remained at the bottom of the socio-economic ladder, and the vast majority remained illiterate through this period. Emancipation assisted in their movement from the South to the Northeast and Northwest, where there was a demand for labour and marginally better wages, particularly in the urban centres. The period witnessed the rise of Black churches like the Negro Baptist Church, along with Presbyterian and Methodist churches that provided close communion and relief, and raised funds for schools for Black children. These congregations also allowed for the emergence of Black ministers, some of whom later became leaders of the African American movement. Gradually, such religious institutions became a centre of support for Republican policies. They aimed to empower the Reconstruction process by uniting three crucial elements of upliftment—education, political participation, and fostering a community and social life. Most Black Americans were part of Protestant Churches, with Catholic denominations in a few places like Maryland and New Orleans.

The rise of Black-led educational and technical education institutions from 1866 to 1867 like the Hampton Institute furthered the cause of education. Unfortunately, higher educational institutions largely remained inaccessible for the rural Black population. In their pursuit of modern education, Black Americans had to continuously negotiate a delicate balance between the desire to become economically independent, and to remove the stereotyped images of Black people—and anti-Black bias in general—from the minds of people.[21] The Freedmen's Bureau and the American Missionary Association, in a joint and concerted effort, established Fisk University in Nashville, Tennessee (1865); Howard University in Washington DC (1867); Atlanta University in Atlanta, Georgia (1867); St. Augustine's College in Raleigh, North Carolina (1867) and Hampton Institute in Hampton, Virginia (1868) with the result that by 1900, the illiteracy rate had come down to 44.5 per cent.[22]

Another hurdle encountered by the Black community in their everyday life was the **policy of racial segregation,** practised in public transport, accommodation, and public spaces, which represented a rejection of demands for racial integration and equality. Although segregation was prohibited by the **Civil Rights Act of 1875**, the provisions of the Act remained confined to paper. Proposals to confiscate or redistribute Confederate property failed in Congress and the southern state legislatures. **In 1866, the Southern Homestead Act** provided 44 million acres of land with inferior soil to the Black and 'loyal' White populations. An inability to buy land, lack of capital resources, and constraints on mobility meant that the White landowner maintained a hold over Black workers. The Freedmen's Bureau Act of 1865 had made a provision to provide a land redistribution process, under which free Black people would acquire 40-acre plots from lands left empty by, or confiscated from, ex-Confederate officials. However, under President Johnson's plan, the land was returned to the ex-Confederates, with the result that till 1910, about two-thirds of the Black population remained landless, indicating the state's refusal to give them equal economic or social status.

The South also practised a new system of **convict leasing**. Under this system, southern employers were given the right to rent out Black prisoners and use their labour in various ways, and in due course, these practices culminated in a new and oppressive labour system.

In the southern states, various methods were adopted based on disenfranchisement, segregation, and physical brutality to maintain White supremacy. All three aspects were carried out legally and legislatively in the period from 1890 to 1908, through successive judgements by the Supreme Court and the states, with the clear motive of preventing Black citizens from voting. These methods were cleverly crafted: **poll taxes** were applied, and payment was made compulsory for exercising the right to vote. This law was separate from another restriction: Black men were required to show that they had been paying taxes every year after the age of 21. Another method was to restrict membership into political parties, effectively turning them into private clubs and restricting the entry of Black people into the political mainstream in the South. Further, only Black men who could pass **literacy tests** that involved reading and comprehension would be eligible to vote. Since such a provision would also disenfranchise poor White men, a '**grandfather's clause**' was inserted to the effect that if a man's grandfather had been on the electoral roll, he would be exempt from the literacy test. Since voting rights were conferred on Black people only after the Civil War, this effectively meant that the grandfather clause exemption could only be availed by White men. Multiple state legislatures implemented Jim Crow laws that instituted racial segregation in railway coaches, streetcars, and all public spaces and accommodations, including libraries, colleges, parks, and swimming pools. Black schools operated for shorter hours, staffed by less qualified and underpaid teachers. Localities with a majority Black population were deliberately neglected, with no sewage, sanitation, water, or street systems. If all these discriminatory practices failed to deter Black Americans, White supremacist groups fell to more brazen tactics. Black people were targeted in increasingly prevalent cases of lynching, ostensibly triggered by perceived infractions like robbery or murder accusations, or even simply for 'answering back' or 'insubordination'. Black communities had to organise their anti-lynching campaigns to counter social repression, control, and violence.

In the ***Plessy v. Ferguson* case**, the provision of 'separate but equal' status was mandated by the Supreme Court, and the South took advantage of this ruling by adopting the policy of 'separate' but wholly ignoring the requirement of 'equal' status. Black people had to follow a rigid code of social conduct to avoid persecution, resulting in the Great Migration, as discussed earlier. However, migration did not spell an end to racism by any means, and in their new locales they came into competition with White workers. However, the actions and collective organising of Black people saw the rise of African American leaders and movements. Their combined efforts and initiatives spurred the growth of colleges, technical institutes, organisations, schools, and businesses specifically for Black Americans, and also encouraged the entry of Black women in the public space.

South Carolina, Mississippi, Alabama, and Louisiana had the largest Black populations, and this demographic advantage allowed for effective lobbying on the issues of land, education, civil rights, and political equality. One out of every five posts in these states was held by a Black representative, and they were represented in state legislatures as well. These leaders and officials comprised the new Black elite, but very few could secure higher offices like governorship. When the Republican Party came to power in the southern states, in 1868, they drew up a new constitution for each state as required by the Reconstruction Act. These constitutions were liberal and democratic in character, instituted checks to the power of the privileged, and increased political participation. Additionally, they provided government services previously lacking in the southern states. These state governments abolished the property qualification for office-bearers, introduced elections for a number of posts, brought in suffrage for adult men regardless of race or property, and initiated programmes of public works to improve the infrastructure of the war-ravaged South (development and construction of roads, bridges and buildings, along with opening up of institutions for orphans, those with severe psychological impairment, and persons with disabilities). The state bureaucracies were expanded and salaries improved, and enlistment within the state military opened up across race lines. To fund the government's public works, taxes on luxury sales, occupation taxes, and property taxes were imposed.

Fig. 1.3: First senators and representatives of colour, 41st and 42nd Congress of the USA (1872)
Source: Wikimedia Commons.

The government saw reason to create and fund institutions and became more active than ever before. The Republicans promoted three initiatives: (*i*) creating a viable school system, (*ii*) protecting the civil rights system, and (*iii*) developing the region's railroad system. W. E. B. Du Bois, in his work *Black Reconstruction*, emphasised that the charges of extreme corruption against the southern Republicans were driven by a covert agenda not to provide any power to free Black people, which led to the eventual failure of the Reconstruction and a failure to establish a democratic tradition in the South. He stated that during this long period of segregation, most of the Black populace lived 'behind the veil', invisible to their White counterparts except in stereotypical images.

By 1868, the South began to resent increased taxes, and the Democratic Party began to win state legislative seats. As we have noted, the reign of terror unleashed by the KKK led to the decline in the prominence of the carpetbaggers and scalawags, and concerted efforts were made to prevent Black people from voting. The federal government did pass the **Enforcement Law in 1870** to tackle this growing problem but could not forestall White segregationist policy and increasing racism. At the same time, in other regions of the US, this period of economic progress, industrial expansion, and unchecked speculation in particulat, led to the 1873 economic depression.

From 1890 to 1910, about 90 per cent of a total 9.8 million African Americans lived in the South, and only 25 per cent lived in cities with a population of 2,500 or greater.[23] Floods, crop destruction by boll weevils, and a demand for workers in war-related industries led to the migration of hundreds of thousands of African Americans to urban areas in the South as well as to cities of the North from 1910–1930. During World War I, the federal government established the Division of Negro Economics within the US Department of Labour to reduce tensions amid entrenched White workers and incoming Black workers in the northern factories. This became a critical concern after race riots in Chicago, Omaha, and Washington DC in the summer of 1919.

Northward migration led to the redefinition of African American identity, manifesting most clearly in the cultural movement that came to be termed the '**Harlem Renaissance**', and the associated concept of the 'New Negro'. The African American scholar Alain Locke, referring to the period from 1886 to 1954, declared that this redefined identity reflected a psychological transformation such that 'the mind' of the Black individual 'seems suddenly to have slipped from under the tyranny of social intimidation and to be shaking off the psychology of imitation and implied inferiority'.[24]

Historiography of the Reconstruction Period

Reconstruction brought about significant shifts and transformations in the southern states that had seceded from the Union, which had a major impact on race dynamics in the region. Reconstruction reunited the North and the South and marked the rise of a new southern world that replaced both the enslaved and their enslavers with landlords, merchants, and sharecroppers. With rapid industrialisation and urbanisation processes setting in around this time, it also marked the end of 'Lincoln's America'. Many of these transformations remained incomplete. Jeffrey R. Hummel has stated that Reconstruction led to the rise of a repressive 'leviathan' state in the persistently racist and conservative southern region, leaving African Americans adrift within a veritable desert with no avenue for social, economic, or political independence and support on the horizon.[25]

The post-Civil War period was, therefore, an era of strife in the political and social life of the southern states and the entire nation in general. The battle began with radical Republicans rejecting the efforts made by President Johnson, whose sole aim was to reintegrate the southern states without providing any rights, recognition, or economic independence to the formerly enslaved. The earliest scholarship on this era, in fact, was critical of the radical programme. They termed the dominance of radical Republicans as a superimposition of 'Black supremacy and power' over the southern White population. This, in their opinion, was an 'extreme measure' that led to an era of an 'orgy of corruption' and 'misgovernance' initiated by the carpetbaggers, scalawags and freedmen, resulting in 'needless suffering'. For early scholars, this was a 'tragic era' that culminated in the rise of secret terror organisations run by White supremacists focusing on their agenda to sabotage attempts at racial equality and to overthrow coloured 'corrupt' governments of the South.

As we shall see, the idea of the Reconstruction as a tragic period persisted in historical scholarship and cut across ideological lines. The traditionalist line of interpretation remained influential for many decades, reflecting a racist mentality that was slow to change. Continued racism, albeit in a different form, led to the eventual resurgence of Democratic governments in the South at the end of the Reconstruction era.

This idea of the Reconstruction as a tragic era was first discussed by William A. Dunning,[26] who used this characterisation for the broader period from 1890 to 1930 based on two assumptions. *First*, he felt that the North did not want 'revenge' on its erstwhile southern foes as its main aim was to restore the Union. *Second*, he assumed that freedmen should bear the responsibility for bringing the southern White people onboard for reform. According to Dunning, this period represented the struggle between the forces of 'good' and 'evil'. Good elements were represented by Democrats, and sympathisers like moderate Republicans (including, importantly, President Johnson), and caught in the middle were Black people. The evil elements were embodied in the radical Republicans, whose 'corrupt practices' and Reconstruction policies were blamed for initiating a destructive phase in American history, with the result that by 1876, all revolutionary governments were overthrown in the South. The **Dunning School** believed that racial integration was difficult to achieve due to entrenched notions of racial hierarchy and the desire of White elites to regain their former status in southern society.

This view carried significant weight in the study of the post-Civil War Reconstruction period. The Dunning School propagated the idea that the South had accepted their military defeat 'with grace' and were willing to pledge their loyalty to the Union for the reunification process, but that their surrender was met with unreasonable demands. Being asked to hand over the reins of government to new social groups in the South who were inept and corrupt administrators and whose policies led to massive government debt turned the governance system of the South into a 'destructive engine'. In a similar vein, Albert Moore in 1942 argued that the North had made a concerted effort to reshape the South in its own image, leaving behind a 'dark legacy' marked by property confiscation of Confederate officials, mental agony to southerners, and imposition of military rule.[27] This low tide stemmed only when the southern White populations managed to consolidate their power and overthrow 'radical' rule to restore 'normalcy'. The bitter legacy, however, reinforced racial tensions and conflicts.

Progressive historians highlighted the changes and conflicts witnessed during this period. In their opinion, the central conflict was between the forces of the North and the South, the White and (newly emancipated) Black population, and between two competing economies of industrial capitalism and agrarianism, in which the former emerged triumphant. The growth and expansion of the industrial economy marked the end of the Reconstruction era.

Historians have now categorised the Reconstruction period into two broad phases. The 'First Reconstruction' was from 1865 to 1877, and the 'Second Reconstruction' was ushered in during the period of the Civil Rights Movement, when historians began a fresh investigation to understand the institution of slavery and its impact from a new and different perspective. This resulted in the development of the **Revisionist School** of historians in the 1960s, which completely repudiated all the earlier notions about Reconstruction. Revisionist scholars were critical of the Dunning School. This debate was initiated by Francis B. Simkins, who termed it a 'constructive' era, but one that failed to provide economic foundations for African Americans to rebuild their lives.[28]

Other historians began to look at this period as a representation of 'national problems' and not sectional problems, in which radical Reconstructionists attempted to form more democratic governments based on racial equality and opportunities for economic growth and development. However, the efforts failed due to resistance in the face of anti-racist reforms. The carpetbaggers and scalawags were seen to play a role in attempts to broaden the state structure and bring about social and economic equality in the southern states. In their opinion, the new southern governments were not corrupt, as projected by other schools of thought, nor did their governance lead to financial bankruptcy and corruption, as alleged by many scholars. They emphasised the question of race, in which the Democrats were not only conservative but rather, an explicitly White supremacist party. In contrast, the Republicans were modern in their outlook, and therefore they secured the support of African American voters. However, when too many impediments were laid on the path of reform, they gave up all their efforts. The ideology of both political parties shifted back to conservatism, and after 1877, the focus of both parties went into economic expansion and growth, with little regard for the issue of race.

Neo-Revisionist scholars have emphasised the 'moral basis' of Reconstruction. They presented the era as representative of moral and ideological elements based on anti-slavery zeal and ideals of equality, natural rights, and democracy. On the other hand, historian Kenneth M. Stampp[29] termed the era 'tragic' as the goals of the Reconstruction could not be achieved. Even the idea of developing an inclusive legislature remained unrealised in the South, and reflected an extremely limited sense of democratic or egalitarian norms. According to **Leftist historians** like Staughton Lynd,[30] freedmen were not given land, and hence could not become economically independent and politically secure. In contrast to these readings, Keith I. Polakoff saw the emergence of decentralised power structures in this period.[31] Other historians looked into the separation of powers, coercion of political action, and inability of political parties to bring about Reconstruction, which were seen to be significant failures.

The era and policies of Andrew Johnson were depicted as both a reflection of racism at the individual and institutional levels, and as a sign of Johnson's personal stubbornness, due to which he was caught in repeated confrontations with Congress. It was this tussle that sparked the rise of the radical Republicans. In this new interpretation, extreme elements were no longer portrayed as vengeful but as 'visionary', imbued with reformist energy that they wanted to introduce into federal politics. Increased prominence was accorded to the radical leaders Charles Sumner and Thaddeus Stevens, both of whom consistently supported full civic and political rights for African Americans. Both leaders took a principled stand during the Reconstruction process, as validated in the constitutional provisions incorporated through the 13th, 14th and 15th Amendments. Most Republicans actively supported granting civil rights to all Americans, including African Americans, and it was this commitment that led to conflict between them and President Andrew Johnson. The prevailing opinion among Neo-Revisionsts about 'Black Reconstruction' under the Radical Republicans was that it was a time of 'spectacular progress' that witnessed the rebuilding of war-shattered public buildings, new public schools, and the beginning of new interracial politics. This revisionist line of thought presented the Reconstruction era as a fight between villains and heroes.

The Neo-Revisionist School attempted to present a more accurate picture of this period wherein their central focus was on the newly emancipated population, who did gain a measure of political power, despite limitations. They have also rejected the notion of a 'Black supremacy' and tie such interpretations to a conservative thought process. These scholars have also reassessed the role of carpetbaggers, who were no longer simply vagabond adventurers, but rather, now understood to be former Union soldiers looking to make their fortune in the war-torn South. Scalawags were presented as 'Old Line' Whigs and poor White farmers who were already opposed to both the institution of slavery and the enslavers. Both groups contributed to establishing a democratic tradition in the South. Seeking to correct the historical biases of White historians, the KKK was portrayed by Neo-Revisionists as a racist White terrorist organisation that deployed undemocratic and frequently violent methods to prevent Black people from exercising their hard-won rights and working to secure a sense of dignity in southern society. Therefore, in this new line of interpretation, the source of the tragedy was that the Reconstruction programme fell short of practical application of the constitutional, politico-economic rights of African Americans. The concerted efforts of former enslavers and the racist attitude of southern White society in general erected social and institutional barriers that proved difficult to scale.

In another significant historiographical shift, this period began to be presented as an era of social and political revolution. According to Eric Foner,[32] it ushered in new systems of labour. As slavery and associated institutions were brought to an end, the US entered a period of exploration in terms of new government policies, and racial and political dynamics. The Emancipation Proclamation brought an end to centuries of slavery and, in one stroke, established that Black and White citizens were equal, at least in constitutional terms. Eric Foner analysed the process of the USA's 'adjustment' to Emancipation within the overall context of external and internal changes that, according to him, made Reconstruction a 'unique' national experience. As previously mentioned, some of the new labour systems were a result of attempts by former enslavers to retain control over, and access to, Black labour. They were aided in this process by President Johnson's vagrancy laws as well as the Black Codes enacted by various state and local governments. African Americans in the South opposed these systems, marking the beginning of a conflict that impacted the South's economy, politics, and race relations. In the cotton plantations, Black families worked on the planter's land and divided crops with the planter at the end of each cultivation season. In the rice-growing region, Black agricultural labourers occupied lands in 1865 and became independent farmers. In the sugar cultivating regions, a 'gang labour' system emerged that survived even after the end of slavery.

In a new light of interpretation, historians like Leon F. Litwack[33] analysed this period from the perspective of emancipated Black people and new forms of sociality that developed as a result of their new-found freedom. Litwack placed particular emphasis on the newly refurbished history of Black churches, which cut themselves loose from the control of White religion and in the process established distinct religious traditions as well as institutions that could assist African Americans in becoming socially and culturally independent. The Freedmen's Bureau played a vital role in this by reuniting family members despite difficulties and financial costs. Litwack also details how the shift in Black women's labour, from formal work to domestic work and childcare resulted in a massive labour shortage in the South. This was a protective measure to prevent White landowners from forcing their children to work in the fields. Black conventions recorded high rates of participation in all the southern states—these were organised to help secure political rights and civic equality. The Reconstruction era was, thus, a 'dramatic experiment'.

According to Dan T. Carter, the central logic of the presidential plan for Reconstruction was to control the Black labour force.[34] This was augmented by the 'Black Codes'. This created a conflict between planters, who sought to rein in the emancipated workers, and Black workers, who were actively working to loosen that control. The result of this tug-of-war was a new system of labour in the South known as sharecropping, which ostensibly offered some freedom. In reality, it did not permit Black people to become independent producers since the credit system was still controlled by White people. Immediately after the Civil War, there was a sharp decline in the prices of crops both within and outside the US, which further impeded the pursuit of economic independence. In this period, planters could no longer control Black labour, keep them tied to the land, or obstruct their mobility, and eventually many Black southerners moved away during the Great Migration. It is this aspect that completely altered labour relations in the South.

The outcome of the Civil War drastically altered the lives of the enslavers and even the common (or 'yeoman') peasantry that had never possessed enslaved people. In the postwar period, more and more White farmers were getting sucked into a debt cycle as they borrowed money for seeds, tools, and animals that forced them to shift to cotton cultivation for better returns, and this further trapped them in a cycle of debt and poverty due to overproduction of cotton, fall in demand, and decline in selling price.

'New Historians' began to investigate changes brought in by the Republican governments in the South that gave the sharecroppers the first claim on the crop produced. Historians also started to investigate whether the radical Republicans' effort to expand the railway brought about any significant economic change in the South. A study by Mark W. Summers showed that railway aid provided by the federal government did not bring about any economic gain.[35] On the contrary, it resulted in worsening the situation of yeomen farmers due to an increase in taxes, which led to the beginning of the decline in support of the Republican Party amongst southern White voters. It also resulted in the rise of massive scandals of corruption and misappropriation of funds that further tarnished the image of the Reconstruction governments in the South.[36]

From the perspective of emancipated Black people, the period of Reconstruction was the first opportunity they got to participate in civic affairs and operate within the context of governments that were working for their interests. However, in his analysis of Black politics in South Carolina, Thomas Halt showed how even Black leaders who began to emerge at this juncture failed to provide avenues that could eliminate the economic barriers facing African

Americans. Halt observed that most Black politicians belonged to relatively elite classes and had a conservative economic outlook. Further, the prevalence of traditionalist and racist attitudes among the southern White population prevented the implementation of measures to promote economic independence and equality and end racial oppression. At the local levels, freedmen, particularly Church ministers and skilled Black artisans did attempt to foster egalitarianism: for instance, they would lobby for equality of law when participating in jury trials, provide relief to impoverished Black families, and open schools focused on Black education. However, these local officials and community leaders were targeted by the KKK and other White supremacist organisations. Scholars have also worked on a neglected aspect: How the Civil Rights Law of 1866 and the 14th Constitutional Amendment transformed the nature of federal–state relations. These provisions gave the federal government power to prevent civil rights violations by the southern state governments.[37] Earlier, the state governments looked after their citizens and safeguarded their rights. With the coming of the 15th Constitutional Amendment, states were also barred from rescinding the right to vote on grounds of race.

Along with the Enforcement Acts of 1870–1871, the federal government secured more powers to safeguard against racial violence and secure full civil and political rights. When the racist violence and brutality of supremacist organisations increased in spite of these laws, the federal government was forced to withdraw from its intended goals and focus on providing rightful dignity and space to African Americans. The resurgence of racist discourses in response to African American assertion also led to revisionist narratives—the Civil War acquired a new meaning for the conservative White population. It began to be termed a conflict within the 'family', fought for noble reasons. It ended in the reunification of the Union and resulted in the abolishment of slavery, thereby creating conditions and a foundation to build a new nation.

By the early 1870s, the governments formed under the provisions of the Reconstruction Acts were faced with such immense opposition and hostility from the former Confederate officials that it became untenable for them to stay in power. After the hotly-contested presidential elections of 1876, the federal government, in a significant electoral compromise, withdrew its political support to Reconstruction efforts and its troops from the South, bringing the Reconstruction experiment to an early end. Ultimately, the Republican governments at the centre and in the states failed to implement the 14th and 15th Amendments, which provided national citizenship and equality before the law and protected suffrage for Black men. The impunity of supremacist and racist organisations on the ground, and later the abandonment by the federal government of any will to safeguard civil rights in the South, spelt an end to state-led efforts at bringing about racial equality. From this perspective, in the words of African American leader W. E. B. Du Bois, the Reconstruction era was 'a splendid failure'.

Conclusion

Reconstruction, as a period of wide-ranging reform, brought with it significant changes and turbulence, particularly in terms of the efforts undertaken to integrate African Americans into the political system. This resulted in the development of a substantial social and political programme, along with the promotion of economic development, to repair the damages of the Civil War, move away from enslavement, and, through the introduction of modern technology, develop railroads for regional growth.[38] All efforts to free the southern region after two centuries of dependence on the institution of slavery failed, and the term 'reconstruction' gave way to the rise of 'progressive reforms' based on 'scientific' and 'rational' methods. It was a new form of social politics to cope with the impact of modern industrial life in American society.[39]

The use of slave labour in the colonial era, as a proposed solution to labour shortages, evolved over the course of two centuries into a foundation of life that birthed a unique economic and social system. The structure of the settler colonial state was a paradox as the USA was the 'land of the free', and yet slavery was in itself a barbaric institution based on injustice, inhumanity, brutality, and oppression. African Americans resisted enslavement throughout its history, and in the Reconstruction era there was finally a space to build one's own communities, mobilise for full citizenship rights, and to lead one's people out of lifelong bondage.

Notes

1. Eric Foner, *Forever Free: The Story of Emancipation and Reconstruction* (New York, 2005), p. 107.
2. According to Bruce Levine, the Emancipation Proclamation and the 13th Amendment brought about a seismic shift in southern life. Prior to this, southern society, which was built on human bondage, had come to control national wealth, the American economy, and political power at all levels. See Bruce Levine, *The Fall of the House of Dixie: The Civil War and the Social Revolution That Transformed the South* (New York, 2013), p. 439.
3. Levine, *The Fall of the House of Dixie*, p. 105.
4. See Clarence L. Mohr, *On the Threshold of Freedom: Masters and Slaves in Civil War Georgia* (Athens, Georgia, 1986); and C. Peter Ripley, *Slaves and Freedmen in Civil War Louisiana* (Baton Rouge, 1976).
5. Eric Foner, *Reconstruction: America's Unfinished Revolution, 1863–1877* (New York, 1988).
6. Rayford W. Logan, *The Betrayal of the Negro: From Rutherford B. Hayes to Woodrow Wilson*, 2nd ed. (New York, 1967).
7. Herbert G. Gutman, *The Black Family in Slavery and Freedom, 1750–1925* (New York, 1976).
8. The Civil Rights Act of 1866 declared that all persons born in the US (except Indigenous people) are American citizens with equal rights. Foner, *Forever Free*, p. 115.
9. This amendment, a 'moderate measure', was pivotal in American history. One scholar concludes that it established a 'perfect republic', rising from the ashes of slavery that had deeply affected American institutions built on the foundation of 'inequality of rights'. Foner, *Forever Free*, p. 118.
10. This term is generally used to refer to a series of Acts passed in quick succession: the Military Reconstruction Act, as well as supplementary Acts that laid down mechanisms for its implementation.
11. This amendment transformed the American Constitution into an instrument through which minorities could demand freedom and protection against the excesses of state power. Ibid., p.122.
12. David R. Roediger, *Seizing Freedom: Slave Emancipation and Liberty for All* (London and New York, 1994), pp. 175–177.
13. W. E. B. Du Bois, 'The Shape of Fear', *North Atlantic Review* 223 (831), 1926, pp. 291–304.
14. Joel Williamson, *After Slavery: The Negro in South Carolina during Reconstruction, 1861–1877* (Chapel Hill, 1965).

15. Leon F. Litwack, *Been in the Storm for So Long: The Aftermath of Slavery* (New York, 1979).
16. Willie Lee Rose, *Rehearsal for Reconstruction: The Port Royal Experiment* (New York, 1976).
17. James L. Roark, *Masters without Slaves: Southern Planters in the Civil War and Reconstruction* (Stanford. 1973).
18. Roger L. Ransom and Richard Sutch, *One Kind of Freedom: The Economic Consequences of Emancipation*, reprint ed. (New York, 2001).
19. Ronald L. F. Davis, *Good and Faithful Labour: From Slavery to Sharecropping in the Natchez District, 1860–1890* (Westport, 1982).
20. Gerald Jayne, *Branches without Roots: Genesis of the Black Working Class in the American South, 1862–1882* (New York. 1986).
21. Michael David Cohen, *Reconstructing the Campus: Higher Education and the American Civil War* (Charlottesville, 2012).
22. See the National Assessment of Adult Literacy (NAAL), a nationally representative and continuing assessment of English language literary skills of American adults. See nces.ed.gov (accessed October 2025).
23. See https://www.encyclopedia.com/history/united-states-and-canada/us-history/african-americans (accessed October 2025).
24. Alain Locke, *The New Negro: An Interpretation* (New York, 1925), p. 6.
25. Jeffrey R. Hummel, *Emancipating Slaves, Enslaving Free Men: A History of the American Civil War* (Chicago, 1996).
26. William A. Dunning, *Essays on the Civil War and Reconstruction and Related Topics*, 2nd ed. (Ann Arbor, Michigan, 1904).
27. Albert Moore. 'One Hundred Years of Reconstruction of the South', *Journal of Southern History* 9 (May 1943), pp. 153–165.
28. Francis B. Simkins, *South Carolina during Reconstruction* (Chapel Hill, 1932).
29. Kenneth M. Stampp, *The Era of Reconstruction: 1865–1977* (New York. 1965).
30. Staughton Lynd, ed., *Reconstruction* (New York, 1967).
31. Keith I. Polakoff, *The Politics of Inertia: The Election of 1876 and the End of Reconstruction* (Baton Rouge, 1973).
32. Foner, *Reconstruction: America's Unfinished Revolution*.
33. Litwack, *Been in the Storm For So Long*.
34. Dan T. Carter, *When the War was Over: The Failure of Self-Reconstruction in the South, 1865–1867* (Baton Rouge, 1985).
35. Mark W. Summers, *Railroads, Reconstruction, and the Gospel of the Radical Republicans, 1865–1877* (New Jersey, 1984).
36. Eric Foner, *Give Me Liberty! An American History*, 3rd ed. (New York, 2011), p. 100.
37. Ibid., p. 101.
38. Foner, *Reconstruction: America's Unfinished Revolution*.
39. Menand Louis, *The Metaphysical Club* (New York, 2001), pp. 372–375.

Chapter 2

The Rise of Big Business Corporations

In the aftermath of the Civil War, until the beginning of World War I, America saw extraordinary economic transformations and remarkable self-sufficiency. In Europe and North America, the period from 1870 to 1914 is generally classified as the **Second Industrial Revolution**, or the **Technological Revolution**—a period marked by scientific advancements and technical innovation that led to unprecedented advancements in manufacture, infrastructure, and industrial output. Apart from this, several factors particular to the US contributed to its phenomenal economic growth: lessons learnt from the War of 1812,[1] the rise of textile mills, gradual adoption of European factory technology, demands of the Civil War, availability of natural resources, and an ever-expanding workforce. Markets for manufactured goods expanded steadily due to the easy availability of capital for investment in industrial corporations. This was facilitated by a new cultural ethos in America, which encouraged the embrace of technological innovation and the inculcation of an '**entrepreneurial spirit**'. This new ethos prioritised rapidly accepting and applying new technologies for business gains, without delving into either legal or ethical aspects of the manner in which new businesses were being conducted.[2] The principle of *laissez faire*, which emphasised free market competition with little or no state intervention, was an influential aspect of this policy.

However, *laissez faire* notwithstanding, historians emphasise the role of federal assistance in facilitating this rapidly changing work and business culture. The Republican Party, which remained the ruling party for successive terms after the Civil War, introduced the **National Banking Acts** (of particular note are the ones passed in 1863 and 1864) and legal systems that encouraged the growth and expansion of commercial, industrial, and agricultural economies without any hindrances. To provide further impetus to **American capitalism**, the federal government used the military to forcibly remove Indigenous peoples and open up their sacred lands in the West. For greater economic integration of the country, railroad companies were given federal subsidies to expand railway lines and stimulate internal markets. A **protectionist policy** was adopted under which high tariffs were imposed to prevent the entry of European goods.[3] During the Civil War, the demand for arms, ammunition, and woollen clothing became a significant stimulus that forced the introduction of new technologies and scientific methods to the industry, leading to the rise of big businesses in America.[4] These businesses created new employment avenues, thus fuelling internal migration from rural to urban regions and attracting immigrants from different parts of the world, and especially from Europe, to America. Industrial progress in America had raced so far ahead by 1913 that it had left behind France, Britain, and Germany in industrial manufacturing.[5]

The rise of big business organisations and monopolies resulted from **economic rationalism** and is a testament to strategic thinking, innovative approaches, and the inventive and resourceful nature of the capitalist manufacturing classes, along with the rise of research labs (both government and university facilities, and private labs developed by corporations).[6] Westward expansion provided both land and resources to sustain a burgeoning industrial capitalism that primarily aimed to secure ever-growing profits. This propelled capitalists to seek new internal and external markets, and in doing so, they showcased remarkable prescience and a sophisticated understanding of the global economy.

The economy grew in scale and complexity. The rise of industrial cities like New York, Philadelphia, Cincinnati, Cleveland, Indianapolis, Atlanta, Kansas City, Dallas, Chicago, and the region around the Great Lakes marked another significant shift brought in by big businesses.[7] However, increasing competition created tensions within the capitalist economy and eventually gave way to an **oligopoly** in many important sectors. Conversely, another significant feature of the post-1860s period was the emergence of labour unions, whose mobilisation aimed to secure better wages, fixed working hours, and better work environments, thereby coming into conflict with profit-driven industrialists. The **'scientific management' system of labour** was developed by Frederick Winslow Taylor, who introduced labour efficiency in the work process and allowed business organisations to expand their reach in the global markets. All of these factors fuelled unprecedented economic growth, leading to the emergence of **American imperialism** in the last decades of the 1890s.[8]

Expansion of the rail network from 1850–1870 assisted in the rise of national markets for agricultural and manufactured goods. The railroad required significant capital investment and had substantial

FIG. 2.1: The cover of a train timetable advertising the Union and Central Pacific Railroad Line (1881)

Source: Wikimedia Commons.

operative costs. Moreover, the smooth operation of this system required not only a bureaucratic management system, but also the employment of highly specialised kinds of workers. The application of new business methods, specifically the creation of monopolistic companies to control fares and maximise revenue generation, made this an extremely lucrative sector. By 1860, railroad companies had overtaken blacksmiths as the primary market for iron products and generated the greatest demand for heavy engineering industries. The first **transcontinental railroad** began operations in 1869, reducing travel times from months to days. By the end of the nineteenth century, the US had the largest rail network anywhere in the world. The railways fuelled the emergence of new urban centres, and this rapid urban expansion, in turn, intensified the demand for products like cotton and food materials. Railways thus opened up new internal markets.

Consolidation of Businesses

The rise of big business corporations brought economic prosperity and had a positive impact on American society. The increase in population led to the development of new markets, and this created the demand necessary for the beginning of production, distribution, and marketing of goods at a mass scale, a production model made possible by large corporations.[9] However, the continuous application of new technologies, combined with increasing competition among business firms, brought down the prices of manufactured goods. This necessitated eliminating competitors from the market, and long-term business survival became possible only by establishing substantial financial resources, instituting management systems and, more significantly, securing monopolies to capture the market. These monopolies emerged in the form of corporate 'trusts', holding companies, mergers, and cartels. Another prominent strategy deployed by large corporations was to deliberately squeeze the money supply in the market. This increased interest rates for bank loans and restricted credit availability for small and rival competitors. This process led to a decline in production by small and medium-sized

The Rise of Big Business Corporations

firms, prompting big businesses to intervene and capture the market, thereby maximising their profits. These corporations came to control a range of economic sectors, from consumer to capital goods and infrastructure, including farm machines, petroleum, railroad, steel, industrial construction, cables, telegraph, electricity, electric motors, soaps, shampoo, toothpaste, toothbrush, oats, cornflakes, meat, cigarettes, and sewing machines, to name just a few. The newly invented sewing machine and typewriter, in particular, generated new modes of distribution and marketing, respectively.

With the expansion of the rail network, there were perceptible shifts in landscape and settlement patterns by the 1840s. New types of big businesses that emerged at this point were associated with agricultural products: the meat industry, cigarettes (reliant on tobacco cultivation), flour, and large-scale banana cultivation. Some well-established small-scale industries for commodities like sugar, salt, leather, whiskey, glucose, starch, biscuits, and fertiliser, saw a process of consolidation where many small manufacturers came together to establish large business units; these were further enlarged by developing marketing and purchasing companies to secure the essential product. New technologies provided further encouragement to these industries. Gustavus F. Swift, a key figure in the meat industry, understood the importance of the refrigerator, a recent invention, in establishing and marketing fresh meat. Even though he faced opposition from the National Butchers' Protective Association, he successfully applied modern management techniques to establish his company. By the end of the 1890s, he had developed marketing, processing, and accounting units controlled by the company's central office in Chicago, Illinois.

Another example can be drawn from the tobacco industry. James B. Duke, realising the potential of the tobacco crop, established a company in 1884. It used advertisements to generate people's interest and popularise the habit of smoking, which ultimately resulted in the creation of a national and then multi-national organisation. By 1890, he managed a merger and acquisition with five smaller competitors, thus establishing the **American Tobacco Company**, which had a monopoly in the market. By 1895 the corporation had reached a new milestone: it successfully consolidated all aspects of the business within its operations, including manufacturing, marketing, purchasing, and finance. The American Tobacco Company thereby came to dominate the world's tobacco business.

James S. Bell led the **Washburn-Crosby Company**, which made and sold high-grade flour for urban bakeries, to massive success. Andrew J. Preston, realising the potential of bananas, began growing, transporting, and selling them for the urban market. All these businesses prospered due to the innovations they introduced in marketing. Later, they carried out **vertical integration** (also known as **vertical consolidation**), where all aspects of the supply chain were brought under the control of one company, allowing it much greater control over the product and ensuring that they were selling directly to the consumer.[10]

Two developments related to power production fuelled the Second Industrial Revolution. The first was the invention of the internal combustion engine, which became the preferred driver for transportation by the 1920s in America. The second was widespread electrification, which brought unprecedented changes in the running of industries and modes of transportation.[11] These inventions were made possible by institutionalising research and associated activities, particularly in the natural and physical sciences, with a specific emphasis on chemistry and physics.

A significant feature of American big business was widespread consolidation: vertical integration (which, as we have discussed, brought different stages of the supply chain under one firm) and **horizontal integration** (which refers to the merging of different firms at the same stage of production, often resulting in large monopolistic entities). The **Standard Oil Company**, founded by John D. Rockefeller, used horizontal integration of business by developing pools, trusts, and holding companies to completely monopolise oil production in the USA and remove competitors from the market. It was also vertically integrated and controlled all processes associated with extracting crude oil to produce petroleum as well as the marketing and distribution of the product inside and outside America. The company also strategically used advertising and transportation networks to cut costs and make its product more attractive to consumers. It owned pipelines, shipped its own oil, operated its own retail outlets, manufactured tank wagons for local distribution, and used consumer-friendly packages to distinguish itself and encourage consumers to buy only its products. By the 1880s, Standard Oil Company had monopolised 90 per cent of the American oil market.

Andrew Carnegie, in 1875, set up the vertically integrated **Thomson Steels Works** in Braddock, Pennsylvania, where he introduced the **Bessemer steel manufacturing process.** This enabled the mass production of steel and application of a new controlling business strategy where all stages of production, from mining, to manufacture, transportation, distribution, and sale of steel and its associated components were under the control of one company. By 1889, Carnegie had acquired rival steel companies as well as railroad and steamship companies, and in 1892 formed the **Carnegie Steel Company.** The company's transportation networks enabled Carnegie to distribute steel to the developing urban centres on the eastern starboard by transporting it via the Mississippi River on steamship barges. Later, the **United States Steel Corporation**, which was the result of an even bigger merger, controlled all aspects of the steel business, from the procurement of raw materials to its transportation, manufacturing and distribution. These business systems enabled the United States to become the world's primary producer of steel.[12] The development of the **Bessemer technique** and later the **open hearth process** pioneered the use of iron and steel in the railroad industry, the manufacture of structural steel for the construction of tall urban buildings, and arm plates for naval vessels; later, steel began to be used in automobile manufacturing.[13]

Another unique aspect of American business was that inventors established companies. One such example was Thomas A. Edison, who invented several devices in the fields of telegraphy, electricity, and cinema, including the mimeograph machine and the microphone. By 1931, he had patented 1,093 inventions. Edison received financial assistance from J. P. Morgan, one of the most prominent bankers in the USA, in 1892 to set up the **General Electric Company**. After a few years, he agreed to exchange his patent with George Westinghouse under a joint board of control known as the **Corporate Patent Agreement**, which quickly became another technique to dominate the market. Nikola Tesla, another innovator, through his electric motor, made it possible to use electricity for industrial and commercial purposes, which boosted the rise of big businesses in the US.[14]

Historians mention the invention of the **Singer sewing machine** as one of the finest examples of mass production and mass marketing. This machine was invented and patented by Isaac Merit Singer. He brought iron foundries and cabinet-making operations under his control and even manufactured interchangeable parts through his corporation. The firm also controlled advertising, purchases on the basis of instalment plans, regional distribution, and ran retail stores. At Singer's shops, hired personnel taught consumers how to use the sewing machine and even gave the product on credit. Two other prominent business examples are **Procter and Gamble** of Cincinnati, which produced soap and other products. It used trading cards, circular prizes, testimonials, and scientific endorsements to advertise its product.

Similarly, when George Eastman developed a paper-based photographic film and founded the **Kodak Film Company**, which also sold cheap cameras, customers returned the film made by the company after using it, and the camera was reloaded for ten dollars. Many other prominent business organisations became equally powerful and experienced broad-based operational expansion, like the textile and shoemaking industries. George Seldon invented the car that the Ford Company would later manufacture, along with corporations that paid for agricultural equipment and tools.

Rise of Mass Consumer Capitalism

In the period after 1890, American society transformed into a materialistic society governed by a '**culture of desire**'[15] that eventually birthed mass consumer capitalism. This was facilitated in major part not only by the big corporations, but also due to the emergence of the mass market retailers and banks. This process received further stimulus with the emergence of novel advertisement and promotion techniques, a new generation of artists and the increasingly influential fashion world in America, and the proliferation of brokers and professional classes who sought to project consumerism as aspirational, that is, as a desirable part of modern life. The new American consumerist culture was based on the twin foundations of capital acquisition, which was the base value of society, and consumption. This fuelled a process of the democratisation of desire. By 1900, the land of desire and plenty had been completely transformed, urbanised and commercialised, and American Market Capitalism had been institutionalised. By this time, capital had become the foundation of 'business and consumption'. This led to the growth of a new American aesthetic that compelled President Herbert Hoover to expand the Department of Commerce. The US became the first country in the world whose economic foundations were established on the basis of mass production, mass consumer institutions, and mass consumer enticements to sell mass-produced goods in the markets.

One of the finest examples of modern merchandising was the emergence of **large department stores** that specialised in mass retail businesses. These stores offered numerous services as they had a vast inventory and emerged at the juncture when America had begun to produce machine-made mass commodities, and this change was supported by the rise of a new White middle class who had the capital to buy new material comforts and were looking for leisure activities. The department stores offered public telephones, postal services, shopping assistance, free delivery, beauty salons, dining places, and more. They utilised well-lit spaces with glass storefronts and mirrors to display and advertise products, providing a polished experience replete with the latest fashions and services to attract more consumers. These consumer items began to be sold throughout the country and with easy availability of capital for investment provided by the emergence of commercial and state banks, including insurance companies. These stores encouraged consumption, which quickly became associated with the American brand of democracy and citizenship. The stores often had no bar in terms of race, gender, age, and class. For women in particular, they offered free and safe public spaces, as they did for people of colour. Department stores remained popular until the emergence of malls after World War II.

Big corporations have also developed new forms of display, using colour, glass, and light to display their products. They introduced billboards, electrical signage, signboards, and display windows. The emergence of advertising 'geniuses' heralded the arrival of new professional classes and experts adept at decoration and display. The rise of promotional one-liners or 'taglines' shaped the way Americans visualised businesses and commodities. Newspapers and magazines like *Cosmopolitan* became mass-market items, resulting in the growth of copywriters and advertising experts, who invented catchy phrases and attractive visual images. New sales promotion methods began using magazines, newspapers, door-to-door free demonstrations, and free samples, which became a new norm in America. 'Eye appeal' became necessary. The rise of registered trademarks was another hallmark, along with an increase in children's clothing stores and toys, and fashion industries. Alongside these significant changes, there was also the rise of the service industry, with the beginning of consumer credit, instalment buying, as well as an increase in art galleries, art exhibitions, auctions, musical concerts and entertainment industries. New hotel chains and skyscrapers all pointed towards the US as a land that fulfilled all desires that human beings could possibly imagine.

These changes would not have been possible without the emergence of educational institutions, particularly commercial art schools and new universities and colleges, along with new types of museums and methods of organising industrial exhibitions to showcase the latest technologies to the world. The assistance provided by the federal and municipal governments, and non-governmental institutions like the American church, lent further support to this new consumer culture. The opposition that came from the labour unions and supporters of the Populist Movement (see Chapters 3 and 5) further whetted the great American desire and appetite for the latest consumer and luxury goods and gadgets—all that money could buy.[16]

In this way, the extensive use of machines, inventions, technical improvements, and new industrial processes assisted mass production. Along with the growth of the population, the availability of capital, and ever-expanding internal and external markets, the rapid rise of business corporations in the US facilitated the process of the Second Industrial Revolution.

The Structure of Monopolistic Companies

Over time, big business organisations evolved a mechanism of fierce competitive spirit to manipulate markets, prices, labour, and mediators to their advantage and remove small competitors from the field. Monopoly companies were established to secure complete freedom to dominate essential aspects of the business. Another hidden aim was to make them look like legal entities with limited liabilities and continuity of ownership beyond the lifetime of the original corporate builder. However, there were frequent economic depressions from the 1870s to 1890s.

Industrialists evolved different types of monopoly companies and methods to maintain control over the market. The first of these were the **pools**. They were loose forms of business organisation where companies agreed to control specific portions of the market, rather than competing with each other. Thus, pools were written agreements associated with market areas, price, production, quotas, or profit shares. In their simpler forms, pooling applied only to output, sale, and distribution of profits on pre-determined prices. Pools were, therefore, specialised business units whose members collaborated to control prices by keeping competitors at bay. Pools partitioned markets between competitive firms and fixed costs to their advantage. American railroad companies were one of the best examples of this type of monopoly. This was very popular in the 1880s and 1890s, and eventually gave way to trusts.[17]

Trusts were rigid forms of business organisation in which stockholders deposited their stock under agreement with trustees. In the US, such deposits had relatively little legal oversight and they came to be identified with large-scale business combinations and consolidation. (The term business combination, here, refers to one company gaining control over another through manoeuvres like acquisitions or mergers, to establish a single entity with a greater market share, thereby controlling markets.) In other words, stockholders under a trust agreement deposited a controlling portion of their stock with a board of trustees and received a trustee certificate in return. The trusts were legal devices by which the workings of competitive companies were brought under the management of a single director. Some examples of these types of companies were Standard Oil Company, Whiskey Trust, Sugar Trust, Lead Trust, Cotton Trust, and Oil Trust.

When trusts were declared unlawful, corporations came up with **holding companies**, organisations in which a corporation holds enough shares of other companies to control their operations. Within such a pyramid, costs were reduced and the last company created could handle all of them. Because the stock was scattered among many smallholders, stakeholders owning no more than 10 to 20 per cent of the inventory available could assume control of an entire industry. In other words, these organisations were created to dominate other business corporations by owning or managing a portion of their stock. For many years, the United States Steel Corporation was the largest holding company in the US. Holding companies were partially curbed after the **Supreme Court dissolution of the Northern Securities Company in 1904**. Over time, other holding companies were dissolved, too, including the American Tobacco Company and the Standard Oil Company in 1911.

The end of holding companies led to the rise of **mergers**. In the 1890s, the merger movement among industrialists aimed to secure monopolies over markets for final products (also known as **horizontal integration**). Firms that provided similar products and sold in comparable markets would merge together. The aim was to establish firms to increase profits or decrease losses, and it became widespread from around World War I. During the 1920s, more than 3,700 utility companies were absorbed in mergers, and in the following decades, the automobile, aluminium, chemical, motion picture, and communication industries saw similar moves.

While a tremendous economic boom was taking shape in the northern and western states, the southern states continued to languish, as evidenced by their annual per capita income, which stood at US $509 when compared with the rest of America at US $1,165. The reasons for slow economic development in the South were devastation caused by the Civil War, lack of capital for investment, northern control of financial markets and patents, and limited urbanisation. Added to this were the problems of growing illiteracy, a low rate of technological innovation (due to an inadequate number

The Rise of Big Business Corporations

of higher educational institutions), and the prevalence of systemic racism and associated conflict. Due to the demonetisation of silver, there was limited capital availability in the markets. With capital and banking in short supply, the South depended on sharecropping and a crop-lien system (see Chapter 1). The South emphasised commercial agriculture, which is generally vulnerable to fluctuations in the national and international markets. The federal government's decision to maintain high tariffs on imported goods, which inflated the prices for imported machines, was seen as a sign that the government favoured industrialists in the North. Discriminatory

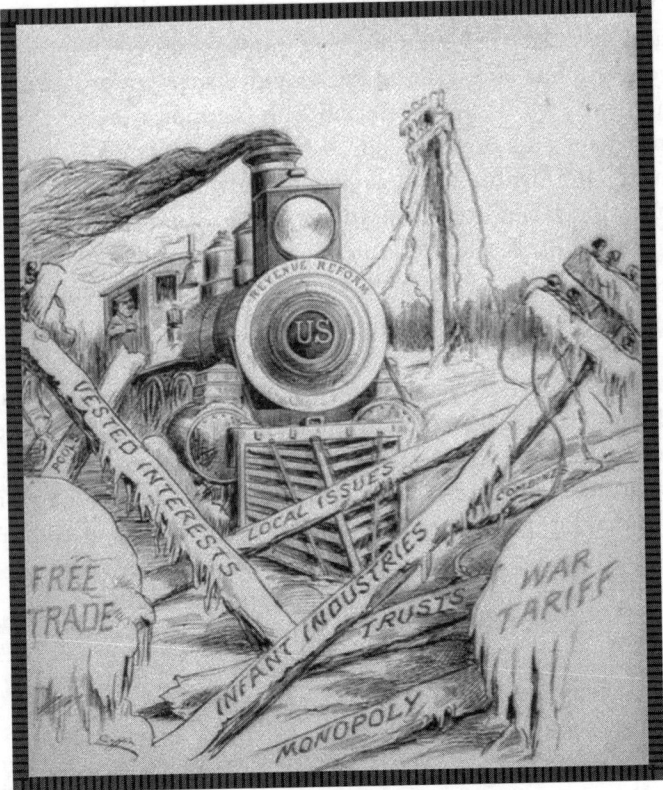

FIG. 2.2: Barriers in the path of the 'revenue reform' train, cartoon, by George Yost Coffin (c. 1880–1890)

Source: Wikimedia Commons.

railroad freight rates hiked costs of transporting finished goods and raw materials to outside markets. Giving pensions to war veterans also led to a shortage of government funds for public works.

The industrialisation process gained momentum in the South only after the 1880s, when tax exemptions were given to develop new businesses and raise business awareness; industrial and agricultural expositions were organised; and attempts were made to overcome labour shortages by using prison convicts. It should be noted that, as discussed in Chapter 1, the last measure was a new form of enslavement, as Black prisoners were leased out and not paid any wages. In Florida and Texas, state lands were given to railroad companies, while forests and mineral rights were sold to land speculators. Gradually, the South increased its production of iron, sulphur and coal, taking tentative steps towards a modern economy. By 1871, limestone and iron ore industries developed in Birmingham and Alabama due to the availability of rich mineral deposits. In Piedmont, Georgia and Alabama, the cotton mill industry grew. But even here, industrial development differed from that of the North. The mill operator built the mill and owned the workers' housing as well as the company's store. The operator also supported the village church, financed local elementary schools, and was responsible for his workers' moral and social behaviour. The mill workers were paid in **scrip**, a certificate redeemable only in goods supplied by the company store, which created another cycle of indebtedness. Such industries exploited cheap, rural labour and drew farmers into paternalistic, company-run villages. The workers had to develop gardens to supply their food, similar to communal farms cultivated under conditions of slavery. The South depended on the North for finance, technology and expertise.

The Gilded Age

The wealth and resources of the American economy rapidly passed into the hands of a privileged minority. This is one reason why the period from the 1870s to the 1890s has often been characterised as '**The Gilded Age**'. The term Gilded Age was used by Mark Twain and Charles Dudley Warner in their 1873 novel, *The Gilded Age: A Tale of Today*, which revolved around the rise of materialism, fuelling political corruption, growing poverty, and social inequalities that were obscured by a thin veneer of gold. While the USA certainly became a formidable economic power, supported by heavy industries and consumer capitalism, it also saw rising wealth inequality, persistent poverty, and rural resentment. This transformed American society to a great extent. The half-century following the Civil War was thus defined by a combination of the economic philosophy of *laissez faire* and the reaction against it.

The Civil War immensely sped up all the processes of the Second Industrial Revolution, but the principles of unbridled freedom and competition remained supreme. The spirit of enterprise and an atmosphere of postwar optimism also added to the swift transformation of the national economy. The US possessed abundant raw materials, labour, transport facilities, and market and technical know-how, which were the main bases of American industrial development. Therefore, the Civil War was a vital factor in US commercial history. It sped up the development of a distinct, American model of capitalism.

The consolidation of business enterprises in the late nineteenth and early twentieth centuries led to immense public resentment, and the federal government was compelled to control unfair business practices to preserve competition and prevent monopolies. The government response was the **Sherman Act (1890)**, and later the **Clayton Act (1914)** and the **Federal Trade Commission Act (1914)**.[18]

Historiography: Understanding the USA's Economic History

From 1850 to 1877, the USA underwent an industrial and urban transformation that resulted in profound changes in its social structure. The growth and development were so rapid that when scholars began to research this period, there was a polarisation of opinions. There were critiques of the methods used to monopolise capital, power, and resources. For some scholars, these smacked of despotism, using blatantly unfair and unethical tactics to ruthlessly crush competition and labour unions, to the extent that doubts began to be raised that such business practices were impeding the nation's political and economic freedom.

The first attempt to evaluate the impact of industrial progress was written by journalist Henry Demarest Lloyd who, in *Wealth against Commonwealth* (1894), analysed the Standard Oil Company and the techniques used by John D. Rockefeller to gain a virtual monopoly over the petroleum industry.[19] According to Lloyd, American industrialists paid lip service to the idea of competition, but their true purpose was to secure a monopoly. Taking this logic further, Thorstein Veblen[20] and E. A. Ross[21] denounced prominent industrialists as predatory, profit-seeking, amoral people whose only purpose was to earn profit at any cost. Gustavus Myers and Algie Simons portrayed businesspersons as malefactors of wealth; however, they were optimistic about the eventual extinction of this economic class as the historical process reached its 'inevitable destiny' and arrived at a socialist utopia.[22]

Many of these writers and scholars popularised the term '**robber baron**' to refer to monopolistic industrialists. Charles and Mary Beard justified this analysis by delineating similarities between the medieval baron and modern-day industry captains.[23] Modern barons were 'aggressive men' who wished to rise higher in the economic ranks by exploiting natural resources without restraint, waging financial war on one another, entering into combinations, making immense fortunes, and, like victorious feudal chieftains or medieval merchants, branching out as patrons of learning, divinity and charity. They indulged in highly irregular and lawless methods, ruthless competition, intrigues, and pitiless destruction of rivals.

Vernon L. Parrington considered the predatory and materialistic industry tycoon as the greatest threat to the humane and democratic values that had made America great.[24] Lewis Corey, a socialist scholar, interrogated the techniques whereby J. P. Morgan, the major banking and investment concern, exercised near-dictatorial control over corporations having assets well above US $20 million.[25] Corey aimed to marshal as much evidence as possible to demonstrate industrial capitalism's evil, selfish, and corrupting nature. Matthew Josephson, in a somewhat different perspective, credited the new industrialist class with bringing changes in large-scale production, but also showed how wealth came to be concentrated in the hands of a few people. For Josephson, the negative aspects of this progress outweighed the positive.[26]

John Tipple[27] noted that a relatively small number of nineteenth-century entrepreneurs used the corporate form of organisation to amass great wealth and, in so doing, contributed to the decline of individualistic institutions and values. Special privileges and the corporation went hand in hand, transferring politico-economic power to a relatively small economic elite.

Allan Nevins published an influential revisionist biography of John D. Rockefeller in 1940; he argued that much of the blame heaped on the man was unwarranted.[28] Nevins conceded that Rockefeller often used methods that were morally dubious, but argued that the monopoly attained by Standard Oil Company was a natural response to the anarchical cutthroat competition of the period. It reflected the trend in all industrial nations toward consolidation. For Nevins, Rockefeller was a great innovator who imposed a more rational and efficient pattern on American industry. Rockefeller's objective was not merely the accumulation of wealth; he was also motivated by a competitive drive towards achievement, a sense of self-expression, and championed the imposition of the American will on a given environment. Nevins pushed his analysis further when he published his second biography[29] of Rockefeller where the latter was described as an 'innovator, thinker, planner, and bold entrepreneur'.

Alfred D. Chandler identified four stages in the development of a large industrial enterprise in the late nineteenth and early twentieth centuries. First came a period of expansion and the accumulation of resources. In the second phase, these resources were rationalised. In the third phase, the organisation expanded its operation to include new products, ensuring the most efficient use of existing resources. In the fourth and final phase, new structures were created to promote the effective use of resources to meet immediate and long-term demands.

Chandler saw large corporations as complex economic, political, and social systems. He also insisted that these corporations required continuous changes in strategy, and the result would be the growth of large, decentralised, multidivisional corporations. This analysis emphasised the forces that led industrialists to develop new products, new markets, and new sources of raw materials. Industry leaders created the **modern corporation**, which integrated the functions of purchasing, manufacturing, marketing, and finance. A separate department managed each central process; a primary office coordinated and controlled all of them. Such a complex organisation evolved in response to the new urban market, which in turn was sustained by the national transportation system. Minimising the role of technological innovation, Chandler concluded that entrepreneurs like Rockefeller and others were successful because they accurately analysed the economic situation and responded creatively to it. Their contributions, he suggested, played an essential role in the dramatic growth of the American economy and the creation of an affluent society.

In his second book, Chandler discussed the development of large-scale vertical organisations, which was seen as a profoundly transformative phenomenon and situated between the Civil War and the Depression of the 1930s.[30] He emphasised the critical role of management and business executives in bringing about consolidation. This shift overturned Adam Smith's long-held belief that markets were the single most important factor in economic growth.

Carl Kaysen, an economist, along with Donald Turner noted that American society possessed two ways of controlling business power: (*i*) promoting competitive markets held by an agency external to the business, and (*ii*) institutionalising responsibility for exercising power within the firm.[31] Traditionally, the US relied on the first, in the form of antitrust activities, although far more could have been done along this line. In their opinion, the effective control of business power remained an unfinished task.

Among the **New Left** scholars, Gabriel Kolko argued that certain distinctive features of American society, which he designated 'political capitalism', dated only from the first two decades of the twentieth century.[32] Rejecting the belief that large-scale business enterprise was inevitable, Kolko maintained that competition was increasing at the turn of the century. Even the merger movement and the capitalisation of new combinations on an unprecedented scale failed to stem the tide of competitive growth. Therefore, corporate leaders turned to the government to control competition and prevent the possibility of a formal political democracy that might lead to a redistribution of wealth. The result was a synthesis of business and government, with the former emerging as the dominant element. Unlike Chandler, Kolko believed that large-scale units turned to government regulation because of their inefficiency. However, Edward A. Purcell. Jr. offered a critique of this view,[33] stating that diverse economic groups who felt threatened by the national economy and rate discrimination turned to the federal government in the hopes of receiving economic safeguards. Political control of the economy was not their ultimate goal; they wanted to protect their interests.

David F. Noble has argued that technology served the needs of corporate capitalism. To benefit the masses, it was essential to liberate workers from an economic system that degraded them rather than enhanced their lives.[34]

In an entirely divergent opinion, Murray N. Rothbard, who believed in anarcho-capitalism, emphasised individual responsibility and self-ownership over state control. In his assessment, the free market works like the government and provides roads, infrastructure, and police protection. Therefore, there is no need to impose taxes, and the government should never interfere in personal economic matters. In short, he believed in self-ownership, minimal state involvement, and complete eradication of a welfare state. Rothbard advocated an extreme example of the principle of laissez-faire to challenge traditional American economic thought.[35]

It becomes challenging to conclude on an authoritative note since so many different views exist on the subject. However, the fact remains that big businesses were a uniquely American enterprise, and the nation had the material, human capital, and economic capacity to produce powerful industrialists. These huge business enterprises were also responsible for the beginning of economic wars in the twentieth century.

Notes

1. Following the War of 1812, the Democratic-Republicans worked to strengthen the economic foundations of the young nation through expansion of cotton production and industry, expansions in trade (the war was fought over neutrality rights during the Napoleonic Wars), and territorial expansion by dispossessing the Indigenous nations (through the ideology of Manifest Destiny). Efforts were also made to strengthen the national banking system and encourage industrialisation. However, these developments pushed the nation towards the Civil War; they also prompted the strengthening of military capabilities in preparation for greater involvement in global affairs (based on the Monroe Doctrine).

2. Harold Underwood Faulkner, *American Economic History*, 8th edition (New York, 1960).

3. Eric Foner, *Give Me Liberty! An American History*, 3rd edition (New York, 2011), p. 586.

4. Paul S. Boyer, et al., *Enduring Vision: A History of the American People*, vol. 2 (New York, 2001).

5. Licht Walter, *Industrializing America: The Nineteenth Century* (Baltimore and London, 1995).

6. Faulkner, *American Economic History*, p. 398.

7. Foner, *Give Me Liberty!*, pp.588–589.

8. William R. Leach, *Land of Desire: Merchants, Power and the Rise of a New American Culture* (New York, 1993).

9. Foner, *Give Me Liberty!*, p. 590.

10. Interestingly, in 1921, General Mills (earlier known as Washburn-Crosby Company) introduced Betty Crocker, an idealised American housewife who would advise consumers on recipes. Crocker was a fictionalised, corporate-created brand image. This introduced a new era in the world of advertisements, which now began to identify and target specific demographic groups.

11. David E. Nye, *Electrifying America: Social Meanings of a New Technology, 1880–1940* (Cambridge, Massachusetts, 1991).

12. Ibid., p. 593.

13. Thomas J. Misa, *A Nation of Steel: The Making of Modern America, 1865–1925* (Baltimore, 1995).

14. Ibid., p. 590.

15. The phrase adapts the famous characterisation of America as the 'land of desire' by John Wanamaker, a prominent nineteenth-century department store owner.

16. Leach, *Land of Desire*.

17. Albert W. Neimi, Jr., *U.S. Economic History* (New York 1980), p. 333.

18. Ibid., p. 335.

19. Henry Demarest Lloyd, *Wealth Against Commonwealth* (New York, 1894).

20. See Thorstein Veblen, *The Theory of Leisure Class: An Economic Study of Institutions* (New York, 1902); also by Veblen, *The Theory of Business Enterprise: Charles Scribner's Sons* (New York, 1932).

21. E. A. Ross, *An Analysis of Latter Day Iniquity* (Boston and New York, 1907).

22. Gustavus Myers, *History of the Great American Fortunes*, vols 1–2 (Chicago, 1910). See also Algie Martin Simons, *Production Management: Control of Men, Material and Machines* (Chicago, 1929).

23. Charles Beard and Mary Beard, *The Rise of American Civilization: The Industrial Era* (New York, 1930).

24. Vernon L. Parrington, *Main Currents in American Thought*, 3 vols (New York, 1927–1930).

25. Lewis Corey, *The Decline of American Civilization* (New Delhi, 2012).

26. Matthew Josephson, *The Robber Barons: The Great American Capitalists, 1861–1901* (New York, 1934).

27. John Tipple, 'The Anatomy of Prejudice: Origins of the Robber Baron Legend'. *Business History Review* 33 (4), 1959, pp. 510–523.

28. Allan Nevins, *John D. Rockefeller: The Heroic Age of American Enterprise*, 2 vols (New York, 1940).

29. Allan Nevins, *Study in Power: John D. Rockefeller, Industrialist and Philanthropist*, 2 vols (New York, 1953).

30. Alfred D. Chandler, *The Visible Hand: The Managerial Revolution in American Business* (Cambridge, Massachusetts, 1977).

31. Carl Kaysen and Donald F. Turner, *Antitrust Policy* (New York, 1959).

32. Gabriel Kolko, *The Triumph of Conservatism: A Reinterpretation of American History, 1900–1916* (Chicago, 1963).

33. Edward A. Purcell, Jr, 'Ideas and Interests: Businessmen and the Interstate Commerce Act', *Journal of American History* 54 (3), 1967, pp. 561–578.

34. David F. Noble, *America by Design: Science, Technology, and the Rise of Corporate Capitalism* (New York, 1977).

35. Murray N. Rothbard, *A History of Money and Banking in the United States: The Colonial Era to World War II*, 2nd ed. (Auburn, Alabama, 2002).

CHAPTER 3

History of the US Labour Movement

Between 1870 and 1900, the United States of America experienced a remarkable surge in industrial and agricultural production, paving the way for the emergence of an industrial nation built on the pillars of new big business organisations. This period was not without its challenges. It was marked by two severe depressions—1873–1878 and 1893–1897—and an economic recession from 1884–1886, that sparked violent strikes in American cities. Despite these hardships, the working class demonstrated remarkable resilience.

These downturns marked a crucial turning point in the American economy, with the growth rate of the gross national product plummeting from 6.5 per cent to 3.6 per cent.[1] They were primarily caused by the over-production of goods, leading to a disbalance between supply and demand. With the USA now stretching from the East to the West coast, frontier expansion came to an end and new lands were no longer available. Additionally, the collapse of the securities market, and competition generated by improvements in transportation and communication exacerbated the situation. The resulting fall in the prices of essential goods and wages led to a significant decrease in the purchasing power of the consumer classes.

One of the most striking aspects of this era was the stark wealth disparity. In 1890, the top 1 per cent of the rich owned a staggering 51 per cent of all property, while the bottom 44 per cent, comprising approximately 5.5 million families, held a mere 1.2 per cent.[2] The stark contrast between the opulent lifestyles of the rich and the struggles of the impoverished working class was a source of deep discontent among the latter, and a powerful motivator for the labour movement.

Technological changes over the late nineteenth century also brought about shifts in work patterns that effectively ended the sense of solidarity previously seen in the handicraft industry. In this context, businesses preferred to employ low-paid workers whose lives were governed by machines and a monotonous routine. It was during this period that contract-based employment emerged, where a subcontractor (generally called a 'pusher' or 'foreman') assumed responsibility for employers' relations with workers. Industrial accidents were commonplace in the late nineteenth century, primarily due to a lack of training for workers operating new machines, and a general disregard for safety standards. In some industries, like coal mines and textile mills, owners preferred to employ 'unskilled' child and women labourers who could be paid abysmally low wages. In case of an industrial accident or death, no financial assistance or compensation was paid to the victim or his family. Some preferred to employ immigrant labourers who were ready to work even on meagre wages. The emergence of working class identity and unionisation therefore emerged from a specific set of socio-economic conditions in American history. The conflict between industry and labour reflected how Americans came to relate to each other as a community and nation.

Labour Relations in the Early Colonial Period

In the formative stages of settler colonialism in North America, there was a shortage of labour in proportion to available land. To overcome this issue, in 1618 the Virginia Company changed its land policy and instituted what came to be known as the **Headright System.** The company began to grant land to new settlers at no cost in the hopes of attracting more immigrants. The system allowed immigrants to come to America if they could pay for the oceanic journey and receive a grant of 50 acres of land. The incentive was to provide them with another 50 acres if they could bring relatives, and another 50 acres if they could also sponsor the journey of indentured servants. The servants worked for a specific period, the purpose being to cover the cost of their passage. Once their debt was cleared, they could secure land. While the early ships had all-male crews, in later years, the Virginia Company also brought young women to Jamestown to 'colonise Virginia properly' by establishing families.

The problem was that survival was difficult in the initial period of colonisation, and on average, 25 per cent of immigrants died within the first year of their arrival in Chesapeake.[3] However, the pace of settlement slowly picked up due to the incentive of free land, an expensive asset in land-starved Europe. As tobacco had become a lucrative commodity, and its cultivation was labour-intensive, there was a rising demand for **indentured labour**. This demand was met by immigrants who lacked the resources to fund the transatlantic voyage and, therefore, entered into a contract of servitude with their masters. The contract typically stipulated a period of four to seven years. The Atlantic voyage was punishing and brutal, with overcrowding and insufficient rations and water, forcing poor immigrants to survive on rats and mice. The rampant commodification of people is reflected in the fact that most ship captains knowingly carried more men than they had provisions for—they were maximising profits, regardless of the human cost. The mortality rate was extremely high, and the cause of death was not only a shortage of food and water, but also disease.[4] Over time, the colonial American labour markets successfully established networks in Europe, using innovative methods developed by the capitalist class. These networks involved buyers, ship captains, or recruiters on the lookout for poor White people willing to risk their lives for a better future in the American colonies. The trade in indentured labour became highly professionalised.

In America, labourers faced the auction block. Prices were decided based on their health, fitness, age, and skill. The 'commodity' had to be fit enough to work and survive in the harsh American conditions. The buyer, the merchant, maintained bookkeeping records, that have now become a valuable source of information for modern historians.

As seen in these records, the contract period ranged from four to seven years, and labourers could be bought and sold during this period, which points to the beginning of the commodification of labour. Gradually, the colonies began to formulate laws that imposed heavy penalties on indentured servants if found neglecting their work. Punitive measures were enacted on those found aiding and abetting runaway servants. This legal system, therefore, protected the economic interests of the elite classes and converted indentured servitude into an involuntary labour system.

The few indentured women servants faced unique challenges and modes of exploitation. Colonists generally considered male servants more valuable. The sexual exploitation of women servants was overlooked, and they were punished if found pregnant, as it meant loss of labour for the master. Any child born to an indentured servant was also forced into indenture till they reached the age of 21 years.

Violence and punishment were considered legitimate modes of maintaining control, and were used to keep servants in check, maintain their non-citizen status, and to deprive contract labour of any legal rights or power. Resistance to this brutal system was generally embodied by runaways, many of whom enlisted in the British army. Suicide was a deeply tragic outcome that many indentured servants turned to, since the system denied all sense of individual dignity.[5] Colonial newspapers of the time were filled with advertisements of runaway servants who, when captured, had to endure harsh punishments and an increased duration of their contractual service.

In 1619, a Dutch ship brought Africans to be sold as indentured servants. By the middle of the seventeenth century, as the flow of White immigrants into America began to dwindle, the institution of racialised enslavement gradually began to take hold. It became an entrenched labour system by the beginning of the eighteenth century. To rationalise multigenerational and inescapable enslavement, White settlers developed a widespread belief that life was determined by 'one's station in life' and, therefore, enslavement was a person's 'misfortune'. Modern theories of racial classification of humans began to circulate in Europe and among White settlers, contributing to the growing dehumanisation of Black people in particular.

A free-wage labour system developed when a labour market emerged in the artisan trades late in the colonial period. Given the history of race relations in the US, this system was only available to the White working class. In this pre-industrial society, work was based on organically blending traditional work methods with the norms of cultural life that had gradually evolved in the colonies. A distinct labour consciousness became visible among the artisans and workers.[6] During the American Revolution, the working classes within settler society wanted to establish a 'just society' based on social equality, freedom, and a 'virtuous' citizenry. The formation of the **Federal Society of Journeymen Cordwainers** (shoemakers) in Philadelphia in 1794 marked the beginnings of trade union organising in the US, and was the first sustained, formal trade union of American workers. They were defending their rights against diluted and cheap labour, and advocating for a shorter workday. This marked the emergence of a job-conscious orientation that brought new elements to the structural organisation of American trade unions. This is evident from early unions such as the **Iron Molders' International Union**, the **Knights of St. Crispin** (shoemakers) and the **Mechanic's Union of Trade Association** in Philadelphia in 1827, through to the **International Typographical Union** founded in 1852, which comprised both American and Canadian workers, thus introducing an international character to union formation. According to John R. Commons and Selig Perlman, the labour unions at this stage served an 'organic purpose' of protecting their employees in a fast-growing and volatile market by securing labour reforms like better wages, limited working hours, and employment security based on collective negotiations, but without disrupting the existing social and economic order.[7] This was also when the factory system gradually gave way to industrial organisations that gave importance to skilled labour. In contrast, the rest of the working classes remained on the margins of the economy, barely eking out enough for their sustenance.

Labour Dynamics after the Civil War: An Overview

The mid-to-late nineteenth century brought in transformative changes, with the rise of industrial capitalism sharpening class divides. By the 1850s, improved transportation and communication systems allowed for greater mobility across the continent, and as discussed in Chapter 2, allowed for expansion of industry and commercial activity. Skilled German, British, French, and Italian labourers migrated to the USA, bringing in trade unionisation experience under socialism and communism. They were an important influence in early strikes during the Civil War as workers tried to keep their wages in line with wartime inflation. However, the American working class was highly fragmented along the lines of race, ethnicity, religion, and gender. They were also divided by unequal skill levels and educational opportunity, the diversity of conditions under which they worked, and the geographical mobility of workers. These factors made it challenging to organise labour around agreed goals. Nevertheless, Alan Dawley contests the idea that only the elite or dominant classes were capable of exerting pressure for social change. His work has shown how different social groups organised themselves into unions and pressure groups.[8] According to Alan Dawley, such collectivisation led to the 'path of power' in three ways:

(i) attempts to bring reform through electoral politics;
(ii) revolutionary forms of direct action,
(iii) efforts to establish a cooperative commonwealth of all producers.[9]

In the post-Civil War period, from 1865 to 1920, there was a substantial increase in the working classes, along with gender differentiation and a clear distinction between the home and the workplace. As jobs in the heavy industries, infrastructure, and factories mainly went to men, women had to limit themselves to working in the domestic sector, the cotton textile industries, or the garment trade. At the same time, historians have seen a significant rise in the share of the labouring classes out of the total population after 1920, primarily due to technological advancements in American industries. The increase in unskilled labourers is also attributed to the rise in immigrants entering America. The demand for skilled workers continued to be high. They were termed 'labour aristocrats' who were proficient and in great demand but remained relatively independent, which assisted their spatial mobility and high wages.[10] Significant changes can be seen with the coming of the industrial age. According to E. P. Thompson, working in the industry required a worker to adhere to discipline in terms of time, which demarcated private life from work and thereby brought about profound changes in the nature and character of American labour. This shift took place over a long period as the new industrial workspace was a more regimented environment with a predictable workflow, where control was exercised not by the family but by an organisation (see, for instance, the discussion on scientific management in Chapter 2).[11] Naturally, this altered the work culture of the working classes. Herbert Gutman first evaluated this aspect when he examined the consequences of industrial progress on both immigrants and long-term European American settlers, which often led to violent clashes, conflicts and spatial segregation in the form of urban ghettos.[12] According to Sidney Pollard, industrialisation in this period brought within its fold a new mechanism and system of labour administration, which allowed industrialists to maintain control over labour and associated state systems of regulation like the courts, state legislators, and the Congress.

From the available sources, historians have concluded that immigrant labour came to America in four great waves: 1843–1857, 1878–1893, 1898–1914, and 1919–1921. It is estimated that about 25 million immigrant families from east and south Europe came to the USA, significantly altering its labour landscape.[13] At the same time, a 'Great Migration' was underway from rural to urban areas within the US, particularly among American-born White men and women who got employment in textile industries. Many skilled American-born workers had moved into iron, steel, coal mining, and railroad industries, and even the English, Welsh, and Scots found space in these industries. Combined with a substantial rise in the African American labour force, these demographic shifts were important facets of labour relations in the US. African Americans were employed in the most dangerous and low-paid jobs and continued to face racism and economic inequality.[14]

On the West Coast and in the Rocky Mountain states, the arrival of Chinese and Japanese labourers as low-paid workers carrying out the most dangerous jobs was met with racial anxieties and resistance on the part of European Americans. This became heavily politicised, to the extent that in 1882 the **Chinese Exclusion Act** was implemented, which barred the entry of Chinese labourers into the USA for 10 years. During the same period, newly immigrated Hispanics of mixed ancestry—including Spanish, Indigenous, and Mexican Americans—formed a large workforce in the Southwest, from Texas to southern California. They worked on sugar, cotton, and fruit plantations and in mining. The experiences of three labour groups—African Americans, Hispanics and East Asians—highlight differences of race and ethnicity within working-class experiences in the US, and reflect the attempts of White Americans to maintain their social and political dominance by institutionalising racial distinctions. W. E. B. Du Bois termed this 'the wages of whiteness',[15] a notion within which even the recent European immigrants sought to accommodate themselves.

The number of women workers also increased from 1870 to 1920, and they were concentrated in sales, service, and clerical jobs. Most of them were either single, widowed or spouses of disabled workers.[16] An increase in the women's labour force, within a wider context that remained patriarchal, led to a gendered division of workspaces wherein women were relegated to 'domesticity' while men alone had full rights to operate in the public space. The position of women, whether they were formally employed or not, deteriorated as meagre wages forced them to take up extra work to support themselves and their families, like sewing garments, making cigars or artificial flowers, shelling nuts, laundry, and operating boarding houses.

The result was the rise of a segmented working class divided along ethnic, regional, and gendered lines, which established multiple layers of complexity and disunity, preventing cooperative labour unions.[17] Another factor that shaped the American working class was social mobility as most unskilled workers moved around for better opportunities, avoiding the emergence of a unified labour front. From 1865 to 1920, America witnessed not only a series of class struggles along with the rise of the Populist and Progressive movements (see Chapter 4), but also the growing influence of socialism. According to Melvyn Dubofsky, there was also the 'tramping artisan', a category that included coal miners, loggers, maritime labourers, and crop harvesters. They were class-conscious and had a reputation for being assertive and even militant in putting forward collective demands and participating in unions. In contrast, the skilled labour class, which was earning more and occupied a relatively privileged position for long, did not join the labour unions as they were 'people of plenty'.[18]

Work Environment

In terms of living and working conditions, the working classes existed at the margins of society. This situation was worse for those living in remote regions and working in the mining industry. Low wages and extreme poverty fostered an environment of persistent deprivations, endangering the labourers' lives, and the long hours of hard labour in unsanitary and unsafe conditions meant that America had the most industrial accidents in the Western world.[19]

Workers faced a constant threat of being thrown out of their jobs due to frequent economic depressions (1873–1878, 1883–1885, and 1897), recessions, and technological changes and shifts. These conditions often created cycles of joblessness, worsened by non-existent relief measures or public sympathy due to the absence of a stable union that could represent all types of labourers. According to Alexander Keyssar, during extreme economic conditions, the working classes organised public protests to make their voices heard in the corridors of power. They even ensured that the labour vote was consolidated to support politicians willing to make their voices and demands heard.[20] This reflected the growth of 'job consciousness' amongst the working classes and their unions, which gradually began to make their presence felt. In *Poverty* (1914), sociologist and progressive writer Robert Hunter analysed the growing problem of poverty in the USA using statistical and sociological research tools. His analysis pointed to unemployment as a major issue, and he established varied types of dependency ranging from physical and mental illness to difficulties associated with old age. According to Hunter, the conditions exacerbating precarity were cyclical, and only a few underwent a permanent state of persistent poverty.[21]

According to Melvyn Dubofsky, a sterotype of the distressed urban classes emerged during this period and was particularly associated with immigrant workers who were minoritised, like Jewish workers, Italians, Slavs, and Finns.[22] The general perception was that they were immersed in alcoholism, sex crimes, violence, and prone to disease. Still, a very gradual process of acculturation was underway, whereby the immigrant working class blended their old cultural world with the new industrial society they encountered in the US. However, the friction between naturalised Americans and immigrants often erupted in violence and unrest. The immigrant labourers re-established their cultural institutions, kinship networks, ethnic organisations, saloons, and music rooms to maintain their cultural identity and existence in their adopted alien world.[23]

American Working Classes (1865–1897)

Labour relations after the Civil War were marked by increasing tensions, with some of the most violent industrial conflicts erupting in the last decades of the nineteenth century. Influential trade unions that emerged at the national level were pitted against the overall consolidation of industrial might, with big corporations thriving on the back of bureaucratic management and rapid mechanisation, fostering impersonal societal relationships. Three developments, in particular—the widespread adoption of railroads, steamships, and the telegraph—established the national economy and integrated internal markets with the global economy. While rapid changes became frequent and greatly enhanced economic integration, these changes also created a 'chaotic environment'. According to historian Robert Wiebe, this led to the rise of 'island communities' where working-class individuals stitched their lives around family, neighbours, and their respective churches to retain some control over their personal life and working conditions.[24] Still, the fact remains that economic changes were so powerful that 'forces of production' killed the 'relations of production'. Political parties, influenced by powerful business corporations, did nothing for the common masses, and the latter faced difficulties in adapting to the rapid technological and bureaucratisation of economic activities and society. The resultant struggle between the labourers and business corporations culminated in the corporate movement towards concentration of power with a small group of people, moving away from the American ideals of individualism, free and fair competition, and equal opportunity. Work discipline clashed with working class demands for autonomy, forcing them to take steps to control social and political power in their 'island communities'.[25]

Conflicts and Strikes

Conflicts between working class groups and the capitalist class sharpened after the Civil War, frequently erupting in mass protests, for instance, the **railroad strikes and riots in 1877**, and the **Pullman Railroad Boycott in 1884**. In the latter case, the federal government used the army to break the workers' strike, and it soon became a pattern that strikes would be met with military force on the pretext of curbing violence and disorder. There were an estimated 9,668 strikes and lockdowns,[26] which clearly suggest that by the end of the nineteenth century, strikes were the preferred course of action. These were sometimes spontaneous, and later, under the influence of trade unions, became more structured and planned.[27] On **1 May 1886, the Haymarket Affair in Chicago** became a site of labour union demonstrations supporting the eight-hour workday. There was visible agitation amongst the workers in a series of meetings that continued on 3 and 4 May at the McCormick Repair Plant and Haymarket Square. A sudden storm on 4 May 1886 broke up the meeting. By night, only a few strikers were left, since the police had ordered them to disperse, when suddenly a bomb exploded. This was immediately followed by an exchange of gunshots, with many accounts suggesting that the police was first to open fire. Ultimately, the violence resulted in the deaths of seven policemen and four to eight workers; estimates of the wounded range widely, since many went into hiding to avoid persecution. The event is known in the annals of American history as the **Haymarket Tragedy**. Later, in 1889, the International Socialist Conference declared that 1 May would be an International Workers' Day to commemorate the Haymarket Affair.

FIG. 3.1: Two girls don banners calling to 'Abolish Child Slavery' in English and Yiddish, most likely at a Labour Day Parade in New York City (c. 1909)

Source: Wikimedia Commons.

IRISH LABOUR

Labour historians often take up the case of the anthracite miners of northeastern Pennsylvania. This was among the regions where internal transportation systems developed rapidly in the mid-1800s, leading to an economic boom that brought in immigrant miners. The intensifying cut-throat business competition saw a sharp rise in the rate of industrial accidents from the 1860s to 1870s—overinvestment in mining properties led to overproduction, which in turn forced wage cuts and reductions, creating an atmosphere of economic insecurity. Over time, three ethnic groups came to dominate the local society and economy in northeast Pennsylvania. The first were the Scots-Irish, who controlled most of the mines, and the second were the Welsh and English, who worked as mine superintendents and public officials. Both of these were Protestant groups. Then came the Irish Catholics, who already had a history of conflict with the English (owing to the suppression of Ireland by the British empire). These tensions came to the surface in a conflict that had both ethno-religious and socio-economic dimensions.[28]

Irish labourers, prior to migration, had developed secret societies to remain organised even in repressive conditions and prevent being over-exploited by their English overlords. When a surveillance system was put in place to curb labour freedom, workers came together to establish the **Workingmen's Benevolent Association (WBA)** under the leadership of John Siney; the union found some success in limiting the powers of the operators responsible for curbing their freedom. However, a series of unsolved murders, rising crime, strikes, and associated violence, coupled with the economic depression of 1873, brought the simmering conflict out in the open.[29] An important turning point was the rise of Franklin B. Gowen, president of Reading Railroad, who controlled the transport network from the southern fields to the markets and had a close relationship with the rail workers who dominated the northern areas. Gowen took advantage of this when formulating policies concerning prices, wages, and the process of union negotiations. To eliminate small competitors, he bought the coal properties—placing him on a collision course with the increasingly influential WBA.

To strengthen his hold, Gowen had to weaken the WBA. In the meantime, Irish workers had established a secret society, the Ancient Order of Hibernians (AOH), which had an inner circle—the Molly Maguires—that carried out the society's covert activities. Gowen set out to destroy this society using a two-pronged strategy. In the first phase, he mingled with the middle- and upper-middle-class Irish community by associating with the Catholic bishop of Philadelphia in order to create a class divide between the 'polished' and 'primitive' Irish communities. In the second phase, he placed an informer or 'mole' inside the AOH to break the organisation. The reports he received of their intended actions, members, and strategies were put to good use in 1875 when the **Long Strike**, lasting six months, was launched by the WBA. The strike was successfully brought down and the mole made a state witness, resulting in the persecution of suspected Molly Maguires, with the result that 20 labourers were sentenced to death. The court trial was conducted in a manner that forced the WBA to identify Molly Maguires as responsible for disturbing law and order.

The historian Herbert Gutman also found similar patterns replicated in other strikes. In a famous railroad strike in 1877, President Rutherford B. Hayes ordered federal troops to repress the strike and re-impose law and order in society. A system began to emerge whereby industrialists hired 'scabs' (strike breakers), employed security guards, and used politicians and the law to their advantage. They also deliberately exacerbated ethnic and racial divisions by exploiting workers' ignorance and acute poverty. Big business organisations, with their growing economic power and access to new technologies, gradually reduced labour-heavy operations and gained an upper hand even in negotiations with skilled labour. They also successfully created the impression that labour union activities and strikes were 'anti-social' and anarchist, thus garnering greater support among society in general, as well as from the state and federal governments.[30] Even the courts failed to protect the American labouring classes. In the 'Gilded Age', the 'power of money' became the primary reason for labour conflict in the US.[31]

The Rise of Labour Unions

This extreme and adverse situation necessitated the formation of labour unions that could pool together their combined power and establish national unions with the organisational strength and resources to conduct long-duration strikes and challenge employers' economic power, propaganda, and lawsuits. This required a structured administrative apparatus, including membership fees and maintenance of finances. By the end of the nineteenth century, workers were faced with two challenges:

(i) to choose whether to work within the capitalistic system or destroy it; and
(ii) to establish national labour unions and confront an increasingly powerful capitalist class.

The National Labour Union

The **National Labour Union (NLU)** emerged in 1866 in Baltimore, under the leadership of William Sylvis, as America's first national federation of unions. The NLU advocated a key set of demands and measures:

(i) a maximum limit of eight-hour workday;
(ii) government monetary policies that favoured debtors;
(iii) federal land distribution programmes for working people;
(iv) strengthen workers' efforts to organise labour unions;
(v) establish workers' cooperatives for procuring essential commodities at low prices; and
(vi) inclusion of women and Black workers in unions.[32]

According to historians Norman Ware and Gerald Grob, the NLU's social reform agenda enabled its transition into the National Labour Reform Party by 1872. However, it failed to establish an organisational structure and core political alignment, and was unable to bring in marginalised groups like women and unskilled labourers within the working class. Therefore, it faced an early demise. On the other hand, David Montgomery perceived the NLU as a political organisation that strengthened the labour force and allowed it to effectively lobby at the national level.[33] Montgomery also argued that at this juncture, labour unions were influenced by the republican principles of individualism, liberty, and virtuousness as citizens. However, with the rise of big businesses, the growing economic disparity and extreme exploitation of the labouring classes necessitated the formation of labour unions in varied shades, from reformist organisations to political labour-oriented parties and the establishment of the Marxist International Workingmen's Association to secure rightful social and economic power to ensure legal equality.[34]

Sylvis, president of the Molders' Union and later chief executive officer of NLU, drew from Karl Marx's ideology. His now famous pamphlet, 'The Eight-Hour Movement: A Reduction of Hours is an Increase of Wages', was written around the same time that Ira Steward, a theorist of labour goals, founded the **Grand Eight-Hour League of Massachusetts in 1865**. The two worked in tandem, deploying different strategies to achieve the goal of limited working hours. Sylvis wanted to establish a national trade union and bring monetary reform through political action programmes to improve the lives of American labourers. Following his sudden demise in 1869, Steward took up the mantle of advocating for shorter working hours, arguing that this would raise real wages, improve living conditions, and grant more financial resources to the working class to purchase consumer goods.

Sylvis believed that a limited workday would accelerate the growth of the US economy. His years of political lobbying were instrumental in securing a ten-hour workday law for women and child workers in Massachusetts (1874). David Montgomery has argued that these strategies marked a transition from the Jacksonian era, where labour was clamouring for reforms and the end of monopolies, to the establishment of a more humanistic and equal society in the age of industrialisation.[35] However, with its shrinking membership and resources, the NLU could not survive the economic depression of 1873.

THE NOBLE AND HOLY ORDER OF THE KNIGHTS OF LABOUR

In 1869, two garment cutters, Uriah Stephens and James Wright, founded the **Noble and Holy Order of the Knights of Labour** as a secret union of garment cutters in Philadelphia. Thanks to this secrecy, the union survived the depression of 1873, and eventually became public in 1878 as the economy improved. According to Norman Ware, it was the only national-level labour organisation to unite other trade unions on the ideological premise of adherence to republican ideals and critique of the existing industrial order. Dubofsky has characterised the Order of the Knights as an organisation that moulded itself into a labour union to impart knowledge to workers and develop systems to secure labour rights.[36] As we have discussed, this period was marked by the power and excesses of big business corporations, and the Knights of Labour emerged in response to the growing need for trade unions.

Terence V. Powderly, a machinist by trade, became an important union leader and in 1879 was made Grand Master Workman of the Knights. He encouraged all 'producing classes' to join the Knights, without distinction of nationality, race, religion, or gender. The goal, thus, was to establish a new social order by expanding union membership, working to create a broad-based labour solidarity and evolving a programme for economic parity and political activism. The Order barred bankers, stockbrokers, lawyers, liquor dealers, and gamblers from membership.[37]

By the 1880s, the Order had grown substantially throughout America, and a successful strike in 1885 by the Knights' rail workers in the West increased its membership to 750,000. In 1886, the Order began participating in politics and launched independent parties. However, the absence of clear political goals, as well as increased resistance to their activities by employers, resulted in its decline.

The Order stood for the enrolment of all workers, including women and Black workers, in their organisation, though gender and racial divisions persisted, with White workers often scuttling attempts at giving marginalised workers a broader role within the Order. Being inclusive, it upheld the principle of industrial unionism, but some craft unions joined it while still maintaining their autonomy and distinction. The Order successfully carried out strikes in many cities. It supported Temperance (as Powderly was a non-drinker) and inculcated good behaviour as an essential part of the Order. However, some Knights were found to be involved in scams and intrigues that tarnished the group's reputation. They also failed to operate successful cooperative stores. The Knights' leaders, while against socialism, believed in public ownership of financial institutions and transportation systems. Due to Powderly's antipathy for strikes, the Order attempted to resolve contentious issues through negotiation and arbitration; however, it still participated in over a 100 strikes.

Historians are divided on the question of whether the Knights of Labour were backward looking, or just a reform movement that wanted to extend the benefits of capitalism to all sections of society. There is little consensus on whether it wanted to build a 'cooperative commonwealth' or just a democratic movement with broader political participation of the working class. The Knights began to decline due to weak leadership, competition from the craft-oriented American Federation of Labour (AFL), and growing hostility to labour unions among the middle and upper classes. The most significant aspect of its legacy was establishing a national organisation and a nuanced critique of capitalist industrial America.

The American Federation of Labour

Born in England, the founder of the **American Federation of Labour (AFL)**, Samuel Gompers, immigrated to New York when he was 13 years old. Here, he met skilled English and German workers well-versed with Marxist and socialist ideologies. Immersed in this social milieu, Gompers came to understand capitalism's weaknesses and the need to strengthen labour unions through well-oiled organisational structures and to push for the creation of equitable profit distribution between the labour and business organisations.

In 1881, Gompers and other skilled men formed the **Federation of Organized Trades and Labour Unions**, which initially allied with the Knights of Labour but became increasingly disillusioned with the movement. He resented Powderly's attempts to dictate policy and ill-organised strikes, and saw the Knights' entry into electoral politics as misguided and a waste of valuable time and energy. In 1886, Gompers led numerous craft unions from the Knights of Labour into his newly formed American Federation of Labour. Till his death in 1924, Gompers remained the most prominent labour leader in the US, commanding the attention of politicians, industrialists, and the press.

Gompers' strategy for the AFL was guided by the following considerations and goals:

(i) The AFL was envisioned as an association of skilled workers who could extract concessions and labour victories.
(ii) The AFL did not register less skilled or easily replaced workers. However, this meant that the Federation ignored the majority of women and Black workers, and also most immigrants.

(iii) The Federation would build strong organisations with high dues, well-paid officers, strike funds, and other benefits to maintain member loyalty and erect a formidable labour organisation capable of exerting pressure on the media, government, and industry.

(iv) Under Gompers' leadership, the AFL took up only 'bread-and-butter issues', demanding higher wages within reason, shorter working hours, and rules to curtail business managers' arbitrary decisions.

(v) The Federation would not waste organisational resources and finances on independent political action or radical political activity.

(vi) The AFL would support only mainstream politicians of any party who favoured pro-labour legislation.

(vii) The Federation rejected both leadership and advice from the intelligentsia and reformers, and concentrated on building 'job consciousness' to protect the rights and jobs of the working class.

The history of AFL has contradictions. Gompers' approach was influenced by his experience with the Knights of Labour. He decentralised the labour union by offering the constituent units maximum autonomy. However, although he spoke out against racial and sexual prejudice and opposed segregated unions, Gompers provided little or no assistance to women and Black workers, who then struggled to form their own alliances. He warned that without outreach, strikes would be lost to the exclusive craft unions. Gompers also argued that labour unions should be non-partisan and non-reliant on politicians, and advocated voluntary efforts. Despite such beginnings, he later became associated with the Democratic Party.

Notwithstanding the founder's conservative methods based on a belief in moderation and appeasement, the AFL became a militant, socialist, and inclusive organisation. In line with his faith in Marxism, Gompers carried out effective labour strikes, challenging capital, but not the capitalist system.

By the end of the nineteenth century, AFL began to exclude Asian and Black workers, as well as East and South European immigrants, as Black workers were blamed for breaking strikes. The other marginalised groups were labelled 'aliens', and women were cast as 'inferior workers', which led to internal fissures within the labour union based on ethnic, racial, and gender divisions. With the organisation becoming more business-like, AFL shifted its office to Washington.[38] These changes led to a substantial increase in AFL membership, greatly assisting the International Typographical Union in securing their demand for an eight-hour workday. At the same time, business corporations began to fund anti-strike associations like the National Association of Manufacturers and Citizens' Alliances.[39]

By the beginning of the twentieth century, AFL had to build up labour organisations that were run by salaried bureaucracy and organised hierarchically, tranforming it into a labour business institution. It worked to secure material gains for its members by extracting concessions from the big corporation owners and kept the public on its side. Dubofsky has suggested that when big businesses introduced a structured scientific management process to maximise labour efficiency, the AFL, too, began to develop a labour-management system of mutually binding rules that established an 'oligarchic' system of control over the labour organisations under its umbrella, within the parameters of the capitalistic system.[40]

The entry of progressive reformers (see Chapter 5) ushered in an era of arbitration to establish 'industrial peace'. Unions started introducing and assisting in 'voluntarism', which would help them lessen oppression of workers by creating powerful independent partnerships. Scholars like Michael P. Rogin assert that voluntarism was used as a tool by the AFL to protect the interests of the labour classes. However, several contradictions appeared: for example, the concept of labour solidarity and collective action came to be seen as conflicting with the American political culture of individualism and liberty.[41]

Through this trajectory, labour representatives realised their dual role as both economic and sociopolitical entities that required political participation to fight adverse judicial decisions through political actions and programmes.[42] In 1906, the AFL formulated the **Labour's Bill of Grievances**, which was put before President Theodore Roosevelt and the Republican Party, but the party remained non-committal to its demands. Therefore, Gompers established a **Labour Representation Committee**, which in 1908 put their agenda before the dominant political parties. The Democratic Party, sensing the possibility of electoral support from the labour force, entered into an alliance with the AFL that became more open and supportive in 1916, when Woodrow Wilson contested the presidential elections. By World War I, the working class had widened its ethnic and religious backgrounds, and its political support depended on which political party was willing to take up its cause.

World War I sparked more militant labour action due to 'war-induced class consciousness' that impacted relations between the working classes and big business, the state, and even labour organisations. Eventually, the War allowed labour unions to become significant labour corporations as they had the power to pressure the government and secure their goals. Some labour leaders, particularly from the AFL, became part of the national political organisation during the tenure of President Wilson. At this time, the USA was entering yet another period of economic depression; however, its neutral stand during the War resulted in greater European orders for war-related supplies. From the middle of 1915 to 1917, American business and labour both enjoyed a period of prosperity and the demand for workers increased substantially. It also saw increased strikes and industrial disputes, especially among skilled workers in war-associated industries. However, any wage gains from such action became insubstantial as the prices of essential commodities rose higher than the wages earned, leading to food riots in several American cities.

The situation became more complex when the government first introduced voluntary enlistment in the US army, to be followed by national conscription. This immediately affected the availability of labour and big corporations had to tap into new groups. Among them were Black southerners who now began to migrate in great numbers to the North, Mexican Americans and Mexican immigrants, and finally, women across racial and ethnic lines—workers from all three groups were mainly semi-skilled or unskilled. The East Europeans who had migrated much earlier to America had by now acquired the necessary experience to become a class of skilled labourers, and they became not only a legitimate citizen-labour class but also made a significant contribution to national war industries. Gompers' decision to support Wilson on the USA's entry into World War I was vehemently opposed by Irish-American, German-American, and Jewish-American workers and supporters of socialism.

The AFL became a powerful force alongside government and big business as Gompers and other union leaders were appointed to the councils of national committees, thanks to the federal labour policy. Some even went on to represent the USA internationally. The AFL, therefore, continued to expand and became a pressure group close to the federal government, and began to overlook the interests of poor, unskilled workers.[43] This neglect alienated a section of the working class, who then turned to left-oriented labour organisations.

The Socialist Labour Party and Socialist Party of America

The labour unions of the nineteenth century began to make efforts to publicise issues concerning the working class through intense lobbying in the corridors of Washington, and also at the state levels. Electorally, both the Republican and Democratic parties brought sections of the labouring classes with them based on ethnicity, religion, and proximity, but not based on class. The influence of political socialism was not evident in the US as it was in Europe. The result was that after the 1860s, when labour-oriented political parties like the **Greenback Party** emerged, they found little success in the presidential elections and later achieved only mediocre success in municipal, state, and Congressional elections. The Republican Party, in the meantime, expanded its electoral base by securing the support of urban industrial workers.

It was only after 1886 that socialism began to influence American labour unions, with the creation of the **Socialist Labour Party**. The party was supported by German immigrants, and later by Jewish workers. Nevertheless, that party began to lose appeal under the leadership of Daniel De Leon, who got entangled in massive arguments with the AFL. Its decline paved the way for the emergence of the **Socialist Party of America (SPA)** under the supervision of Eugene Debs. The aim was to pressure employers to pay higher wages, inculcate political activism amongst party members, and develop a cooperative commonwealth in publicly owned industries. It was a shifting, moderate, and 'pragmatic' socialist movement. It was more successful with organised workers, but frequently changed direction over the issues of immigration, racism, and war and peace.

The Socialist Labour Party and the SPA declined just around the end of World War I. One of the main reasons behind this was that the American labour force was divided by ethnic, religious, and racial differences. Also, by this time, the provision of universal suffrage had dented the socialists' plank. The Democratic Party maintained good relations with trade unions from 1908 to 1918, which prevented the socialists from gaining power at the grassroots level. The fact that both parties were often in conflict with the AFL did not help the socialists. However, the most important reason for their decline was the emergence of a radical, left-wing socialist group that came to be known as Industrial Workers of the World.

Industrial Workers of the World

The **Industrial Workers of the World (IWW)** was a radical labour organisation formed in June 1905 in Chicago by a diverse group of socialists and militant unionists, including William D. Haywood of the Western Federation of Miners, Eugene V. Debs (who was earlier the leader of the SPA) and Daniel De Leon (of the Socialist Labour Party). At its first convention in Chicago, the delegates constituted, in the words of William D. Haywood, a 'Continental Congress of the American Working Class', a national-level organisation parallel to the AFL that would bring together the industrial working class to fight a class war against the capitalists and destroy bourgeois society and government. They appealed to those trade unions and labour classes that the AFL had neglected. While their leaders always differed over philosophy and strategy, some common tactics deployed by IWW members or 'Wobblies' were on-the-job actions such as strikes and sabotage politics. They eventually hoped to organise all workers into a single union per industry, and all unions into 'one big union' or umbrella organisation. This would work to build labour solidarity and prepare for a mass strike that would topple capitalism. The organisation believed the struggle between employer and employee would go on until the labourers become masters of the world, took charge of production, and abolished the wage system. This militant nature of the IWW prompted historian David Brody to define it as a 'homegrown brand of American syndicalism'.

Fig. 3.2: A promotional 'stickerette' of the IWW
Source: Wikimedia Commons.

Known mainly for its revolutionary goals and its violent reputation, the IWW also organised women, Black workers, 'new' immigrants, and workers across skill levels (skilled and unskilled, including semi-skilled and migratory labourers). All of these groups had been shunned by the AFL. The IWW led strikes in the mines of the Rocky Mountain states, the Pacific Northwest, Massachusetts, and Paterson, as well as in New Jersey lumber camps and the steel foundries of Pennsylvania. During World War I, the IWW was subjected to intelligence attacks and prosecution under the pretext of federal and state espionage, sedition, statutes barring criminal syndicalism. In 1912, it was declared illegal as its violent strikes had frightened middle-class Americans. By 1919, burgeoning communist groups emerged as powerful rivals of the IWW, making it defunct by 1920.

Scholars have differing views about why the Wobblies were feared and declined quickly. There is a lack of agreement on whether they wanted a revolution or just reforms. Their members were eager to gain reforms and success and willing to use violent methods, language, and acts to achieve these. The Wobblies' strikes always followed violence. The general impression was that the Wobblies were a gunslinging union whose songs and the oratory power of whose leaders were more famous than tangible results. However, according to Dubofsky, the Wobblies emerged as a response to the new industrial age and were victims rather than aggressors. They were a combination of reformers committed to industrial unions, and expanded civil liberties, and a socialist coalition that broke many existing American cultural norms to achieve their revolutionary goals.[44] The significance of the Wobblies was that they brought into public consciousness the unequal distribution of economic power and the growing corporate, monopolistic accumulation of wealth. Through this, they hoped for a broader section of society to gain more social and economic control. They highlighted how the law was used to weaken and persecute low-income and disenfranchised people. The IWW also gave voice and strength to recent immigrants, ethnic minorities, and African Americans, showing a new pathway of gaining power by developing their organisations and combining their strengths to achieve their goals. The Wobblies dreamt of creating a society where organised workers' unions, based on their class consciousness and using direct action programmes, would wrest control of industries to eliminate the political party system and bureaucracy. This is the reason for categorising IWW members as syndicalists.

Conclusion

Over time, scholars applied new approaches to studying labour history as they began to explore social and occupational mobility, ethnicity, gender and race, and community history. They studied working-class political behaviour and intersecting issues of race and class. Other facets that caught scholars' attention include women and work, scientific management, technological change, company unionism, welfare capitalism, and labour militancy, making American labour history more in-depth and comprehensive in nature.

Notes

1. Paul W. Rhode and Richard Sutch, Table CA192–207, 'Gross national product: 1869–1909 [Gallman]', in *Historical Statistics of the United States, Earliest Times to the Present: Millenial Edition*, edited by Susan B. Carter, et al. (New York, 2006).
2. Gustavus Myers, *History of the Great American Fortunes*, vol. 1 (Chicago, 1909).
3. See https://encyclopediavirginia.org (accessed October 2025).
4. Ibid.
5. Susan Klepp, *The Unfortunate: The Voyage and Adventures of William Moraley, An Indentured Servant* (Philadelphia, 1992).
6. Sidney Pollard, 'Factory Discipline in the Industrial Revolution', *Economic History Review* 16 (2), 1963, pp. 254–271.
7. John R. Commons, *History of Labor in the United States*, vol. 1 (New York, 1921).
8. Alan Dawley, 'Paths to Power after the Civil War', in *Working for Democracy: American Workers from the Revolution to the Present*, ed. Paul Buhle and Alan Dawley (Madison, 1985), pp. 41–51.
9. Alan Dawley, *Class and Community: The Industrial Revolution in Lynn* (Cambridge, 1976).
10. Melvyn Dubofsky, *Industrialism and the American Worker, 1865–1920*, third ed, (Wheeling, Illinois, 1996), pp. 2–5.
11. Ibid., pp. 5–6.
12. Herbert G, Gutman, *Work, Culture, and Society in Industrializing America: Essays in American Working-Class History* (New York, 1977).
13. Ibid., pp. 7–11.
14. Ibid., pp. 11–12.

15. W. E. B. Du Bois, *Black Reconstruction in America: An Essay Towards a History of the Part Which Black Folk Played in the Attempt to Reconstruct Democracy in America, 1860–1880* (New York, 1935).
16. Alice Kessler-Harris, *Out to Work: A History of Wage-Earning Women in the United States* (New York, 2003).
17. Gutman, *Work, Culture, and Society in Industrializing America*, pp. 12–15.
18. Dubofsky, *Industrialism and the American Worker*, p. 20.
19. Ibid., p. 24.
20. Alexander Keyssar, *Out of Work: The First Century of Unemployment in Massachusetts* (New York, 1986).
21. Robert Hunter, *Poverty* (New York and London, 1914).
22. Dubofsky, *Industrialism and the American Worker*, pp. 28–30.
23. Keyssar, *Out of Work*, pp. 28–30.
24. Robert H. Wiebe, *The Search for Order, 1877–1920* (New York, 1967).
25. Keyssar, *Out of Work*, pp. 36–39.
26. David Montgomery, 'Strikes in Nineteenth Century America', *Social History* 4 (1), 1980, pp. 81–102.
27. Keyssar, *Out of Work*, pp. 39–40.
28. Ibid., p. 42.
29. Ibid., p. 41.
30. Ibid., pp. 48–54.
31. Ibid., pp. 56–59.
32. While William Sylvis favoured an inclusive structure, the National Labour Union continued to be dominated by White male workers, who largely opposed such measures due to prevailing biases and a fear of increased competition from Black workers in particular.
33. David Montgomery, *Citizen Worker: The Experience of Workers in the United States with Democracy and the Free Market during the Nineteenth Century* (New York, 1993).
34. Ibid.
35. Ibid.
36. Dubofsky, *Industrialism and the American Worker*.
37. Montgomery, *Citizen Worker*, pp. 64–65.
38. Ibid., pp. 100–101.
39. Dubofsky, *Industrialism and the American Worker*, p. 103.
40. Ibid., pp. 99–100.
41. Michael Rogin, 'Voluntarism: The Political Functionals of an Antipolitical Doctrine', *ILR Review* 15 (4), 1962, pp. 521–535.
42. Dubofsky, *Industrialism and the American Worker*, pp. 106–107.
43. Ibid., pp. 108–110.
44. Ibid., pp. 114–121.

Chapter 4

The Lowell Textile Mill Girls
The Emergence of Women's Unions and Labour Strikes

In histories of economic and labour relations, there has often been a tendency to privilege the perspectives of men over those of women. In the USA, as in much of the Western world, this usually stems at least partly from the exclusion of women from factories and organised professions. Further, economic sectors that saw high participation of women, including agriculture, textiles, domestic and care work, have often been undervalued. Thus, working-class women not only experienced scarcity and material deprivations on account of their class position but were also constrained by a patriarchal culture both at home and in the workplace. The scenario becomes more complicated due to the prevalence of racial and ethnic discrimination.

Despite these social limitations, women made significant contributions to the struggle for labour rights in the US. The Ten-Hour Strike by women workers of the Lowell Textile Mills presents an important case at the intersection of labour and gender issues. It became an early marker of women's growing labour consciousness and their entry into public spaces, breaking societal barriers for social and gender equality as well as economic independence.

New Spaces of Work

In the **Anglo-American tradition**, women had no legal status, political rights, or freedom of spatial movement. They could not participate in public or civic rituals. Women were expected to be pious, submissive, domesticated, and religious. However, such notions were challenged as rapid transformations in economic and demographic patterns altered the social landscape. By the beginning of the nineteenth century, around 1815, rapid **westward expansion** prompted greater mobility among the population. The beginning of the **transportation and communication revolutions**, which saw the advent of canals and improved postal services, provided further encouragement for the movement of people. The period also witnessed the commercialisation of agriculture, creating a pool of landless farmers who were forced to migrate to urban areas, and also leading to changes in gender roles. This societal shift allowed women, who had hitherto been confined to their homes, to move out and take up formal work.

The Lowell Textile Mills developed in Massachusetts at this juncture. The mill was established by Francis Cabot Lowell, a 'visionary' who not only found a suitable location near the Pawtucket Canal—so that canal water could be used to power the looms—but who also developed the unique **Waltham-Lowell system of production**. This method involved vertical integration of the processes of spinning, weaving, dying, and cutting cloth, all carried out by women workers. In other words, it was a revolutionary approach that brought all aspects of production under a single plant and thereby transformed the textile industry. Under this system, families were incentivised to send their daughters to work within a system characterised by paternalism and 'moral guardianship', bringing them from farms to factories, where they resided in the protective environment of the mill's boarding houses and working for fixed wages. The mill acquired a unique reputation, since women workers not only augmented their families' income, but also had the opportunity to become educated and socialise in a protective environment.

The Development of Textile Mills

The Lowell Textile Mill developed in two phases. In the first phase, from 1800 to 1820, textile mills were set up, drawing in labourers from agricultural families who were searching for work. The work culture was based on the **model of family labour**, where the father worked on a company farm, and the mother and children worked in the mills. According to Barbara M. Tucker, class consciousness had not developed among labourers at this point since the textile factory was based on a traditional pattern of authority and patriarchal regulation.[1] The mill owners established a 'harmonious relationship' based on a management system that worked well for both employer and employee. The father or patriarch controlled members of his family, and the mill used this regulation as a form of social control. This meant that **patriarchal logic** directed the early phase of transition from artisanal production, a traditional form of work, to factory work, a new and emerging socio-economic structure.[2] The second phase, from 1820 onwards, occurred amid a period of rapid immigration to westward territories. More and more people desired economic independence, while mill owners wanted to increase their profit margins. According to Albert Niemi, by the 1820s the rise of large-scale factory production had enabled the entry of those women into the workforce who were earlier concentrated in handicrafts, domestic service, and agriculture.[3] The introduction of the **power loom** in the northern textile industry in 1814 was another significant factor in the shift from handicraft to large-scale factory production. The formal employment of an increasing number of women was crucial to this transition, marking an important shift in societal norms and women's roles.[4]

Until the beginning of the Civil War (1861–1865), the textile industry was the only avenue for women's employment as all other manufacturing industries were male-dominated. Tucker has shown that by 1829, patriarchy gave way to '**competitive capitalism**', a new economic system emphasising profit and competition. This shift brought in new methods of cost accounting and management practices in the period between the 1820s and the Civil War. By the

1840s, textile women workers began to face stiff competition from first-generation immigrants, leading to a decrease in their wages. With the coming of industrialisation, brought on by the entry of immigrant labour, the mills' management began to control labour as a class (that is, the father or patriarch no longer held importance). Labour now became premised on the individual as the basic unit of economic production, who would be paid direct wages, which led to conflicts and competition for jobs—between men and women, young and old, longtime European settlers and new immigrants and religious groups. The textile mill owners took advantage of this to keep wages low and prices competitive. This new system led to an increase in mill workers, who were made to work even on Sundays. New machines with more advanced technology were installed to increase production, and this became the pretext for more stringent control over labour.

It was easy to discipline and control women labourers based on the application of patriarchal control mechanisms. Most of them were in the impressionable age group of 15 to 25 years and were paid low wages. Out of about 1,200 workers, 90 per cent were women. The women were required to enter into a contract that promised: '... regular church attendance, strict moral behaviour, and residence in a corporation boardinghouse'. About 30 to 40 women were made to stay together in each boarding house and were supervised by house 'mothers' who were responsible for their well-being and reported their activities to the mill owners. This supervision was implemented to maintain the 'moral qualities' of the workers and the mill's productivity, as the mill motto was 'Good girls do good work'. The boardinghouse controlled every aspect of the workers' lives, from when they entered the factory for work to meal and curfew time, and information was maintained about their visitors, movements, and daily activities. Nevertheless, even with such restrictions on their spatial movement, the new labour dynamic sparked a subtle change in the American economy and society. In nineteenth-century America, when women were usually relegated to being daughters, wives, and mothers and had no voting or property rights, the textile mills offered women economic independence and a better life.

Work Routine

At the mill, young workers or '**doffers**' were charged with changing the bobbins on the spinning machines. Their slender hands and small frame gave them the advantage of working around the device, a feat impossible for adults. However, they were paid less than the adult workers on the looms. The doffers were made to work around 14 hours daily and were constantly guided by adult workers. Adolescent and adult employees spent the little spare time they had together, playing the piano, reading books, writing letters, and sewing. Over time, doffers who persisted with work increased their rank and became carders, spinners, and weavers. Some of these workers, even after returning home to get married, sought to remain economically independent by pursuing higher education or starting independent businesses or trade.[5]

Fig. 4.1: Two young women of the Lowell Mill, tintype (c. 1870)
Source: Wikimedia Commons.

The Period of Transformative Change

Economic independence was followed by a new sense of freedom from patriarchal control as the workers were far away from parental supervision. With money, they could gain an education and visit public spaces. This manifested in the freedom of expression and spatial movement, a 'transformative change' that, along with economic and technological changes in the working environment of the mill, sparked a growing consciousness of their 'collective identity'.

Between 1830 and 1837, two significant developments took place in the textile industry:

(i) Increased competition led to declining prices of clothes.
(ii) By 1837, there was a sharp decline in consumer demand for clothes due to an economic depression. This forced the mill owners to introduce three new working systems: speed-up, stretch-out, and premium.

To increase output without increasing salaries, the price paid per unit was reduced. The growing pressure to increase production eroded the relationship between mill owners and workers. According to Alfred W. Niemi, Jr., the working conditions became punishing, with workdays extending to 12–13 hours in mills with poor ventilation, unhygienic conditions, and non-existent safety norms. The result was the beginning of verbal opposition from the women workers, who began to demand a limit on working hours.[6]

The protests by women workers at Lowell Mill occurred in three phases. In the first phase of the strike, on 1 March 1834, about 800 workers spontaneously walked out when they received wages with a 12 to 25 per cent reduction. The women workers organised a procession to demonstrate their opposition to wage cuts and issued a statement with the heading, 'Union is Power'. This unorganised procession ended almost as soon as it had begun. The second strike took place in October 1836 with a significantly larger contingent of about 1,500 women, who decided to march in protest against an increase in rent for the boarding houses, which was another method of wage reduction. This was a more prolonged strike that went on for almost a month, and this time, women workers from other textile mills joined hands and marched to Chapel Hill to listen to the speeches of labour leaders, reformers, and one daring woman worker who outlined the problems faced by the mill girls. This was a significantly better-organised strike as, by this time, the women labourers had established the **Factory Girls' Association**. Lessons learnt from these protest marches were carried forward in the third strike at Lowell Textile Mill, which came to be known as the **Ten-Hour Movement**.

The Ten-Hour Movement

In 1845, 1,150 workers signed petitions in Lowell demanding a 10-hour workday, reduced rent for dormitories, better working conditions, and better wages. Three-fifths of these workers were women. In the same year, the newspaper *Voice of Industry* initiated a campaign under the banner of the **Lowell Female Labour Reform Association**, collecting 2,000 signatures to apply pressure on the House of Representatives to investigate working conditions of the textile factories where, on average, workers were required to put in 12.5 to 14.5 hours of labour each day in extreme conditions that impacted their physical and mental well-being and hampered individual growth. William Schouler, the Massachusetts House of Representatives member from Lowell, forced the state legislature to appoint an investigating committee. He heard six of the most experienced women operatives, working between 16 months and eight years,[7] who presented a primary demand and enumerated their workplace difficulties:

(i) Their demand was for a 10-hour workday. They argued that limiting the workday to 10 hours would grant them benefits of an intellectual, moral, and religious nature.
(ii) They complained about an unhealthy working environment inside mills with no proper ventilation, sanitation, or light.
(iii) They complained that they were permitted very short breaks for meals.

This time, the striking women were better organised, and they marched to the state legislative assembly, asserting their right to freedom of space, expression, and gender equality (the last demand is particularly remarkable in a time generally marked by a patriarchal mindset and limitations). The legislative committee, however, concluded that the workers had no adverse health conditions, that they were getting adequate wages, and that their working conditions were satisfactory. They opposed the 10-hour workday as it would put Massachusetts mills at a competitive disadvantage.

The **Female Labour Reform Association (FLRA)** was at the heart of the Ten-Hour Movement. Before this, Lowell Mill labourers had formed the **New England Workingmen Association (NEWA)**, which encouraged the admission of women's labour groups on an equal basis with those of men. The FLRA focused on a host of activities:

(i) Working to generate labour consciousness.

(ii) Organising periodic fairs, picnics, musical evenings, and propaganda.

(iii) FLRA started the pro-labour newspaper *Voice of Industry*, edited by Sarah Bagley, which reported on the activities of the Association and the working conditions of women workers.

(iv) Another newspaper, the *Lowell Offering*, sought to build respect for New England women workers. Harriet Hanson Robinson, Lucy Larcom, and Sarah Bagley elaborated on the working conditions of the Lowell Mill girls. Their articles highlighted that these women were sent to work so that their earnings could put their brothers through college, help their family pay off debts, and support the ever-expanding family. The articles hinted at diseases these workers frequently suffered, like lung inflammation, cholera, measles, dysentery, and inflammation of the brain. In 1844, there were 362 deaths in the mills, of which 200 were child workers under the age of 10 years.

In time, these reports together formed a strong critique of the 'benevolent' paternalism of textile mill managers and owners, highlighting the sexual and economic discrimination against female workers. Eventually, this also led to the development of a shared identity based on the 'sisterhood' of working women. Through their collective action, these workers also developed a critique of the 'cult of womanhood', a highly restrictive social code that confined women to their homes (see Chapter 9). However, some women workers opposed the Ten-Hour Movement as they came to work only for brief periods and earned money expressly for their families and to secure their marriages. They focused only on the short-term implication that the 'Ten-Hour Movement' may lead to a reduction of their wages as working hours were disrupted or reduced. The women opposing the movement were often of an overall conservative orientation, having internalised the belief that domestic labour and marriage made up their whole life. They accepted that men should determine customs, laws and opinions, including those affecting women. This was the dominant ideology that enabled the persistence of women's subordination and confined them to the domestic sphere.

Broader Developments in Women's Activism

New journals began to criticise the prevailing gender ideology in the US. From the 1820s, the journal *Advocate of Moral Reform*—and its most prominent contributors, the Grimke sisters—championed women's rights, condemned sex work, and highlighted women's work and contribution at home. These journals were critical of society's tendencies toward 'protection and paternalism', particularly in the context of rising commercialisation and industrialisation of the economy, which resulted in the devaluation of women's work.

The period saw the development of a newfound consciousness where women began to question why they needed the 'support' of men when they were economically independent. The 'cult of true womanhood' depended on the twin notions of 'dependence' and 'subordination'. Existing norms that governed White American society emphasised four 'virtues' that all women were to inculcate: purity, piety, submission, and domesticity. Thus, women's identity was premised on their status as mothers, daughters, wives, and sisters, and as beings who belonged in the domestic space, beyond which they had no existence. Moving away from such an ideology, new women's journals argued that home and family were limiting influences and accused men of defining womanhood without actually paying heed to women's voices. The Ten-Hour Movement cannot be termed a revolutionary movement, but it was nevertheless one that broadened the scope of women's rights activism. Many women continued to adhere to the cult of womanhood; economic independence was a stepping stone to marriage and reintegration into a system of dependence and subordination. But these developments led American women to realise they had a right to education, self-respect, and an inalienable right to full participation in economic activities, such as working in textile mills. This was indicative of the emergence of a new, empowering consciousness and community-based bond amongst women workers that went against entrenched societal norms. As workers, women shared experiences, helped each other in times of need, and also trained other women apprentices on the machines to get jobs.

Textile mills also forced specific changes on women. They had to change their style of dressing, living, and speaking. The mills created three new elements—the work structure, the boarding system, and workforce homogeneity—all of which were factors in the women's protest movement. However, by 1860, before the concretisation of this newfound consciousness and identity, the age of the 'mill girl' began to fade as mill owners began to prefer European immigrant workers, mainly the Irish, Greek, Polish and Russians, who were ready to work longer hours for much lower wages.

Importance of the Ten-Hour Movement

The significance of the Ten-Hour Movement was manifold. For the first time, women demanded direct political action to reform their working conditions and wage labour system. With the 1837 economic depression looming, the FLRA, which had 600 members, joined the **Lowell Female Industrial Reform and Mutual Aid Society**. The movement raised women's labour consciousness and enabled the growth of a community identity while also empowering women to raise their voices in the public arena.

The most important aspect of the Lowell Mill strikes was that it was women who initiated the movement towards early labour reform, even as they were denied fundamental legal rights to vote, own property, or make decisions about their lives. These working women were not only economically independent but also mentally committed and resilient. They wrote articles and poems. They organised themselves to establish a union, which later played a crucial role in the strike. It was a collective initiative that reflected their efforts at labour reform, their capacity to understand both their strength and the nature of exploitation they faced as a group; it also marked their conscious opposition to exploitation. In the process, the women workers of Lowell Mill became important figures in American history, and especially in assessing the historical exploitation and liberation efforts of women.

Notes

1. Barbara M Tucker, *Samuel Slater and the Origins of the American Textile Industry, 1790–1860* (New York, 1984).
2. Ibid.
3. Albert W. Neimi, Jr. *U.S. Economic History* (Boston, 1980), pp. 305–307.
4. Ibid.
5. Thomas Dublin, 'Women, Work, and Protest in the Early Lowell Mills: "The Oppressing Hand of Avarice Would Enslave US"', *Labor History* 16 (1), 1975, pp. 100–105.
6. Neimi, *U.S. Economic History*, p. 306.
7. Ibid., p. 307.

Chapter 5

The Populist Movement and the Progressive Era

Introduction

This chapter concentrates on the two extremely significant movements in American politics, society, and economy. The **Populist Movement** collectively emerged in the background of prolonged agrarian problems encountered by the southern and western farmers who, in the postbellum period, faced the twin problems of debt and economic hardship. They blamed the powerful big businesses, in particular railroad companies and banking institutions, for using unfair business practices to usurp wealth. Various farmers' alliances came together in 1892 to establish the **Populist Party**, also known as the **People's Party**, focused on unifying American farmers against political and economic corruption. The main aim of this party was to initiate reforms, particularly on issues of taxation and government regulation of railroads, and to demand direct elections of senators to the US Congress.

Many of the Populist Party programmes were implemented during the **Progressive era** that emerged in the late nineteenth and early twentieth centuries. This was a period of intense social activism and political reform; a wave of methodical research, scholarship, popular writings (novels, magazine articles, etc.), films, and paintings emerged highlighting major problems of American society and economy. These sparked different political initiatives. The Progressives brought public attention to the problems associated with rapid urbanisation and industrialisation, particularly increasing corruption, widening wealth inequity and growing poverty, unsafe working conditions, and extremely low wages that further widened economic disparities. Progressive reformers ushered in a new era of social reform measures, highlighting the need for welfare programmes, better sanitation, public healthcare, and government intervention to rein in the big corporations. Crucially, they also engaged with the question of women's rights. This period in US history was significant due to the impact it had on social advocacy and political reform, particularly during the presidencies of Theodore Roosevelt and Woodrow Wilson.

The Populist Movement

The agrarian movement that came to be known as **Populism** emerged in the 1890s and is considered a turning point in American history. This was an era of large-scale immigration from southern and eastern Europe, in the wake of rapid economic growth and the emergence of big business corporations. However, this coincided with the economic depression from 1893 to 1897, which led to large-scale unemployment and pushed many into poverty and hunger. The federal government was insensitive to these hardships: President Grover Cleveland brought down organised public protests and industrial strikes with military deployment and legal persecution (1885–1889; 1893–1897).

At this critical juncture, many Americans questioned the compatibility between democracy and business, leading to the rise of the **Progressive Movement**. Some began to take the initiative of setting up settlement houses in low-income areas. Christian ministers organised church activities to provide community assistance and alleviate suffering. Newly emergent women's clubs became forums to discuss social problems. Even big businesses felt compelled to contribute to municipal reforms aimed at improving urban living conditions. As we have discussed, new transportation and communication systems were developed in this period, and increasing mechanisation reduced human labour; however, machines were expensive and required large capital investments. In agriculture, this effectively widened the gaps between rich and poor farmers, adversely affecting the rural economy, which was already suffering due to monopolies in the banking and railroad sectors.

Discontent in rural USA was many years in the making. The government had made some interventions in the preceding decades. During the Civil War, the federal government had begun to pump money into developing agricultural colleges and education centres through the **Morrill Land-Grant Act (1862)**, which encouraged research projects and created new crops like soybeans. Eligible states were allocated 30,000 acres of federal land for every member of Congress that they had as of 1860.[1] The land was to be sold, and money was put into the endowment fund to support applied fields like agriculture, mechanical arts, and home economics. For these reasons, it is also known as the **Land Grant College Act**. Nevertheless, farmers were faced with mounting problems as the prices of staple crops like cotton, wheat and corn had been declining. Technological advances may have increased farm productivity, but overproduction decreased agricultural incomes worldwide. In the cotton-dependent South, White and Black families, landowners, and tenants alike struggled to repay the merchants who held liens on their crops. The farmers also faced problems due to unfavourable climatic conditions, soil erosion, faulty credit systems, stiff international competition, and attempts by the northern industries and financial institutions to monopolise the southern markets.

The National Grange of the Order of Patrons of Husbandry

Compared to factory workers, America's farmers had certain advantages in forming associations. White rural Americans were all native-born Protestants and their conditions of life and labour were tied to the land they worked, fostering a sense of cultural homogeneity. The predecessors of the Populist Movement were the **National Grange of the Order of Patrons of Husbandry**, generally known as the **National Grange,** founded in 1867 by Oliver Hudson

The Populist Movement and the Progressive Era 115

Kelley as a response to the negative impacts of technological progress and capital investment on the rural economy and the established social fabric of the rural community.[2] It was not a political movement at the time of its inception, and aimed primarily to highlight and address the issues of rural communities. However, it later shifted goals to improving farmers' social and economic conditions and introducing new cost-effective and efficient techniques of cultivation (for instance, it supported the use of the cast-iron plough, which increased productivity by 50 per cent). It also established farming cooperatives and marketing associations where small farmers could open general stores and get northern industrial products at competitive rates, thus contributing to the modernisation of the agricultural economy (which had so far been highly localised and dependent on kin networks and community-based social relations). To bring the rural community together, the Grange organised social events like the Grange Fairs and picnics. These spaces allowed farmers to exchange knowledge about new agricultural practices, and public lectures were organised on different aspects of rural life and economy, eventually resulting in the emergence of agricultural journals and periodicals. Additionally, fairs and picnics were a popular means of socialisation and to discuss organisational and economic matters.

The **Granger movement**, therefore, began as a social and educational association of midwestern farmers and later became an organised protest against economic exploitation. Its membership peaked in 1875 (partly due to the financial crisis of 1873), and the first Grange-backed legislation was passed in 1871 in Illinois, which empowered a **Railroad and Warehouse Commission** to fix maximum rates chargeable for short- and long-haul trains and for using warehouses to store grain. Later, Wisconsin and Iowa regulated interstate railroad freight rates in 1874, and by 1876, independent farmer associations had been organised in nine American states. One remarkable aspect of this movement was the inclusion of women, as the Head Council reserved four of the elected posts for women. According to Charles M. Gardner, one of the slogans adopted at St. Louis Grange was, 'Give women in the Grange equal voice and vote'.[3] However, the organisation was not racially inclusive: Black agriculturalists were mostly excluded, with the predictable outcome that racist attitudes became widespread within the White-dominated association. A prevalent anxiety among Grangers was that if Black farmers were given opportunities, they would outperform their White counterparts. After the Civil War, Black sharecroppers, tenant farmers, and independent farmers formed the **Colored Farmers' National Alliance and Cooperative Union** since they were excluded from White-dominated farmer alliances. The primary goal of the **Colored Alliance** was to improve farmers' economic position through cooperative organisation. This approach enabled Black farmers to be competitive in the markets and actively participate in the farmers' movement and reform processes of the era. Significantly, the Alliance also helped blur racial differences in rural America.

The Grange-backed laws implemented in some states outlawed pooling arrangements and discriminatory rate practices, favouring some railroad companies to ship crops over others. These laws were a historic first step toward more effective government regulation of business in the US, which later led to the **Interstate Commerce Commission Act of 1887**, which established the Interstate Commerce Commission, the nation's first federal regulatory agency to prevent railroad companies' monopolistic tendencies.

The Greenback Party

The beginnings of political collectivisation of American farmers, which would come to power the Granger movement, can be traced to the financial panic of 1837, the Civil War, and the Franco-Persian War in Europe. Taken together, these factors led to price collapse and economic pressure on rural communities in the US, eventually prompting the Grange to focus on the economic interests of rural communities. The period also marked the beginning of an outmigration where increasing numbers of African Americans, and also some marginal White farmers, began to move North and West in search of economic opportunities and a better life. This necessitated the turn to mainstream politics.

The **Greenback Party** emerged in the mid-1870s, primarily supported by politically active farmers and trade unionists. During the Civil War, the federal government issued paper currency that was not backed by or redeemable in gold (this is generally termed **fiat currency**). These were popularly called '**greenbacks**' due to the green ink used on the reverse side of the notes. The issuance of greenbacks fueled extreme inflation during the Civil War, prompting calls for a ban. However, labour and farm groups wanted to keep them because a loose money system provided easier access to credit, allowed for repayment of debts in depreciated currency, and offered a chance to combat a deflationary cycle that kept farm prices and wages low. Despite the farmers' struggle to maintain greenbacks, their lobbying pressures resulted in the federal government adopting silver as a basis for issuing more redeemable paper currency instead of gold.

The Rise of the Farmers' Alliance

In the 1880s, agricultural protest reached a new phase with the emergence of the **Farmers' Alliance**, an economic movement that grew out of the National Grange and brought together multiple independent organisations, notably the **Northern Alliance**, the **Southern Alliance**,[4] and the **Colored Farmers' National Alliance**. It encouraged the formation of local farmers' purchasing and marketing cooperatives. The Alliance also called for greater support to farmers as they were facing adverse economic conditions due to repeated crop failures, drought, high storage and warehouse fees, falling prices of agricultural produce, poor marketing, and credit avenues. The Farmers' Alliance began in Texas in the mid-1870s and had spread throughout the South by the 1880s. The first concrete organisational structure was formed in 1880 by Chicago farm journalist Milton George. Later, several local chapters were established and consolidated into state-wide groups. The movement saw cooperative purchasing and marketing enterprises as a solution to financial hardship in rural America. Among their demands was a new fiat currency, the introduction of a federal income tax on wealthy farmers, direct elections of Senators, and nationalisation of transportation and communication companies, along with government warehouses where farmers could deposit their harvested crops and borrow capital at a low rate of interest. Compared with the Grange movement, Farmers' Alliances were more politicised.

Fig. 5.1: US Post stamp commemorating the National Grange (1967)

Source: Wikimedia Commons.

The Alliance assisted farmers in mobilising to buy seeds and other supplies at wholesale prices and invest together in expensive farm machinery. They also pooled their harvests together and marketed in concert, waiting for the best prices. The cooperative movement became a crusade, enrolling, educating, and politicising farmers.

The farm cooperatives established in the 1880s needed easier access to credit, and the money supply issue became linked to the cause of cooperatives. The Alliance pushed the sub-treasury plan, or the **Federal Farm Credit and Marketing Scheme**, an ambitious scheme that called for the federal government to establish a nationwide system of agricultural warehouses. Under the programme, individual farmers or their cooperatives would store their crops in government storage facilities, thus avoiding the exorbitant fees charged by private operators, and, in turn, their crops would serve as collateral against low-interest government loans. The farm cooperatives' supporters hinged the movement's success on the enactment of the sub-treasury plan. However, when the Republicans and Democrats alike ignored

The Rise of the Populist Party

The Populist Party was established on 4 July 1892. According to John D. Hicks, the party pitted itself against the rising power of 'eastern plutocracy'.⁵ Similarly, Adam Slez describes the party as a response to an emerging urban hierarchy that created stark material and spatial inequalities, and wanted political actions to remedy the condition of farmers in debt.⁶ At the party's national platform in 1892, a strong critique of political and economic institutions was advanced and reforms proposed to bring equitable economic benefits to the farmers. 'We meet in the midst of a nation brought to the verge of moral, political and material ruin', stated the party's preamble. They then put forward the following demands:

(i) Introduction of a stable currency and increased circulation in terms of free and unlimited coinage of silver.
(ii) Cancellation of railroad land grants to the northern railroad companies.
(iii) Debarring foreigners and recent immigrants from securing land ownership.
(iv) Nationalisation of railroad, telegraph, telephone, postal services, and banks.
(v) Limit on the working hours of agricultural labourers to eight hours per day.
(vi) Restrictions on immigration to the USA.
(vii) Curbs on monopolisation of land by wealthy farmers.
(viii) Implementation of a graduated income tax on wealthy farmers, using the money for the growth and development of the rural economy and tariffs for revenue only.
(ix) Initiation of federal poverty alleviation programmes and instituting preventive measures to stop the exploitation of small farmers.
(x) Direct election of Senators.

According to Lawrence Goodwyn,[7] the Populists' demands required 'structural alteration' of hierarchical economic structures. They were meant to bring about significant but moderate changes within the existing capitalist system and provide farmers with economic growth at par with business and industry.

The rapid growth and popularity of the Populist Party was also due to an economic depression that had hit the agricultural sector in the 1870s. This setback led to a fall in the prices of corn and wheat and, to make matters worse, a drastic drop in cotton prices in the international markets. The rise in railroad freight charges compounded rural distress, and in the post-Civil War period, most southern banks had declared bankruptcy. All these factors created financial and economic woes, particularly for the small farmers, who gradually began to gravitate towards urban areas for employment opportunities and hope for a better life.

In November 1892, the Populist Party candidate for president, James B. Weaver, received 8.5 per cent of the total vote and the Electoral College votes of six states.[8] This was the most successful insurgent political effort up to that point in US history. However, the party began to weaken and could not capitalise on this success for a number of reasons:

(i) Popular discontent, which was fuelled by the economic depression of 1893, could not hold ground for long.
(ii) The Populist Party's decision to concentrate on the issue of silver-back currency blunted its appeal.
(iii) The party's entry into electoral politics lessened its grassroots engagements. Where earlier it had supported Granger farm protests through the Farmers' Alliance, it began to withdraw that support after 1897.
(iv) After 1897, demand for US agricultural products grew due to crop failures in Europe. This was accompanied by the large-scale immigration of southern and eastern European migrants to industrial cities in the North, along with an increase in the money supply due to gold discoveries in Alaska and South Africa. All these factors led to an inflationary cycle that boosted farm prices and incomes and brought 20 years of prosperity to the American agricultural community.

The Populist Party was perceived as a party of nativists that supported a backward-looking cultural movement. In other words, it was a misguided endeavour to return the nation to an 'ancient' and mythical age of yeomen farmers. Richard Hofstadter, in his book *Age of Reform*, has characterised farmers as small businessmen.[9] Analysing their attempts to form a suitable alternative and the struggle for broader political participation, he criticised the Populist Movement for being provincial and moralistic, marked by xenophobia and a hatred of urban and cosmopolitan culture. On the other hand, Lawrence Goodwyn credits the farmers' 'movement culture' with ushering in a culture of participatory democracy, and notes that it challenged an economic system that allowed corporations to accumulate wealth and corporate politics.[10] Goodwyn also questioned the notion that the Populist Party was against industrial and capitalist society—a claim that some historians made based on the party's demand for greater state intervention in the economy. In his assessment, the party required 'structural alteration of hierarchical economic reforms', and not the end of the capitalist system.[11] Peter Argersinger has characterised the farmers as reformers.[12] According to Marilyn Watkins, the Populists were rooted in rural social radicalism and reform and were more popular in the Rocky Mountains than in the Great Plains region.[13]

In Connie L. Lester's[14] assessment, populism was a rural social movement that evolved from non-partisan Grangers and the Farmers' Alliances to promote better agricultural practices. Later, the Populists shifted their focus to increasing commodity prices, reducing costs, and promoting agricultural interests. Farmers' alliances were the foundation for developing grassroots organisations, and the Populist Party was a national organisation. Unlike the Grangers and Alliance farmers, the Populists demanded a more 'human' capitalism to protect the rights of labour and small producers against the excessiveness of industrial capitalism.

Another question that confounded historians was why industrial labourers did not join the cause of the Populist Party. Although the Populist platform celebrated 'the union of the labour forces of the United States' in 1892, that union never materialised. Most labour unions continued to support either the Democrats or the

Republicans. Goodwyn's explanation for this is that the American labour movement had not been schooled in the 'movement culture' of populism and 'was simply not yet ready for mass insurgent politics'.[15] The farmers' cooperative movement was more successful when compared with working class movements of the period. However, it is important to note that these two groups did not occupy an equivalent class position. While many farmers in the Populist Movement were landowners and employed labour, the working class was a producer and did not own assets; this critical difference kept the labour unions away from the farmers' alliances. Melvyn Dubofsky has suggested that farmers and workers had incompatible demands: farmers pinned their hopes for economic upliftment on free silver, cheap money, and market inflation, while wage workers prioritised demands for affordable food, hard currency, and high wages.[16] The Populists could not extend their mass base into the cities. They were gradually absorbed by the Democrats and branded as dangerous radicals among middle-class Americans. For this reason, they slowly faded away after their electoral defeat in 1892.

In recent decades, historians have begun to re-evaluate the Populist Movement. According to Charles Postel, small farmers and labourers were committed to opening up the market and carving out a space for themselves in it.[17] They used the language of popular sovereignty, which, according to Chip Berlet and Matthew Lyons, had been in use since the Jacksonian period, when the 'producing' classes supported hard work and the ideals of the American Revolution.[18] Postel has also argued that the Populists attempted to apply new technologies, innovative methods, and scientific and technical knowledge to reform the agricultural economy through a centralised organisational structure, a cooperative movement and by pushing for reforms in central government organisations.[19] Miners, railroad workers, and women involved in the movement hoped to get better jobs in schools and offices and live a better, 'modern' life.

The Populists impacted American public life by forcing both Republicans and Democrats to incoporate popular demands in their political agenda. With the economic depression of the 1890s, leaders across the two parties had to accept populist demands. The Republicans, in particular, incorporated the populist ideology into their framework of progressive reforms, which allowed them to stay in power for a long time, apart from Wilson's tenure in office. Therefore, the Populists did manage to bring about political upheaval in America.

One of the consequences of this political upheaval was a decline in the incentive to vote as a clear divide emerged in the US, with Democrats winning the South and the Republicans remaining dominant in the North and the West. The party voting lost its privileged position in American public life. Elite southern Democrats were alarmed by the interracial Populist Movement, and by the active political participation of African Americans in the southern politics of the period. Democrat governments therefore continued to institute measures to disenfranchise Black voters through the 1890s (see Chapter 1).

The vacuum created by this was filled up by the **Anti-Saloon League**, established in 1895 to protest against alcoholism and lobby for national prohibition on the consumption of alcoholic beverages. Women entered the public space to secure employment and increase their household earnings. As we shall discuss, urban reform movements sprang up that aimed to transform city governments to be more responsive to the needs of ordinary people. The period also saw the emergence of the Socialist Party of America under the leadership of Eugene V. Debs (see Chapter 3), and just like the Populists, they, too, lobbied for a stable and actively interventionist government. These reform movements disagreed on their approaches and agenda, but their impact profoundly impacted public life in the early 1900s.

The Progressive Era (1890–1917)

The **Progressive Movement**, led by influential figures such as Theodore Roosevelt and Woodrow Wilson, was an ideological and political response to the transformation of America from a rural, commercial economy to an urban, industrial one. It was a concerted effort to provide the fundamental political, social, and economic reforms necessary for the new economy.[20] The enormous advances made in the nineteenth century came at the cost of multiple forms of dislocation, inhumane labour conditions, and brutal economic exploitation—concentration of economic power, inequitable taxation, wasteful resource consumption, political corruption, sweatshops, high rates of child labour, and crowded slums.

The Progressive era was characterised by a series of organised reform efforts, including those led by voluntary associations, and advocacy sparked by public-interest investigations. These were analysed through the lens of nascent 'social science methods' that sought to remedy the problems and contradictions of modern, industrial society. Initially, the reformers placed their faith in private organisations, but later, they looked towards public agencies to carry out progressive reforms. At one level, progressivism manifested in attempts to eradicate corruption; this was followed by **populist progressivism**, which highlighted the issues of farmers and workers. Then there was 'elitist' **conservative progressivism** under the leadership of US presidents Roosevelt and Wilson. They ushered in an era of increased 'regulatory powers' of the federal government and demonstrated an avowed concern for 'social justice' aimed at safeguarding the rights of women, children, and disadvantaged social groups.[21]

Progressivism was developed primarily by the native-born, urban middle and upper-middle classes, including doctors, lawyers, ministers, business people, editors, teachers, professors, engineers, and social workers. In terms of political ideology, historians have found it difficult to distinguish 'progressives' from 'conservatives'—the present-day binary between these two terms is not necessarily relevant to the idea of *progressivism* as a particular period in American political thought. Still, the fact remains that as a movement, it received substantial support from the leaders of big business corporations, rural Americans, and immigrant working classes. It was deeply rooted in evangelical Protestantism and advocated greater collectivism and state interventionism even while remaining within the fold of capitalism and American notions of individualism. One remarkable aspect of this reform movement was the pivotal role played by women, who, empowered by their education, began to apply innovative solutions to social problems.

MUCKRAKERS

The term '**muckracker**' applied after 1906 to the 'literature of exposure and protest' that had become prevalent in the US towards the end of the nineteenth century. The movement was inaugurated in 1881 by Henry Demarest Lloyd in *The Atlantic Monthly*, with 'The Story of a Great Monopoly', which portrayed the methods of the Standard Oil Company. His book *Wealth against Commonwealth* (1894), was another critical study of corporate power in America. The movement gained momentum in the 1890s, amid rural revolt and mounting protest against monopolies, and it aroused public sentiment to the point that, by 1910, there was public support at both local and national levels for such vital reforms as consumer protection, direct election of senators, municipal ownership of utilities, and the city-manager system.[22]

President Roosevelt, who took office in 1901, used the term 'muckraker' in a 1906 speech to criticise journalists' continued investigations into corruption. (He was alluding to a character in John Bunyan's classic, *Pilgrim's Progress*, who was so intent on raking muck that he could not look up to see a celestial crown being offered to him.) While it had negative connotations, the term soon became almost a title of distinction. Muckrakers set themselves the task of 'saving' political and economic democracy. According to Michael E. McGerr, a mass churn was underway in the early 1900s, and this spurred an era of 'radicalism'.[23] Every aspect of social life began to be questioned: family life, the role of sexes, race relations, conceptions of morality, forms of leisure, and formal politics. Alcoholism reportedly reduced due to the Temperance Movement; women secured the right to vote; and with the introduction of income tax, a long-held demand of the Populists was fulfilled.[24] The US began to intervene in global geopolitics by participating in multiple wars, projecting this as an effort to 'make the world safe for liberal democracy'.

Muckrakers were important drivers of reforms and social change. The Progressive era was supported by many influential critics of American life, novelists, historians, economists, sociologists, and philosophers. However, the credit for the advancement of progressive politics before World War I belongs to the muckrakers. The public became aware of the issues after 1900 when such popular magazines as *McClure's, Everybody's, Collier's, Cosmopolitan,* and *The Independent* opened their pages to different aspects of human life. Contributors included Lincoln Steffens, Ida Tarbell, T. W. Lawson and R. S. Baker. Newspaper photographers also created vivid portraits of exploitative working conditions and squalid circumstances.

During this period, middle-class, educated women began to move out of the domestic sphere. These pioneers realised the need to provide settlement houses for women who had recently migrated to the cities. There was also a need to establish community centres that provided working women with various services, including medical care, legal assistance, vocational training, and recreational activities. They also promoted a public playground movement and campaigned to abolish child labour while advocating for better wages for women. These working women used their experiences and education to launch surveys to examine the working and living conditions of other women and undertake appropriate steps to mitigate the problems of working women in urban areas. They forced Americans to think about the social rather than personal causes of poverty and the necessity of public relief programmes. Social activists like Jane Addams and Florence Kelley later played a crucial role in lobbying for and shaping the nation's first government welfare programme, despite the continued denial of the franchise and political office to women. All this led to the growth of the women's club, which discussed civic affairs and began to campaign for child labour laws, assistance to working women, establishment of kindergartens, and other reform measures. Women began to use progressive methods of organisation, education, and lobbying to secure the right to vote in a graded but focused manner. At this point in the 1890s, Black women began to highlight issues specific to the dual burden of race and gender bias, thereby creating a parallel movement. They began to oppose unsafe working conditions in factories and living conditions that promoted the spread of disease. They also opposed prostitution and other 'social ills'.

In historian Robert H. Wiebe's opinion, the Progressives had set out to achieve reform goals based on 'middle-class values'.[25] Medical doctors used their expertise to eradicate community diseases like dysentery, cholera, tuberculosis, hookworm, and venereal disease. Educated people in new and specialised professional roles, for instance social workers, educators, city planners, and criminal justice experts, assisted ordinary people in the cities.

The Progressive era, however, saw continued racial inequality and hate crimes, with Jim Crow laws still in force, leading to racial segregation in politics, law, and public and private facilities. Progressive reformers did little to address race riots and lynching. C. Vann Woodward believed that White progressive reformers in the South contributed to the 'White supremacy movement'.[26] Institutional racism against Black people went unchecked, and many efforts led by White reformers reflected persistent racist prejudice and attitudes. Black communities launched their own reform efforts. An interracial organisation, the National Association for the Advancement of Coloured People (NAACP) was formed in 1909 for political equality and to end racial violence. Another point of recurrent debate was over immigration into the United States, as workers from both Europe and the Asia-Pacific region arrived in increasing numbers. The progressive focus on overcrowding and epidemics contributed to anxieties around immigration, and their investigations were used to lobby for a literacy test for admission into America to limit the entry of 'unskilled' and 'less desirable' immigrants. This became law with the **Immigration Act of 1917**, followed by a system of exclusionary national quotas in the **Immigration Act of 1924**. Businesses began to strategically support or oppose government regulations, seeking to manipulate government agencies and machinery to their advantage.

In American universities, new departments were established for economics, political science, and other social sciences. Scholars and students associated with these departments began surveying contemporary urban and industrial conditions to evolve 'social policies'. The John Hopkins Institute for Research was established for graduate studies. Harvard University introduced elective study subjects at this time, reflecting a move towards specialised research. The period witnessed the growth of high schools, kindergartens, industrial schools, and schools for adult education under the **Chautauqua Movement**.

The '**Social Gospel**' also emerged in this period—this was a social movement among the Protestant clergy that strongly advocated concerted programmes of care and assistance to the 'less fortunate'. The post-Civil War period saw opposition to the rapidly spreading habit of alcoholism, which led to the beginning of the **Prohibition Party**, the **Women's Christian Temperance Union**, and the Anti-Saloon League.

The Progressive era was accompanied by intensified intellectual labour and scholarship; while much of this literature was ephemeral, some had a long-term impact. Henry George and Thorstein Veblen made lasting contributions to economic thought. Muckrackers made impressive critiques of social conditions and exposed political corruption. Frank Norris, Edward Bellamy, and Upton Sinclair were some of the novelists of this period. The American idea of pragmatism was developed by William James and John Dewey, drawing on English naturalist Charles Darwin's landmark work, *On the Origin of Species*. They judged human institutions by their consequences. Whatever worked satisfactorily was the answer to that particular social problem; therefore, there were no absolute answers. Then came Frederick Jackson Turner, who, through his paper 'The Significance of the Frontier in American History in 1890', pointed to the sociological impact of the USA's centuries-spanning experience of expanding along new geographic frontiers. The existence of frontiers, Turner famously argued, made Americans democratic, individualistic, and distinct from their European ancestors.

However, cycles of economic depression, recession, and the dislocations produced by massive immigration and urbanisation demanded a political response in the US. The protests of workers and farmers and the dissenting literature of social commentators and activists forced the political leadership to take action. For this reason, Vernon L. Parrington of the **Progressive School** of historians has termed this period the '**Democratic Renaissance**', a movement of the masses against a 'plutocracy' that aimed to democratise both political and economic structures.[27] It was a broad-based movement in which the middle classes, including journalists and scholars, joined in. For John D. Hicks, it was a movement borrowed from Jeffersonian agrarian traditions, which were carried forward by the

Populists. The Progressive Movement was an organised protest of the masses against the encroachments of a monopolistic plutocracy.

Despite its spectacular influence, the movement collapsed after World War I as the US experienced frequent race riots, industrial strikes, high inflation, and the 'Red Scare'.

Theodore Roosevelt and a Newfound Nationalism

Theodore Roosevelt became president in 1901 following the assassination of President William McKinley. Over the course of Roosevelt's six-year tenure, the White House became the centre of a storm of political activism. He skillfully used public opinion as a political weapon in pursuing his progressive goals of labour mediation, consumer protection, conservation, business ethics, and activism abroad. Roosevelt enlarged the presidential office as a public forum and a centre of legislative initiative. The first among three progressive presidents, including William Taft and Woodrow Wilson, Roosevelt projected himself as a guardian of the people and their constitutional rights and interests. Roosevelt's brand of '**new nationalism**' envisioned the expansion of the powers of the federal government as necessary in order to effectively execute this function, and significantly enhanced the role of the President and introduced government regulation of economic affairs. Roosevelt's re-election in 1904 has been viewed as public support for his progressive agenda. He attempted to protect public interests by leveraging the federal government's power to balance business corporations and labour unions. He approached this based on his theory of the 'Square Deal', which centred on three Cs: control of corporations, consumer protection, and conservation.

At the beginning of the twentieth century, Americans were concerned about the fast-growing power of corporate trusts, which was seen to be responsible for the continuously rising prices from 1897 to the 1900s. Roosevelt activated the **Sherman Antitrust Act of 1890**—the first federal act that outlawed monopolistic business practices. Although it had been on the statues for over a decade, the Act had remained dormant due to the reluctance of

Presidents Cleveland and McKinley to enforce it, based on their understanding of a Supreme Court ruling in 1895 stipulating that the measure did not apply to combinations in manufacturing. In 1902, Roosevelt dissolved the northwestern railroad monopoly, and the Beef Trust, then proceeded to dismantle existing monopolies in the manufacture of oil, tobacco, and other goods. He forced Congress to establish a Bureau of Corporations that was given powers to investigate corporate practices, and exposed many cases against trusts. Consolidating the federal government's control over US industries, Roosevelt, in his capacity as President, intervened on behalf of labour associations in 1902 to bring about arbitration in a strike organised by the **United Mine Workers of America** against the Pennsylvania anthracite coal operators.

After his re-election in 1904, there was growing public pressure to regulate interstate railroad rates, which sparked Roosevelt's conflict with Congress from 1905–1906 and culminated in the formulation of the **Hepburn Act of 1906**. This law granted more powers to the **Interstate Commerce Commission (ICC)** and prevented railroads from enhancing freight rates without its approval. Next, he introduced the **Meat Inspection Act** (partly influenced by Upton Sinclair's novel, *The Jungle*) and the **Pure Food and Drug Act** (both were passed in 1906). He brought substantial forest and mineral lands under the federal government's jurisdiction to safeguard environmental concerns, including hydropower projects. In his first term, Roosevelt implemented the **National Reclamation Act of 1902**, which initiated the federal programme of irrigation and hydroelectric projects in the western regions.

In the presidential elections of 1909, William Howard Taft of the Republican Party secured a clear majority. The primary planks of his campaign were reduced tariff rates, the imposition of income tax, direct elections of senators, and more regulations on railroad companies. However, his tariff reform resulted in an increase rather than decrease, sparking outrage within his party, which was increasingly split between conservative and progressive politicians. An insurgent group of Republicans lobbied to increase the authority of the ICC. When Taft publicly supported a free trade accord, or tariff reciprocity, with Canada (still under the control of Britain), many Canadians opposed the accord. This was a controversial move and opened the path for a Republican defeat and the election of the Democratic Party candidate Woodrow Wilson.

Woodrow Wilson: New Kinds of Freedom

Wilson won the 1912 presidential election and was in office from 1913 to 1917. In his election campaign he had promised a brand of progressivism known as the 'New Freedom'—it guaranteed to lower tariffs, dissolve trusts, give the banks back to the people, and destroy all special privileges enjoyed by big business organisations like trusts. Wilson was against Roosevelt's plan to monitor trusts, as he believed that watching trusts meant adding the power of the government to those of the monopolists. Removing all restrictions on private enterprise, Wilson argued, would herald an era of liberty, justice, and progress. By invoking these concepts, he was drawing from the Christian principles of obligation, service, and righteousness—pillars of the Populist Party's belief system.

During this period the US faced multiple challenges, especially with a continuous stream of migrants entering its increasingly crowded cities, exacerbating ethnic divides and problems from growing poverty, coupled with a sectional pattern of racial discrimination against Black people. At the national level, persistent bigotry and prejudice was visible in a general disregard for the needs of marginalised groups, scuttling any hopes for an inclusive federal programme that would expand political rights and economic opportunity. Labour movements were gaining ground; women's organisations were demanding equal opportunities, and the masses wanted more economic employment avenues.

Wilson realised that the USA's problems were too complex to be resolved through Roosevelt's 'new nationalism', which espoused active federal intervention to promote social justice. He instead believed that American politics should be viewed in terms of individual rights and pluralistic values. Therefore, he reinterpreted Jeffersonian values to integrate modernisation, industrialisation, and urbanisation, which he felt would release the creative impulses of a free people, while also preserving the traditional values of small-town and rural America. In the elections, Wilson had won the working-class vote, but he ultimately failed to deliver on his promises to this section of the electorate. As far as race relations were concerned, Wilson's southern upbringing had given him a generally unenlightened view on race and he tacitly supported the South's anti-Black bias.

The chief architect of Wilson's 'New Freedom' was Louis Brandeis, a progressive lawyer who had challenged big business corporations. Brandeis had worked out a complete alternative to Roosevelt's New Nationalism. The core element of his programme was to break up big business corporations, ensuring the survival of regulated business competition by small industrialists. The fragmentation of big business corporations would return the market to free enterprise, which would help spread wealth more widely and evenly, and give the workingmen a helping hand.

The first item on Wilson's agenda was tariff reform. The **Underwood-Simmons Tariff Act of 1913** reduced rates from 40 to 25 per cent, added more items to the tariff-free list (iron and steel), and introduced a modest income tax authorised by the newly ratified **16th Constitutional Amendment**.

Banking and currency reform came next with the **Federal Reserve Act of 1913**. This is widely considered to be Wilson's most outstanding legislative achievement. The Act created a network of 12 regional Federal Reserve Banks under mixed public and private control. Each regional bank was authorised to issue federal reserve currency notes to the private banks in its districts. The banks, in turn, could use this money to offer loans to corporations and individual borrowers. Overarching control of the system was placed in the hands of the presidents of the regional banks and a Washington-based **Federal Reserve Board** (comprising the secretary of the Treasury, the comptroller of currency, and seven other members appointed by the President for a 14-year term).

Wilson then turned his attention to business regulation. The **Federal Trade Commission Act of 1914** created a new five-member federal 'watchdog' agency called the **Federal Trade Commission**, which was empowered to investigate suspected violations of federal regulatory statutes, demand regular reports from corporations, and issue 'cease and desist' orders (subject to court review) if it found unfair methods of business competition. The **Clayton Antitrust Act of 1914** listed specific illegal activities for which it could issue cease and desist orders. While the earlier Sherman Antitrust Act of 1890 had outlawed all business practices 'in restraint of trade', it had remained vague about details. The Clayton Act instituted measures to curb monopolies, limit unethical practices like price discrimination, deals and mergers that undermined competition, and allow labour unions the power to organise strikes, picketing, and other labour actions.

FIG. 5.2: Woodrow Wilson priming the pump of prosperity, cartoon by Clifford Berryman (1914)

Source: Wikimedia Commons.

Sympathetic to labour and leading a party historically identified with working people, Woodrow Wilson supported the American Federation of Labour (AFL), defended workers' right to organise and endorsed a clause in the Clayton Act that explicitly exempted strikes, boycotts, and peaceful picketing from being interpreted as actions 'in restraint of trade'. Woodrow Wilson pushed through three other crucial laws:

(i) the **Keating-Owen Act**, which barred inter-state commercial products manufactured using child labour (later outlawed and finally accepted only in 1938);
(ii) the **Adamson Act**, establishing an eight-hour workday for inter-state railway workers and federal aid for education; and
(iii) the **Workmen's Compensation Act** providing accident and injury protection to federal workers.

Wilson also supported the **Federal Farm Loan Act** and the Federal **Warehouse Act of 1916**, allowing farmers to use land or crops to secure long-term, low-interest credit from a regional Farm Loan Banks network. The **Federal Highway Act of 1916**, which matched federal funds with state funding for highway construction, benefited not only the new automobile industry but also farmers plagued by bad roads.

Four constitutional amendments were passed during Woodrow's term:

(i) the 16th Constitutional Amendment that granted the Congress the authority to tax incomes;
(ii) the 17th Constitutional Amendment, which initiated direct election of the senators in each state;
(iii) the 18th Constitutional Amendment instituting nationwide alcohol prohibition; and
(iv) the 19th Constitutional Amendment, granting women the right to vote.

Nature of the Progressive Movement

Richard Hofstadter[28] has opined that rapid industrialisation and growth of corporate business in America displaced farmers due to the commercialisation of agriculture. Members of the clergy, intellectual elites like lawyers and professors, and prominent White Protestant families had lost their traditional social status, privilege and authority, and were now demanding restoration of the old order. The Populists and Progressives wanted to maintain the homogeneity of US civilisation. Therefore, these were not liberal movements, as sometimes argued by progressive historians. Instead, they were movements led by a relatively affluent middle class alienated from society because of technological and industrial changes. On similar lines, George E. Mowry has also examined this movement as class-oriented, with privileged classes aiming to reassert their declining political clout. In other words, for both historians the tensions and insecurities of the American middle class emerge as a chief cause of the Progressive Movement. Other scholars have disagreed with this conclusion and surmised that a series of depressions in the late nineteenth century exposed the weaknesses of industrialisation, which then generated progressive thought and a demand for reform that cut across class lines. Moreover, this was a period of weakening party loyalty, and the development of pressure groups commanded greater attention among the public. As we have discussed, there was a considerable decline in voter turnout in the USA.

Neo-Conservative historians saw the Progressive Movement as a conservative—not radical—attempt to strengthen the USA internally and socially. Others have emphasised the dominance of big business corporations and the bureaucracy. The Progressive Movement brought a shift in the national value system where the stress was now more on efficiency, order, rationality, and systematic control. What the two presidents did, according to Samuel P. Hays, was to govern society under the new ideals of scientific management and efficiency.[29] Economic regulations were meant to facilitate an 'age of organisation' that would establish order and equilibrium in an increasingly urbanised and industrialised society, which now had a sizeable middle class. This new, urbane and educated middle class wanted economic power and national welfare programmes for low-income groups. In contrast, Left historians view the Progressive Movement as one primarily concerned with the control of government, and argue that since the movement accepted the political capitalist logic of the business class, it was a reactionary rather than a reform movement.

Aileen S. Kraditor, analysing women's progressivism, concurs that it is wrong to assume that progressivism was a radical movement; it would be more accurately described as pragmatic and conservative.[30] Women, for example, were only seeking to preserve middle-class values against rapid changes triggered by the processes of industrialisation and urbanisation. Nancy Woloch, however, has suggested that although it may not have been radical, the period was undoubtedly an era of 'reformulation' of women's approaches towards life and social problems.[31]

At the end of the Progressive era, some expected and unexpected shifts brought about changes in the status quo. Women's suffrage did not spark the desired change in American politics and gender relations. Class conflicts continued to plague industrial America as specific interest groups fought to reinforce their dominance in the corridors of political power. In the South, the White establishment's attempts to keep freedmen suppressed under the weight of racial violence, poverty, and discrimination received a crushing blow with the rise of African American leaders who brought in the **Second Reconstruction**. In all this, the bitter truth was that women, African Americans, new immigrants, Indigenous peoples, and the working classes continued to encounter grave inequalities in American public life.

Notes

1. Much of this land had been appropriated from the Indigenous nations, who were driven out from their ancestral lands from the mid-nineteenth century onwards in a process of internal colonisation.

2. Noam Maggor, 'To Coddle and Caress These Great Capitalists: Eastern Money, Frontier Populism, and the Politics of Market Making in the American West', *American Historical Review* 122 (1), pp. 55–84.

3. Charles M. Gardner, *The Grange, Friend of the Farmer: A Concise Reference History of America's Oldest Farm Organization, and the Only Rural Fraternity in the World, 1867–1947* (Washington, 1950), p. 196.

4. The National Farmers' Alliance and Industrial Union, generally known as the Southern Alliance, did not open membership to non-White farmers. This forced Black farmers in the South to form their own association.

5. John Donald Hicks, *The Populist Revolt: A History of the Farmer's Alliance and the People's Party* (Minneapolis, 1931).

6. Adam Slez, *The Making of the Populist Movement: State, Market and Party on Western Frontier* (New York, 2020).

7. Lawrence Goodwyn, *The Populist Moment: A Short History of the Agrarian Revolt in America* (New York, 1978).

8. See https://www.presidency.ucsb.edu/statistics/elections/1892 (accessed October 2025).

9. Richard Hofstadter, *The Age of Reform: From Bryan to F. D. R.* (New York, 1955).

10. Goodwyn, *The Populist Moment*.

11. Ibid.

12. Peter H. Argersinger, *The Limits of Agrarian Radicalism: Western Populism and American Politics* (Kansas City, 1995).

13. Marilyn P. Watkins, *Rural Democracy: Family Farmers and Politics Western Washington, 1890–1925.* (New York, 1996).

14. Connie L. Lester, *Up from the Mudsills of Hell: The Farmers' Alliance, Populism and Progressive Agriculture in Tennessee, 1870–1915* (Athens, Georgia, 2006).

15. Goodwyn, *The Populist Moment*.

16. Melvyn Dubofsky, *The State and Labor in Modern America* (Chapel Hill, 1994).

17. Charles Postel, *The Populist Vision* (New York, 2007).

18. Chip Berlet and Matthew N. Lyons, *Right-Wing Populism in America: Too Close for Comfort* (New York, 2000).

19. Postel, *The Populist Vision*.

20. Arthur S. Link and Richard L. McCormick, *Progressivism* (Arlington Heights, Illinois, 1983), p. 3.

21. Stephen J. Whitfield ed., *A Companion to 20th-Century America* (New York, 2004), p. 5.

22. The 'city-manager system' emerged in the USA from the late nineteenth century onwards, during the period of urbanisation and the development of municipal government. Managers were appointed in urban areas and had the authority to oversee the city's legislative and administrative functions through various departmental divisions. The city-manager, therefore, was a professional responsible for handling the city's affairs on behalf of its representative body.

See Herman G. James, 'The City Manager Plan, the Latest in American City Government', *American Political Science Review* 8 (4), 1914, pp. 602–613.

23. Michael E. McGerr, *A Fierce Discontent: The Rise and Fall of the Progressive Movement in America* (New York, 2005).

24. Ibid.

25. Robert H. Wiebe, *The Search for Order, 1877–1920* (New York, 1967).

26. C. Van Woodward, *The Burden of Southern History* (Baton Rouge, 1960).

27. Vernon L. Parrington, *Main Currents in American Thought: An Interpretation of American Literature from the Beginning to 1920*, vol. 3, *The Beginnings of Critical Realism in America, 1860–1920*, reprint ed. (New York, 1984).

28. Hofstadter, *The Age of Reform*.

29. Samuel P. Hays, *The Response to Industrialism, 1885–1914* (Chicago, 1957).

30. Aileen S. Kraditor, *The Ideas of the Women Suffrage Movement, 1890–1920* (New York, 1981).

31. Nancy Woloch, *Women and the American Experience* (New York, 1984).

Chapter 6

The New Deal

Introduction

On 24 October 1929, the **Great Depression** began with panic in the stock market, and by 29 October, the share market was falling rapidly, leading to a complete economic and financial collapse. American businesses and banks collapsed, throwing millions of people into a dark abyss of unemployment, drastic reduction in wages, and a decline in the value of the American dollar. According to historian William E. Leuchtenburg, during the presidency of Herbert Hoover, not only did financial markets take a significant hit, but industrial production came to a grinding halt.[1] By 1932, about 13 million Americans were unemployed.[2] The condition of the agricultural economy was equally bad, and it had already been facing reversals for many years. The Great Depression and the drought of the 1930s in the Great Plains further worsened the situation. (The term '**Dust Bowl**' was used to refer to the severe dust storms that developed partly due to the droughts in this decade, causing extensive environmental and agricultural damage.) The federal government was faced with the prospect of bankruptcy due to a sharp fall in the collection of taxes and began to show signs of a massive economic crisis and an inability to handle or even comprehend the seriousness of the economic situation. World trade collapsed along with the US and most European nations began to impose high tariffs on imported goods to protect their domestic industries.

FIG. 6.1: 'Migrant Mother, Nipomo, California', one of the most famous portraits of the Great Depression era, by Dorothea Lange (6 March 1936)

Source: Wikimedia Commons.

By 1932, millions of Americans were left with no avenue of sustenance due to the absence of unemployment insurance. There was a further reduction in hourly wages, and more banks and businesses began to collapse, along with the drastic fall in the prices of agricultural produce. The immediate impact was food scarcity and hunger, material deprivation, and immense psychological pressure, which resulted in a high rate of suicide. The blame lay at least in part with the Hoover government, which had refused to provide even basic welfare measures. As a result, liberal capitalism began to collapse, forcing people to seek alternative solutions across the political spectrum.

In 1932, Franklin D. Roosevelt from the Democratic Party won the presidential campaign. During his campaign, Roosevelt had made a case for action by outlining steps for provide immediate relief and economic recovery, based on the ideological tenets of the Progressive Movement and its philosophy of social welfare, foundations of which had already been laid by earlier presidents Theodore Roosevelt and Woodrow Wilson. His advisors believed that the Great Depression had occurred because the economic surplus from production was invested in savings and speculative ventures, when they should have been invested in expanding the disposable income of the consumer class (by increasing workers' wages and providing higher prices to farmers). On assuming office in 1933, Roosevelt declared a four-day national 'bank holiday' that temporarily halted all banking operations. A special session of Congress was convened in March 1933 for the passage of the **Emergency Banking Act**, releasing funds to restart the banks and reinstate people's confidence in the banking institutions. The **Economy Act of 1933** aimed to reduce the federal deficit by reducing the salaries of federal workers and cutting benefits for war veterans. Simultaneously, Roosevelt took the first step to repeal nationwide **Prohibition**[3] through the **Cullen-Harrison Act of 1933**, which allowed the manufacture and sale of light wines and beer with 3.2 per cent alcohol by weight. In December 1933, the 21st Amendment, to repeal the 18th Amendment that had introduced Prohibition, was ratified by the requisite number of states. Then, in two phases, the programme of the New Deal was inaugurated: The **First New Deal** comprised relief, recovery, and reform measures within the broader political framework of democracy and individual liberty; in the **Second New Deal** the federal government introduced state economic planning. The aim was to prevent the spread of socialism, Nazism, and unrestrained capitalism in the United States.

Table 6.1: The New Deal

S. No.	Year	Programme of the New Deal	Purpose/Goal
1	1933	National Recovery Administration (NRA)	To revive industrial production, eliminate unfair trade practices, reduce unemployment, provide a minimum wage, set maximum working hours and the right of labour to bargain.
		Civilian Conservation Corps (CCC)	To alleviate unemployment, especially amongst the youth.
		Tennessee Valley Authority (TVA)	To provide electric power to the people through hydropower projects on the Tennessee River and control floods.
		Agricultural Adjustment Administration (AAA)	To provide subsidies and loans directly to US farmers and control the production of key crops.
		Public Works Administration (PWA)	To employ people in large-scale construction projects, such as highways, bridges, dams, and construction of public buildings, and to revive the economy and enhance consumer purchasing power.
		Commodity Credit Corporation	To stabilise farm income and prices to support US farmers.
		Farm Credit Administration (FCA)	To provide financial relief to farmers by refinancing mortgages at a lower interest rate and providing new loans.
		Federal Deposit Insurance Corporation	To ensure deposits against bank failure and regulate bank practices.

(Contd)

Table 6.1: *(Contd)*

S. No.	Year	Programme of the New Deal	Purpose/Goal
		Federal Emergency Relief Administration	To provide federal grants to states for relief and work programmes in the aftermath of the Great Depression.
		Home Owners Loan Corporation	To facilitate home financing.
2	1934	Securities and Exchange Commission	To regulate financial institutions, restore investors' confidence, and protect the public from fraudulent market prices.
		Federal Communications Commission (FCC)	To regulate all interstate and international communication, including radio, telegraph, and telephone.
		Federal Housing Administration (FHA)	To improve housing standards and increase employment in the home construction industry.
3	1935	Works Progress Administration (WPA)	To generate employment in public art, restoration, landscaping, and public beautification. This was meant as a short-term aid programme to provide immediate relief.
		National Youth Administration (NYA)	To employ youth in national forests and government-aided programmes.
		National Labour Relations Board (Wagner Act)	To create legal recognition of the right of labour to organise labour unions and utilise the power of collective bargaining.

(Contd)

Table 6.1: *(Contd)*

S. No.	Year	Programme of the New Deal	Purpose/Goal
		Social Security Board (SSB)	To provide a safety net to older adults and widows, create provisions for disability insurance, unemployment benefits, etc.
		Rural Electrification Administration (REA)	To provide low-cost loans for the construction of power lines in order to bring electricity to rural areas.
4	1937	Farm Security Administration (FSA)	To deal with rural poverty by providing loans and assistance to poor farmers, tenants, and sharecroppers.
		United States Housing Authority	To provide federal aid to states and localities for the removal of slums and to build low-rent housing.
5	1938	Federal Crop Insurance Corporation (FCIC)	To implement the federal crop insurance programme.

Source: Author.

The First New Deal: Relief Measures

The first aim of the New Deal was to provide immediate relief to both agriculture and industrial sectors. For the agricultural economy, Congress passed the **Agricultural Adjustment Act (AAA) in 1933** to provide relief to US farmers, raise farm income, and destroy overproduced crops and even animals to cut down agricultural production. These steps were taken by raising crop prices through government subsidies to compensate for voluntary cutbacks in agricultural production. It was proposed that a tax be imposed on industries associated with processing crops to generate funds for this programme. The central idea was 'agricultural adjustment', aiming to increase farm income by controlling production and providing benefit payments to farmers who agreed to regulate their cultivation according to a national plan. The Act also empowered the government to maintain prices through loans or purchase of non-perishable crops deposited in cold storage. This would help decrease costs borne by the farmer and decrease the total agricultural output. The government also acquired the power to stop land cultivation through leasing and control over the sale of agricultural commodities. Farmers had to adhere to marketing agreements and strict quotas. The US dollar was taken off from gold to reduce inflation. Special measures were undertaken to support the price of silver and stabilise the currency at 60 per cent of its former value. The purpose was to increase commodity production, aid recovery of manufacturing processes and, in turn, farm exports, and enable a rise in income by almost 50 per cent (from 1932 to 1935).[4] However, these measures adversely impacted tenants and sharecroppers. Further, as mentioned earlier, from 1935 to 1938 drought hit the region of the Great Plains, forcing people from many farming states to migrate, particularly to California. Here, too, employment was not readily available, leading to further impoverishment, hunger, and suicides. The programme was abandoned by 1936 when it was declared unconstitutional by the Supreme Court.

Reform Measures

The economic downturn had rendered many millions unemployed, sharply reducing the total industrial output and further reducing the purchasing power of the consumer class. To stimulate American industries and overcome this crisis, the **National Industrial Recovery Act (NIRA)** was passed in 1933, under which two agencies were set up: The **National Recovery Administration (NRA)** and the **Public Works Administration (PWA)**.

The NRA aimed to restore lost jobs and aid regeneration of industries by applying a 'blanket code'—employers would pledge to adhere to NRA standards on minimum wages and maximum hours.

In the economic sphere, it attempted to bring about re-employment by raising salaries and reducing working hours. At the same time, the Act introduced some social reform measures such as the abolition of child labour, general improvement in working conditions, and more incentives to labour union under Section 7A of the NIRA (which accorded unions the right to bargain collectively and organise their representation). Section 7A led to the establishment of a **National Labour Board** to assist in the mediation, conciliation, and arbitration of industrial disputes, and the application of fair-trade practices by federal machinery to check business practices, investigate prices, and ensure that maximum benefits should reach small businesses. The main task of the NRA was to work with the business classes to frame an outline of codes that would set the standards of output, prices, working conditions, and hours, thereby eliminating possibilities of establishing monopolistic companies. However, in the long run, these measures proved to be ineffective.

Federal grants to states for unemployment relief programmes and public works were known as the **Federal Emergency Relief Administration (FERA)**, to which Roosevelt added the **Civil Works Administration (CWA, 1934)** in the Second New Deal. The PWA concentrated on heavy and durable projects. The government took active steps to generate employment by constructing dams and bridges, irrigation projects, and aircraft carriers.

The New Deal initiatives were unprecedented in US legislative history and played a pivotal role in the economic recovery during the Great Depression. The **Home Owners Loan Corporation** and **Federal Housing Administration (FHA)** provided avenues for refinancing mortgages, while the **Federal Emergency Relief Act** established a system of federal relief. The **National Housing Act, passed in 1934**, made buying a house cheaper than renting it out. Another significant measure was conserving natural resources under the **Civilian Conservation Corps (CCC)**, as well as reforestation and conservation projects. The CCC programme aimed to bring immediate relief to young workers aged 18 to 25 years. Under this scheme, unemployed youth were made to work in camps in return for a salary of US $30 per month. The corps were engaged in wide-ranging programmes like prevention of soil erosion by planting soil-improving crops, planting trees to preserve national forests, cleaning rivers, lakes and streams, preservation efforts to save animals and birds in their respective sanctuaries, along with steps were initiated to conserve natural resources like coal, gas, and other resources. The **Tennessee Valley Authority (TVA)**, the largest government-owned industrial undertaking at the time, managed the construction of dams and powerhouses that brought electricity to far-flung parts of Tennessee. Rivers in the area were cleaned, soil erosion was stopped, forests were rebuilt and, with electricity reaching even the remotest parts, wholly transformed lives and assisted in the development of the American West. Additionally, it brought the government into the field of selling electricity, along with private players.

RECOVERY MEASURES

Various trade agreement acts were passed that granted powers to the President to negotiate a low-tariff agreement to revive foreign trade. Reform measures were introduced to regulate stock exchange and investment banking, which was separated from commercial banking to stop speculation. This was done through the **Glass-Steagall Banking Act**. The **Federal Deposit Insurance Corporation (FDIC)** gave government assurance to individual depositors' accounts. As we have discussed, the US dollar was taken off the gold standard to stimulate economic activity, which assisted the federal government in bringing more currency into the market. The **Security Act of 1933** brought new securities issues to be registered with the **Federal Trade Commission** and the company's financial position statement. The statement was made available to the purchasers in the market. The **Federal Communication Commission** was established to supervise broadcast airwaves and telephone communication, and the **Securities and Exchange Commission** was established to watch the stock and bond markets. These measures, though challenging, brought a glimmer of hope to the nation, signaling the beginning of economic recovery.[5]

While providing relief and reform, the First New Deal could not produce recovery as the gross national product remained low, and millions of workers were still unemployed. The other problem was that the Supreme Court declared both NIRA and AAA unconstitutional. This period saw massive labour unrest and around 2,000 strikes against what was termed 'corporate dictatorship'. A federation of unions called the **Congress of Industrial Organization (CIO)** was established in 1935 and quickly became an important pressure group in all the major industrial centres of the USA. The CIO's focus was on achieving 'economic freedom and industrial democracy' by bringing about parity between wealth and income with assistance from the federal government that would, in turn, generate consumer demand which in turn would raise labour income and thereby bring a more equitable distribution of wealth.[6] Actions by organised labour were part of a wider churn among the public for economic justice, demanding a more proactive government role in generating employment and facilitating better transportation, education, and health facilities. Growing demands to increase taxation on high-income individuals and groups, and to nationalise essential industries helped shape the Second New Deal.[7]

The Second New Deal

Despite the Roosevelt administration's best efforts, the tentacles of the Depression continued to hold the nation in a tight grip. The government shifted its attention to providing economic equality by giving people a sense of economic security against unemployment and poverty through the redistribution of national income to increase people's purchasing power, which would, in turn, stimulate the consumer economy.

The **National Labour Relations Act of 1935**, or the **Wagner Act**, replaced Section 7A of the NIRA. It provided more reliable guarantees for collective bargaining and empowered the National Labour Relations Board to supervise union elections. The Act outlawed 'unfair labour practices' like arbitrarily dismissing workers or blocking unions. The government aimed to assist in unionisation and ensure better wages for the working class to increase their purchasing power. The **Public Contracts Act** applied government-sanctioned salaries and working hours to firms working with the federal government. The **Guffey-Snyder Coal Act of 1935** established provisions for a **Bituminous Coal Labour Board** to regulate wages and working hours as well as fix prices. Although it was ruled unconstitutional, in 1937 it was replaced with the **Guffey-Vinson Coal Act** which had fewer provisions for labour practices.

The **Rural Electrification Agency (REA)** was established to extend the power grid to rural and remote areas. The aim was to increase the purchasing power of average Americans so that they could buy household tools and appliances, and it ultimately proved to be one of the most successful programmes of the Second New Deal. Congress passed the **Farm Relief Act**, under which the government paid farmers through subsidies to achieve 'parity' with the exchange value that these crops had held before World War I. The subsidy was provided to those farmers who agreed not to plant crops that led to soil depletion, in a bid to promote soil conservation practices and environment-friendly techniques. By 1940, about 6 million farmers had received federal subsidies. The Act went a long way in assisting farmers avail loans on surplus crops and insurance on wheat, and provided more affordable ways of storing produce to enable a more stable supply chain of essential farm products. The prices of agricultural commodities increased due to these provisions. Wastelands were bought up by the federal government and developed into national grasslands and parks.

Roosevelt's government also established the **Works Progress Administration (WPA)**. The aim was to provide work, rather than simply welfare. Millions of Americans were employed in construction projects for government buildings, bridges, roads and airports, stadiums, sewage treatment plants, and public swimming pools. This programme sought to use the skills of professional workers who had lost jobs during the Great Depression. This included not only doctors and engineers but also artists, painters, and writers, who were made to research local histories and guidebooks and included in schemes like the Federal Theatre Project, the Federal Music Project, and the Federal Dance Project. These projects not only granted talented people a space to perform and earn money, but also greatly enhanced the USA's cultural capital. These remarkable changes were accompanied by the creation of an agency called the **National Youth Administration (1935)**, which provided economic relief to students and the youth by creating training programmes and distributing aid to the unemployed.

FIG. 6.2: 'New Deal' WPA art, mural in New Jersey by Charles Ward (c. 1932), photographed by Carol M. Highsmith in 2010
Source: Wikimedia Commons.

In Roosevelt's assessment, his **Social Security Act of 1935** was the cornerstone of the government's policies as it secured citizens' right of social support. It was made law on 14 August 1935, which created a system of insurance for the aged, unemployed, and disabled based on employer and employee contributions. The aim was to reduce unemployment and growing poverty, and initiated the beginning of a 'welfare state'. Old age pensions were controlled by the federal government and paid by taxes on employers and employees. The states provided relief to the unemployed through the Aid to Dependent Children programme. However, a notable drawback of the Act was the exclusion of domestic and agricultural workers, Black people, and unmarried women, even though these groups comprised a large segment of the population and faced economic disadvantages.

The **Public Utilities Holding Company Act** was passed to restore competition in the US economy, prevent monopolies from controlling financial markets, and restrict the buying and selling of companies. The **Revenue Act** taxed high-income corporations and estates to assist small businesses. The **Banking Act of 1935** increased the power of the Federal Reserve Board to control open market operations.

Long-Term Impact

The First and Second New Deal had many commonalities, as their respective aims were to revive the American economy and initiate social reform measures. The public mood, however, had shifted between 1933 and 1935. In 1933, people wanted the government to introduce measures to stem the economy's downward spiral. The actions of the First New Deal established a government-controlled market economy and the rise of new institutions was meant to keep the economy in equilibrium. By 1935, economic conservatism had set in, and it reignited a demand for the classical model of a free market economy, where free competition under the watchful eyes of the government. The First New Deal initiated programmes for reform and recovery of the economy.

In contrast, in the Second New Deal, the focus was only on reform (and not relief measures), with a greater share of the federal budget being utilised towards increase public spending that would generate employment. These measures were formulated under the influence of Keynesian ideas. More and more court cases were being filed in the Supreme Court against New Deal laws, which were in many cases declared unconstitutional. The **American Federation of Labour (AFL)** declined in the same period, and the CIO, as noted earlier, rose in prominence. The Black population was the worst affected by the Great Depression as it faced systemic disadvantages. In the southern states, for instance, most of the welfare benefits were cornered by European Americans, pushing African Americans deeper into the grip of poverty and racial segregation. Violence and discrimination in securing jobs as well as housing were becoming evident.[8] Faced with economic hardship and routine exclusion from state welfare programmes, the Black community increasingly began to mobilise for their rights, which culminated in the Civil Rights Movement. The New Deal brought more American women into the government workforce, but overall, many more women also lost their jobs in the interwar period (see Chapter 9). They were denied the benefits of the Second New Deal, including social security assistance. An idealised image of the male-dominated family was popularised amid an atmosphere of increased gender conservatism, which also impacted social policies.[9] The position of Indigenous peoples improved marginally with the implementation of the **Indian Reorganization Act**. However, on close inspection, the programmes of the New Deal could not stem the tide of poverty nor properly address Indigenous interests.[10] At the same time, with war clouds looming over Europe by 1938, public demand for reform in the US began to dissipate. Circumstances forced Roosevelt to shift his focus from internal to external matters.

The New Deal brought about significant changes, many of which sparked debate and disagreement. While the policies did not necessarily bring prosperity, the fact remains that it did prevent the US economy from complete collapse. The wide-ranging programme established a pattern of governance for a new plural society where even immigrants could find their voice, and it transformed the physical environment through the electrification process. The federal government learnt the hard lesson that it would have to ensure economic security and maintain democratic values through welfare programmes and by constantly working to mitigate economic inequalities. Ultimately, it managed to save American capitalism through proper management while respecting the core values of personal freedom, economic growth, and faith in a free society.

Historiography: Assessing the New Deal

Historians have examined the New Deal as a conflict between the forces of liberalism and conservatism on the one hand, and between people and vested business interests on the other. The New Deal may thus be summarised as another phase in a struggle against monopoly, entrenched privilege, and special economic interests. Scholars also identify the Jeffersonian and Jacksonian models of democracy as important historical antecedents to the policies of this period, even as they acknowledge the impact of the Populist and Progressive movements where the US began to make rapid strides to secure political, economic, and social equality and security through the efforts of both government and non-government organisations.

Scholarly assessments of the New Deal vary greatly. In *The Shaping of American Tradition*, Louis M. Hacker termed the New Deal the 'third American Revolution' and stated that it led to government intervention for the general welfare of the people.[11] On the other end of the spectrum was Henry Steele Commager, who felt that the Roosevelt presidency was not 'revolutionary', but rather, simply a process of shuffling a new hand from an old pack of cards.[12] In other words, the New Deal drew from ideas already in circulation in both the USA and Europe. Commager asserted that the New Deal was based on the foundations of the Progressive Movement. Its primary focus was to restore the self-confidence of the people in liberal democratic values and individualism, along with a restoration of people's faith in constitutional equality and conservation of the USA's natural and human resources through welfare programmes and policies of government regulation, supervision, and reforms. According to Commager, the programme seemed radical mainly due to the rapid pace of its implementation, and in comparison with the period of the Harding-Coolidge and Hoover administrations where no effort was made to stem the economic downslide.

Historian Arthur M. Schlesinger, Jr., in *The Age of Roosevelt*, posited that US history moves in a cyclical pattern,[13] with alternating periods of vigorous public reform for 20–30 years followed by increased conservatism where 'personal goals' become more important. After the Progressive Movement, individual interests took centrestage in the 1920s, which later gave way to the emergence of liberal energies in the 1930s as the New Deal. The New Deal was a liberal movement marked by pragmatism and dynamism, offering practical solutions to problems based on the belief that the 'managed and modified capitalist order achieved by piecemeal experiment could combine personal freedom and economic growth'.[14]

Frank Freidel has argued that the New Deal programme was envisaged within the parameters of 'American tradition'. Unlike Schlesinger, Freidel finds that its main goals were conservative, and he further states that it attempted to conserve the existing economic and social system by eliminating its weaknesses without introducing radical reforms.[15] Roosevelt, thus, did not present a radical line of thought and was guided by political arithmetic rather than an ideological or principled position.

In *The Age of Reform*, Richard Hofstadter makes the case that the New Deal reformers saw a sick society that had to be reformed through active federal action, placing the New Deal within the reform tradition. In nature and magnitude, it marked a departure in American life, representing a triumph of economic emergency and human needs over the values earlier cherished by conservatives and reformers. He believed the New Deal was based primarily on political expediency and gratification of immediate human needs at any cost.

Rexford G. Tugwell has pointed out that the US economy's productive capacity had outrun purchasing power by the 1920s, and this is what resulted in the Great Depression. Since his predecessors failed to undertake emergent steps, Roosevelt introduced measures aiming to strike a balance between the interests of competing pressure groups.[16]

Conservative historians like John T. Flynn, author of *In the Roosevelt Myth*, criticised liberal and progressive perspectives on the New Deal.[17] Flynn was critical of Roosevelt's measures which, in his assessment, threw the principles of free enterprise, individual freedom, and free competition into permanent crisis. The steps restricted the powers of the state governments and even led to a decline in the authority of Congress. Conversely, the President's powers increased as a result of new legislation, federal debt grew, and economic inflation increased. Neo-conservative historian Heinz Eulau considered the New Deal a symbol and evidence of the nation's political maturity.[18] Problems were solved politically through adjustment, compromise, and integration. The New Deal was, therefore, an attempt to cope with unique issues in a manner Eulau characterised as 'simple, sensible, and American'.

In New Left scholarship, represented by historians Barton J. Bernstein,[19] Ronald Radosh,[20] and Howard Zinn,[21] the focus was on weaknesses, limits, and recourse to conventional instincts in policymaking. This was a clear departure from scholars like William E. Leuchtenburg. The New Deal was committed to capitalism, benefiting only the upper and middle classes and doing nothing for the working classes and African Americans. Paul K. Conkin said the New Deal solved very few problems but created multiple new ones.[22] In the 1980s, Left historians came out with a more nuanced critique of the New Deal: Thomas Ferguson, for instance, emphasised the role played by an emerging group of internationalist capitalists responsible for shaping and controlling the New Deal agenda.[23] In the Revisionist evaluation of the New Deal, Colin Gordon also noted the role of corporate forces in developing and managing New Deal programmes.[24]

Since the 1990s, most historians have tended to accept Leuchtenburg's interpretation. However, new studies have also brought fresh insights on the New Deal's form and the political changes it brought in. James MacGregor Burns was critical of Roosevelt and felt that the President did not use his popularity to effectively challenge his opponents. He made no effort to change the American two-party system and find ways to accommodate the Progressives.[25] Others disagree on the extent of Roosevelt's popularity—James Paterson argued that there was massive opposition to the New Deal in Congress, and their voices became more vocal over time.[26] Frank Friedel,[27] Harvard Sitkoff,[28] Nancy Weiss,[29] and John Kirby[30] have all argued that the President, Congress and the federal administration could have used the New Deal programme to bring racial equality in the South. In a similar vein, Alan Brinkly[31] and Bruce Schulman[32] have highlighted the inability of New Deal liberalism to establish itself in southern politics.

Some scholars believe that the New Deal was conservative, as evident in the work of Frank Friedel. Looking at the implementation of the New Deal, Barry Karl and Otis Graham have emphasised that some liberals within the administration insisted on the application of better planning and organisation but failed to garner support.[33] Similarly, according to Mark Leff, the administration could have applied a progressive tax system to finance the New Deal programmes instead of relying on a regressive taxation system.[34] Herbert Stein, Robert Lekachman, and Margaret Weir believe that instead of depending on Keynesian economics, the administration could have made better use of federal spending to overcome the Great Depression. Jill Quadagno highlighted that the government welfare or social security programme left out those jobs where there was greater representation of African Americans and women.[35] Theda Skocpol[36] and Linda Gordon[37] developed the argument about gendered exclusion further: Social security, they suggested, was designed on the premise that if men were provided with benefits, the programme would assist the entire family. Therefore, women were only given 'Aid to Dependent Children', which was later changed to 'Aid to Families with Dependent Children'.

David Montgomery, Bruce Nelson, James Atleson,[38] David Brody,[39] Karl Klare,[40] Ronald Schatz,[41] and Katherine Stone came to the same conclusion from a different perspective. While labour groups did achieve small victories, the New Deal programmes failed to bring about industrial democracy in its most tangible form. Still, the struggles of labour classes did bring about class consciousness, and the question of ethnicity receded to the background.

Sociologists and political scientists whose arguments revolved around the notion of 'state-capacity'—including Kenneth Finegold, Anna Shola Orloff, Karen Orren, Theda Skocpol, and Margret Weir—argue that the New Deal failed to bring about comprehensive reforms as the state was not capable.[42] This was due to the inability of the federal bureaucracy, which was inexperienced in undertaking such an arduous task. The failure of the NRA is attributed to this factor, while the success of the AAA was due to the administrative abilities of the Department of Agriculture, which had extensive experience in handling farm economy and had forged a close association with farm organisations. Historians like Lyle Dorset, Bruce Stave and Charles Trout had examined these aspects in the 1960s and 1970s,[43] and they concluded that some New Deal programmes were given to traditional, urban political functionaries both as a political choice and due to the absence of capable bureaucrats.

Ellis Hawley, in *The New Deal and the Problem of Monopoly*,[44] evolved the theory of the rise of the 'broker state'. Federal government policies worked to ensure the protection of a variety of interest groups, leading to increasing pluralistic competition in the marketplace and therefore creating the broker state. This shift, Hawley theorised, was not intentional. By analysing the NRA, he concluded that the programme had failed to establish stable prices and markets and balance industrial relations. However, it did help organise the industrial workforce, allowing for their rise as competitive actors in the labour markets. Similarly, while the New Deal could not establish a balanced economic world, it provided a platform where economically weaker groups could mobilise and confront stronger groups and directly challenge the centres of power.

Other organisational historians emphasise that the achievements of the New Deal were based on long-term social transformations in which the organisation of the managerial system played a significant role in both public and private life. Joseph Huthmacher, Mark Gelfand, and Bruce Stave[45] have placed importance on urbanisation and the increased political power of the cities—the fact that public housing, labour standards, and public health were given priority was a mark of the political influence that urban elements now wielded. Jordon Schwarz evolved the term 'state capitalism' to describe the reconfiguration of neglected areas in the US. The development of national parks is one example of this process, wherein public investment was used to establish the infrastructure of regions that had hitherto been neglected.

Historians like Herbert Stein, Dean Mary, and Alan Brinkly believed that the New Deal introduced Keynesianism to American governance based on the culture of consumption in the American economy.[46] Roosevelt's economic and welfare policies were tuned to adapt to those changes politically.

In the end, most scholars considered Roosevelt a pragmatic leader whose policies were meant to produce immediate results, without much thought about their long-term impact. Leuchtenburg believed that the New Deal was a movement led by men who wanted to make human life more tolerable and show that the Great Depression was not the end. It was only later that historians and scholars began to look into the long-term transformative changes brought in by the New Deal policies.

Notes

1. William E. Leuchtenburg, *Franklin D. Roosevelt and the New Deal, 1932–1940* (New York, 1963).

2. Bureau of Labour Statistics, 'Graph of US Employment Rate, 1930–1945', *SHEC Resources for Teachers*. Available at https://shec.ashp.cuny.edu/items/show/1510 (accessed October 2025).

3. The term Prohibition Era refers to a nationwide ban on the sale and manufacture of most types of alcohol across the United States, effected through the Volstead Act and the 18th Amendment. It was a result of years of lobbying by the Temperance Movement; another factor was the desire to conserve foodgrain during World War I. However, continued demand for alcohol led to a sharp rise in organised crime and bootlegging, eventually resulting in an overwhelming consensus to repeal the Prohibition laws.

4. Presidential Proclamation (no. 2029) of Franklin D. Roosevelt to facilitate the coinage of silver.

5. Eric Foner, *Give Me Liberty! An American History*, third ed. (New York, 2011), p. 805.

6. Foner, *Give Me Liberty!*, pp. 806–809.

7. Ibid., pp. 809–810.

8. Ibid., pp. 821–826.

9. Ibid., pp. 820–821.

10. Ibid., p. 823.

11. Louis M. Hacker, *The Shaping of the American Tradition* (New York, 1947).

12. Henry Steele Commager, *The New Deal in History*. Available at https://www.tesd.net/cmc/lib/PA01001259/Centricity/Domain/314/GD%20Critics.pdf (accessed October 2025).

13. Arthur M. Schlesinger, Jr., *The Cycles of American History* (Boston, 1986).

14. Schlesinger, Jr., *The Age of Roosevelt*, 3 vols (Boston, 1957–1960).

15. Frank Friedel, *Franklin D. Roosevelt*, 4 vols (Boston, 1952–1973).

16. Rexford G. Tugwell, *The Diary of Rexford G. Tugwell: The New Deal, 1932–1935* (New York, 1992).

17. John T. Flynn, *The Roosevelt Myth*, revised ed., (New York, 1956), pp. 414–445.

18. Heinz Eulau, 'Neither Ideology Nor Utopia: The New Deal in Retrospect', *Antioch Review* 19 (Winter), 1959–1960, pp. 523–537.

19. Barton J. Bernstein, 'The New Deal: The Conservative Achievements of Liberal Reform', in *Towards a New Past: Dissenting Essays in American History* (New York, 1968), pp. 263–288.

20. Ronald Radosh, 'The Myth of the New Deal', in *A New History of the Leviathan*, ed. Ronald Radosh and Murray Rothbard (New York, 1972), pp. 146–187.

21. Howard Zinn, ed., *New Deal Thought* (Indianapolis, 1966).

22. Paul K. Conkin, *The New Deal* (Arlington Heights, Illinois, 1967).

23. Thomas Ferguson, 'From Normalcy to New Deal: Industrial Structure, Party Competition, and American Public Policy in the Great Depression', *International Organization* 38 (1984), pp. 41–94.

24. Colin Gordon, *New Deals: Business, Labour, and Politics in America, 1920–1935* (New York, 1994).

25. James MacGregor Burns, *Roosevelt: The Lion and the Fox* (New York, 1956).

26. James T. Patterson, *Congressional Conservatism and the New Deal: The Growth of the Conservative Coalition in Congress, 1933–1939* (Lexington, 1967).

27. Friedel, *Franklin D. Roosevelt*.

28. Harvard Sitkoff, *Fifty Years Later: The New Deal Evaluated* (New York, 1985).

29. Nancy J. Weiss, *Farewell to the Party of Lincoln: Black Politics in the Age of FDR* (Princeton, 1983).

30. John B. Kirby, *Black Americans in the Roosevelt Era: Liberalism and Race* (Knoxville, 1980).

31. Alan Brinkly, 'The New Deal and Southern Politics', in *The New Deal and the South*, ed. James C. Cobb and Michael V. Namarato (New York, 1982).

32. Bruce Schulman, *From Cotton Belt to Sunbelt: Federal Policy, Economic Development, and the Transformation of the South, 1938–1980* (New York, 1991).

33. Barry D. Karl, *Executive Reorganization and Reform in the New Deal: The Genesis of Administrative Management, 1900–1939* (Chicago, 1963).

34. Mark Leff, *The Limits of Symbolic Reform: The New Deal and Taxation, 1933–1939* (New York, 1994).

35. Jill S. Quadagno, *The Transformation of Old Age Security: Class and Politics in the American Welfare State* (Chicago, 1988).

36. Theda Skocpol, *Protecting Soldiers and Mothers: The Political Origins of Social Policy in the United States* (Cambridge, Massachusetts, 1992).

37. Linda Gordon, *Pitied But Not Entitled: Single Mothers and the History of Welfare* (New York, 1994).

38. For Montgomery, Nelson, and Atleson, see Chapter 4, 'Prosperity', in Eric Foner, *The New American History*, revised and expanded edition (Philadelphia, 1997).

39. David Brody, *Workers in Industrial America: Essays on Twentieth-Century Struggle* (New York, 1980).

40. Karl E. Klare, 'Judicial Deradicalization of the Wagner Act and the Origins of Modern Legal Consciousness, 1937–1941', *Minnesota Law Review* 65, 1978, pp. 265–239.

41. Ronald W. Schatz, *The Electrical Workers: A History of Labor at General Electric and Westinghouse, 1923–1960* (Urbana, 1983).

42. See Foner, *The New American History*.

43. Ibid.

44. Ellis Hawley, *The New Deal and the Problem of Monopoly: A Study in Economic Ambivalence* (Princeton, 1996).

45. See Foner, *The New American History*.

46. Ibid.

CHAPTER 7

A Struggle for Equality
The African American Movement

Introduction

In the foundational years of the United States, freedom was a limited notion: Practices of enslavement and indenture were normalised and legal, and enslavement in particular was a racialised system. Only very few enslaved persons were given freedom in the early years of the **Revolutionary War** as a reward for rendering military service; some others managed to buy their independence; in some cases, enslavers offered '**manumission**', that is, they themselves freed the people that they had enslaved.[1] Even these limited avenues were foreclosed once westward expansion was in full swing, as the importance of slave labour increased manifold. Before the Civil War, freedmen in the South were generally of mixed-race ancestry and worked as farmhands, craftsmen, artisans, and small traders. They lived in constant fear of being sucked into slave labour. According to John White, free Black persons managed to retain their free status by becoming a distinctive elite class within the Black community, with a relatively higher social and economic status, particularly during the period of Reconstruction when some of them became Congressmen and others were elected to state legislatures. This class used their newfound status to adopt a 'middle path' approach to formulate conservative and amiable racial policies.[2]

The status of enslaved people in the northern states was considerably different. While it is important to note that the North had relied on slave labour as well, and that racist attitudes were entrenched among the northern White population, the region never developed a slave society. By 1804, most northern states had abolished slavery. Racism persisted through policies of segregation that kept the Black population isolated, and through other laws and hurdles to deny African Americans the right to vote, prevent their entry into the military, and deny access to education. Segregation was practised religiously in transportation, hotels, restaurants, prisons, hospitals, and even in death, with the creation of segregated cemeteries.[3] However, African Americans in the pre-Civil War North had won some limited rights, such as the right to lodge petitions, print their journals and newspapers, and carry out political protest and related activities. Their activities gradually gave rise to different types of resistance and activism. Richard Allen, who was from Philadelphia, converted to Methodism in 1777 and purchased his freedom three years later. He founded the African Methodist Episcopal Church (AME) in 1794 and was elected its first bishop in 1816. The aim and purpose behind the AME, the first independent Black denomination in the US, was to create organised support for **abolitionism** and inspire other free Black Christians to disassociate from White churches, initiating tentative steps towards racial justice. Allen was also an important organiser of the first National Colored Convention. Over time, this movement became more assertive, engaging with issues of disenfranchisement and segregation to secure racial equality and integration in the US.[4]

In 1827, **Freedom's Journal**, the first newspaper owned and run by African Americans, began publication in New York City. It was edited by John Brown Russwurm and Samuel Cornish. The paper published letters by Richard Allen and another prominent Black abolitionist denouncing the establishment of the American Colonization Society (ACS) in 1816, which they saw as an attempt to propagate and further entrench slavery. One of the agents of this newspaper in Boston, David Walker, published *An Appeal to the Colored Citizens of the World* (1829), which instantly became a widely-read treatise against White supremacy and slavery, and it has been seen as a nineteenth-century 'Black Power' manifesto. The *Appeal* added to growing mobilisation for Black rights—the USA had already seen numerous rebellions by enslaved people. The year 1830 marked the emergence of a new strand of militant, moral abolitionism under the leadership of William Lloyd Garrison and his newspaper *The Liberator*, which advocated for the abolition of slavery and racial bias, helping bring the issue of slavery into the national discourse. However, the publication of the *Appeal* also highlighted the differences between Black leaders and White abolitionists, as many of the latter group condemned the *Appeal* and its advocacy for a 'bloody insurrection' against slavery. Such 'radical' Black writings, which focused on the rights of Black people to combat any system that oppressed and enslaved them, ran contrary to the 'moderate' approach of White abolitionists, which was based on moral persuasion to enslavers to 'gradually' end slavery.

Despite these differences, Black leaders actively supported interracial abolitionist efforts, establishing a platform of working groups that became extremely important after the Civil War, when the establishment of the NAACP and the National Urban League carried forward the goal of securing civil rights for Black Americans. Cracks began to appear in this interracial abolitionist movement when some Black leaders began to tilt towards more radical political activism instead of pursuing the goal of freedom within the moral framework of the settler colonial state.[5] In this atmosphere, another group of opinion emerged in the 1850s, represented by Black leaders like Alexander Crummel, Samuel Ringgold Ward, Henry Highland Garnet, and Martin R. Delany, who strongly stressed the emigration and colonisation of Black Americans in East Africa and later shifted their focus towards West Indies, Central and South America. This led to the establishment of the American Colonization Society (ACS) in 1816, which aimed to send freedmen and emancipated persons from the US to the colony of Liberia in Africa. However, this idea did not find many takers, and was in fact strongly opposed by abolitionist leaders who had begun to advocate for racial equality in the US during the Civil War, and to assert a positive, empowered, and culturally distinct Black identity. To achieve the goal of racial emancipation, they began to develop Black-led schools, churches, and organisations.[6] After the Civil War, many of these leaders became active members of the Freedmen's Bureau, established by the federal government to assist and extend Black rights and freedom as secured through the 13th Constitutional Amendment (see Chapter 1). These changes gradually sowed the seeds for greater mobility among African Americans and new political ideologies such as **Black separatism**. Affiliation with Africa as a motherland or point of origin was an element in the ideological stances of multiple leaders over the next century, including of W. E. B. Du Bois, Marcus Garvey, and Malcolm X.

Early African American Leadership: Frederick Douglass

In the above context, one needs to situate and evaluate the role of Frederick Douglass (1817–1895), one of the most prominent abolitionists and social reformers of the nineteenth century. Born in Maryland, Douglass was enslaved as a domestic servant in Baltimore. He taught himself to read and write and escaped enslavement with the aid of his future wife, Anna Murray, a free Black woman from New Bedford, Massachusetts. After reading *The Liberator*, he became an abolitionist and was deeply influenced by its proprietor, William Lloyd Garrison. In 1845, he published his most famous work, *Narrative of the Life of Frederick Douglass, an American Slave*, an autobiography.

Once settled in Massachusetts, Douglass became part of an active community of free and formerly enslaved African Americans. He joined the AME and became a licensed preacher in 1839, and soon began a career as an antislavery and pro-reform speaker and activist, taking up the causes of racial equality, civil rights, and suffrage for Black people and women. In 1847, Douglass started the abolitionist newspaper, *The North Star*. He supported the Temperance Movement, pursued an anti-colonial agenda of world peace, and advocated the abolition of capital punishment and the convict lease system, as well as an end to racist violence such as lynchings. Douglass believed that industrial education would make Black people self-reliant and guide them to adhere to strict moral principles. He took an active part in the Colored Convention Movement from the 1840s to 1850, and in 1851, he split from Garrison, citing ideological differences over their response to the problem of slavery. To promote political participation of Black people, Douglass supported John Brown's anti-slavery movement and goals, although he was opposed to the attempted slave rebellion at Harper's Ferry, Virginia, in 1859, and publicly appreciated the Emancipation Proclamation of 1863. He demanded the inclusion of Black soldiers in the Union Army during the Civil War. He later supported the 14th and 15th Constitutional Amendments and exerted all force to implement the Civil Rights Act in 1875. He placed his complete trust in the Republican Party, which gave him prestigious government posts and the Ambassadorship of Haiti. This accommodationist ideology was later adopted by Booker T. Washington, making him an inevitable successor of Frederick Douglass.

The Late Nineteenth Century

The constitutional promise of racial equality was won after a long struggle led by African Americans. The question of slavery as an 'institution of morality' came into play during and after the Civil War and in the period of Reconstruction. However, soon after the compromise of 1877 with the failure of Reconstruction policies, the 13th, 14th, and 15th Constitutional Amendments were made practically ineffective due to the role played by White supremacist armed groups like the KKK and racial policies like the Black Codes (see Chapter 1). Also, industrialising America pursued social segregation with support from the judiciary. At the end of the nineteenth century, the Black intelligentsia began to realise the urgent need for comprehensive education.

By the end of the nineteenth and beginning of the twentieth century, African Americans had begun to develop independent economic institutions like banks, insurance companies, cooperative societies, manufacturing units, newspapers, and retail businesses and were providing a range of services like barbers, tailors, beauty shops, dry cleaners, sewists, and funeral parlours. These developments led to the creation of a separate Black economy. The period also saw the rise of Black towns like Nicodemus in Kansas established in 1879, Langston and Boley, both in Oklahoma, in 1891 and 1904, apart from cities in California, Illinois, Michigan, and New Jersey (though not all towns survived for long). The period also saw the emergence of new Black churches that preached a 'pure life' and promoted the idea that Jesus Christ would soon return to the earth for the Final Judgment. One such church was the Church of Christ (Holiness), which propagated 'pure living' devoid of alcohol, sin, and the use of cosmetic products, and which asked adherents to dress modestly. Gospel music that developed in these churches later assisted in the rise of jazz and other genres of music, such as blues, that completely changed US popular music culture. Practices of music and dance that had developed in the South before Emancipation, and which carried a complex history of racism but also subversion, such as the 'cakewalk' and 'ragtime', remained in circulation. The period also witnessed a diversification in the arena of sports. Black boxers found great success in this period, and many Black players joined professional baseball, later forming their own baseball leagues to combat segregation. Whenever they were not permitted to participate, Black communities created their own spaces: playgrounds, clubs, boxing rings, track and field events, horse racing, and cycling groups, and teams for golf and tennis. By 1900, more than 200 Black newspapers and magazines had been published, and multiple films had been produced.[7]

African American Leadership after Reconstruction

African American leaders who emerged in nineteenth- and twentieth-century USA need to be understood in terms of both their context and the social and political influences that shaped them. This chapter will analyse the rise of a few leaders in particular—Booker T. Washington, W. E. B Du Bois, and Marcus Garvey—focusing on their ideologies and activism. They were pioneers of the postbellum period, and each one had a distinct approach to the task of eliminating racial inequality and segregation. These leaders contributed to larger patterns of mobilisation amongst Black people to secure their rights and dignity, supported by constitutional amendments, to rise beyond the narrow confines of a White-dominated society. Apart from Booker T. Washington, these leaders advocated forms of **racial separatism** to establish two co-existing worlds until a time when racial equality could be achieved.

A study of these leaders also reveals the ideological interconnections between activists within and across generations: For example, Washington drew on Douglass's idea of propagating an industrial education. Washington, in turn, served as a mentor to Marcus Garvey, who adopted his racial and economic philosophy. Garvey influenced Malcolm X, particularly his radicalism and idea of racial separatism. Martin Luther King, Jr. greatly admired Washington, Du Bois and Garvey, and acknowledged Malcolm X's importance in giving momentum to Civil Rights reforms.

Apart from these commonalities, each leader was different in their approach and the path they adopted to achieve equality for the Black community, creating a unique image among the oppressed, exploited minorities within the US and across the world. According to John White, from Douglass to Du Bois, their meteoric rise and popularity was at least partly due to the ample support they received from White public figures who were sympathetic to their cause or wanted the support of a growing Black electorate.[8] Washington and Du Bois emerged as public figures in the Progressive era, and their political trajectory was undoubtedly influenced by other popular discourses on problems associated with social, class, and gender inequalities that comprised the hidden cost of rapid industrialisation. Garvey has been described as the first truly 'mass' leader of the Black rights movement. Malcolm X and King walked the same path, using different ideas, styles, and tactics to secure an equal space and rights regardless of race, as enshrined in the Constitution. However, White concurs with the observations made by Gunnar Myrdal that African American leadership provided both 'accommodation' and 'protest' and carried out their crusade within the confines of a 'politics of limited options'.[9]

Myrdal's *American Dilemma* (1944) was considered a scholarly work that analysed the predicament of African Americans and the need for action at the federal level. Historians have observed that Black leaders in the postbellum period were either those who had been free even before Emancipation, or those who, post-Emancipation, were in an elevated position (for example, in terms of education or means) and could take up the mantle of leadership. He claimed that southern and northern Black leaders were different owing to their distinct circumstances. The southern Black leader, having survived a highly oppressive and exploitative system that had proved difficult to destroy, became 'a consummate manipulator', using covert tactics to get what was needed to advance Black rights.

While many scholars appreciated Myrdal's work, Ralph Ellison highlighted some critical aspects, particularly the lack of in-depth study of Black people's inner worlds that enabled them to survive, sustain, and create an independent world in the US. This critical insight proved influential and fundamentally changed the way historians understood the issue of race. As a result, from the 1970s onwards, new history-writing began to question the centrality of White experiences and perspectives in history and especially in historical analyses of race relations. As the perspectives shifted to Black people's experiences and scholarship, a new understanding evolved of the process of Black enslavement, right from their forced migration from Africa and long period of bondage and enslavement, to the Emancipation Proclamation and continued marginalisation of Black Americans even after slavery was formally abolished. Black leaders played a significant role in both, creating a sense of identity, and in sparking wider movements to end segregation, achieve racial equality, and secure political and economic rights.[10]

The Emergence of 'Black' and 'White' Worlds

While, as we have noted, racism and structural inequalities persisted post-Reconstruction, a marked change was witnessed in the form of the beginning of large-scale protests and a mass 'freedom movement' against the Jim Crow laws that institutionalised segregation in the southern states. Many Black people migrated en masse out of the South, settling in new urban centres. This was part of a process whereby Black communities sought to mobilise and wield political power, eventually culminating in the beginning of the **Civil Rights Movement in the 1950s and 1960s**.[11] Compared with the South, the North did not overtly practice Jim Crow laws and racial societal norms of behaviour. Northern cities provided avenues of employment and education that assisted in the growth of African American culture of literature, poetry, and music and saw new waves of protest. Still, racial discrimination and prejudice in housing, schools, and employment avenues was common.[12] A paradoxical picture was emerging. On the one hand, spatial movement assisted in the development of an African American cultural movement and identity, eventually crystallising in the Harlem Renaissance. On the other hand, with the rise of Black 'ghettos', new structures of exploitation and suppression emerged that deployed subtle and hidden forms of racism, and the mental and physical separation of the two worlds—the Black and the White—persisted.

For the White population, this separation served as a defensive management strategy to limit and restrict the inclusion of Black people and retain a White stronghold over the public sphere. This was done by excluding Black workers from job markets, labour unions, and other associations, which also limited their entry into the political system. Antagonism developed between Black southern migrants and White workers (the latter group included new ethnic groups as well as native-born White settlers). This dynamic of exclusion served to keep African Americans politically weak and economically dependent, creating conditions of continued racial discrimination.[13] These situations assisted in the rise of Black leadership, who mastered the art of utilising both public and private spaces, media, and books. Through their own organisations, these leaders began to write and to raise voices against racism, inequality, oppression, and exploitation. The rise of the African American movement coincided with the period when economic institutions shifted from agricultural to industrial processes, ushering in the era of modernisation and bringing significant structural changes. Black leaders analysing these changes recognised that this was the right time to lend their voices, energies, and lives to an organised movement to bring racial equality and justice to America.

The Great Migration and the Rise of a New Black Identity

The 'Great Migration' (see Chapter 1) was a momentous event that transformed Black society, economy, cultural traditions, and political outlook.[14] While White America underwent a period of reform known as **Progressivism**, Black America moved from rural to urban economy. The Great Migration resulted in the growth of Black-majority urban neighbourhoods, which were often characterised as 'ghettos'.[15] These spaces allowed for new lifestyles and a sense of independence, and became home to a shared consciousness and identity.[16] Harlem in the Upper Manhattan area of New York City is a prime example of how new urban spaces challenged the entrenched race hierarchy.[17] The neighbourhood became a refuge for Black artists and intelligentsia and birthed a vibrant literary and cultural movement.[18] The 'psychological transformation' of African Americans from a dependent and subordinated peasantry, to a community of self-reliant, independent individuals, became the cornerstone of Black political activism in this period. It formed the bedrock of Du Bois's political aspirations. Through the **Niagara Movement**, Du Bois strove for the right to vote, which infused a new spirit in African Americans and found its expression in their political participation in World War I and its aftermath.[19] In the era of segregation, African Americans voted against southern racism 'with the movement of their feet'. In the North, circumstances were better, but slowly, new forms of racial abuse and victimisation began to appear here as well.[20]

From the beginning of the Niagara Movement (1900) to what was then termed the **'New Negro Movement' (the 1920s)**, two organisations, the **National Association for the Advancement of Colored People (NAACP)** and the **National Urban League (NUL)**, played significant roles through print media: the journals *Crisis* and *Opportunity*. They provided avenues for young and educated African Americans to unite, eventually leading to the **Harlem Renaissance**,[21] the period of 'self-discovery' that, according to one its pioneers, Alain Locke, was centred around the need for African Americans to cultivate self-awareness and identity, drawing on their African heritage as well as American traditions to evolve a distinct cultural world. Locke became an important figure in the movement when he published a magazine, *The New Negro*, in 1925, an influential anthology of Black art, music, poetry, and essays that focused on the development of Black culture, a distinct African American identity, and the promotion of racial equality. As Black communities recovered their histories and evolved new forms of artistic expression, jazz music evolved and African sculpture found new expression. The Harlem Renaissance also saw interracial efforts at equality. Van Vechten, a White man, contributed significantly to the spread of the Harlem Renaissance through his literary saloons. His famous 'Know the Negro' campaign brought writers of different races and ethnicities together.[22] In World War I, Black people were drafted and participated in the war effort, but on their return they faced racism, discrimination, racial riots, and brutal attacks. This effectively ended aspirations for 'assimilation' and led to the rise of Black nationalism, also marking the entry of Garvey's programme with its slogan, 'Back to Africa', that offered hope amid an otherwise dismal situation for African Americans.[23]

The **Talented Tenth** (a class of educated elite African Americans who were designated 'leaders' of the new Black communities, as mooted by Du Bois), too, realised that they could never overcome racial barriers unless they evolved a 'mass movement'. A new Black identity was consciously forged using the centuries-old Black folk culture centred around the collective experiences of, and resilience in spite of, enslavement, the environs of the rural South, and new dynamics of marginalisation in urban spaces. This led to the emergence of cultural dualism, where the Black writers turned for inspiration to their African roots, slave culture, and experiences that were completely devoid of the White world. The Harlem School eventually moved towards **Black nationalism**.[24]

The Harlem School relied on popular Black folk traditions and culture in order to debunk and challenge the pervasive stereotyping of Black people as seen by the White, and to build a wholly new, transformed sense of identity. Their writings brought in the tempo and styles of Black speech, that is, African American Vernacular English (AAVE). Instead of advocating for racial equality, the Harlem

School began to uncover the layers of Black culture, writing about Black experiences where racism was relegated to the background to highlight aspects of love and joy, and not dwell on conflict and oppression. There was a conscious move away from 'protest literature' to create a holistic 'non-Western world'. It is significant that this new genre developed in a hostile environment of extreme racism, and that it never advocated integration or assimilation.[25]

The era of the New Negro and the Harlem Renaissance was brought to an abrupt end due to the Great Depression. By the mid-1930s, a majority of Black people were dependent on relief programmes; in some cities, about 80 per cent of African Americans had to shift to government welfare for survival. The inauguration of the New Deal by Roosevelt, according to August Meir and Elliot Rudwick, 'marked a real turning point in the trends of American race relations'.[26] New events marked the rise of Black sportspersons like Joe Louis, a boxer who became a symbol of racial pride. Haile Selassie, the ruler of Ethiopia, fought off an unsuccessful Italian invasion. The emergence of African American religious leader 'Father Divine', who provided food and lodging in a time of extreme deprivation and advocated for the end of racism and the rise of Black religious nationalism, offered a ray of hope. Eugene Brown, who gave himself a new name, Sufi Abdul Hamid, led a new boycott movement in which Black people were urged to boycott all White merchants in Harlem who refused to hire Black staff. This period also saw the rise of Du Bois, who broke off with NAACP in 1934 and began to advocate for a distinct Black economy based on a cooperative programme. He wanted his people to utilise 'segregation' to establish Black businesses, labour unions, and cooperative stores. Du Bois's eventual aim was to secure Black political rights.[27] The 1940s witnessed industrial growth during and after World War II and increased Black migration to urban areas. In 1941, President Franklin D. Roosevelt banned racial discrimination in the defence industries, but this executive order was met with race riots and retaliatory discrimination against Black people; the most severe riot occurred in Detroit in 1943. President Truman continued his goal of racial integration in the US armed forces and remained committed to implementing civil rights.

The Emergence of NAACP

The NAACP contributed immensely to the movement to achieve civil rights. Racial violence in the US became impossible to ignore after the **Springfield race riot of 1908**. The public reckoning with this issue was initiated by William E. Walling, who undertook independent research and published a hard-hitting article in the *Independent*, urging sympathetic Americans to revive the abolitionist movement to secure social and civil rights for all the Black people in America.[28] The call was well-received, also drawing in White supporters such as social worker Mary White Ovington, Oswald Garrison (grandson of William Lloyd Garrison), Villard, who was then editor of the *New York Evening Post*. In a series of organised meetings that extended from 1909 to 1911, the NAACP was created with a clearly outlined agenda: abolition of segregation laws; implementation of the 14th and 15th Constitutional Amendments; and the right to equal education for all. All the member-officials of the NAACP were White except Du Bois, who was appointed the editor of the NAACP's magazine, *Crisis*. Du Bois brought with him all the Black intellectuals of the Niagara Movement.

To achieve its goals, the NAACP initiated legal cases in the courts and generated public pressure. It was NAACP-led court battles that secured many significant victories, like the abolition of the grandfather clause used to disenfranchise Black voters.[29] Carefully crafted court cases assisted in the outlawing of a Louisville ordinance that mandated residential segregation. The NAACP also organised protests against D. W. Griffith's film *Birth of a Nation*, which blamed African Americans for all the problems of the Reconstruction period and presented the Ku Klux Klan in a positive light. The organisation also generated public awareness against lynching—civil rights leader James Weldon Johnson in particular led this thrust, and his appointment marked the inclusion of African American leaders in the organisation. In 1930, the NAACP, under the leadership of Thurgood Marshall, launched a campaign to secure rightful constitutional and political rights and civil equality for African Americans. Later, in 1968, Marshall became the first African American judge to be appointed to the Supreme Court bench. He took up the issue of legal persecution of Black people, the race bar in the jury service of southern states, and the complete disenfranchisement of Black citizens from southern politics, in addition to pursuing steps to ensure equality of education for all by ending segregation.

Understanding Southern Black Activism: The Context of Racial Segregation

Historians disagree about when segregation first appeared in the postwar South—whether it was before, during, or at some point after Reconstruction. What is clear is that segregation was institutionalised as a means of maintaining racial subjugation even while maintaining the farce that racial exploitation had ended with the 13th Constitutional Amendment. As discussed in Chapter 1, new systems of tenancy and sharecropping, along with restrictive laws passed by state legislatures, trapped Black people in cycles of debt and impoverishment. Socially, southern race relations during and after Reconstruction were marked by increasing segregation in public accommodations, hospitals, prisons, schools, and places of entertainment.

CHANGES IN THE LABOUR SYSTEM

We have noted in Chapter 3 that the nineteenth century was a period of industrialisation in the US, with changes in work, labour demand, and education. The fundamental changes taking place in societal relationships as the result of a capital-intensive economy were profound. By the beginning of the twentieth century, the **post-industrial era**, service and information centres expanded. White-collar jobs took precedence over blue-collar ones and brought about another kind of change in labour requirements. The Second Industrial Revolution created the need for a geographically and socially mobile labour force with greater literacy and a demonstrable skill-set.

However, the Black Codes devised in the South had systematically segregated labour. They placed Black workers in an inferior position, with limited avenues and control over the conditions and kind of work. New segregation laws were adopted that modified the voting system, which now mandated literacy tests, poll taxes, and property requirements. These changes effectively disenfranchised most Black people from voting in the 1920s. Also, by 1910, a vast majority of Black workers were in agricultural employment (as tenants and sharecroppers, often with increasing debt) and another significant share was in domestic occupation (see Chapter 1). As a result, the jobs that emerged by the beginning of the twentieth century—at the time when the South began to industrialise—were monopolised by White workers.

In another blow to Black rights mobilisation, the US Supreme Court passed the *Plessy v. Ferguson* case (1896), declaring that the southern states had constitutional rights to segregate public facilities as long as they provided them for both races: this has famously been termed the concept of 'separate but equal' spaces. Even the judiciary, thus, restricted the empowerment of African Americans. The White establishment deliberately and consciously excluded Black folk from the process of industrialisation, modernisation, and social transformation.

During and after the Reconstruction, most Black southerners rejected the option of emigration. Rather than integrated institutions, they hoped to secure better schools and welfare facilities. Aware of their position in a society whose loudest voices had pledged to restore White supremacy, those who attended the first conventions held in the South, immediately after the Civil War, were extremely careful not to offend White sensibilities by demanding Black political rights. This thought process can be seen in Booker T. Washington, whose policy of 'accommodation' allowed African Americans to acquire the skills needed to participate fully in the urban economy. Washington was the first nationally accepted leader of the African American community, and his most outstanding contribution was uplifting the community to a position of economic independence.

Booker T. Washington, Educationist and Accommodationist

Booker T. Washington was born into slavery in Franklin County, Virginia, in 1856. He was the son of an enslaved domestic worker and an unknown White man. He spent his early life in slavery and, during the Reconstruction, studied at the Hampton Institute, which had been recently established by a philanthropic northerner, Samuel Chapman Armstrong, to promote Black students seeking higher education.[29] Armstrong believed that education for emancipated people would help them make a more straightforward transition from slavery to freedom. The same line of thought was extended under the Congressional or radical Reconstruction policies, visible in the creation of the Freedmen's Bureau, which supported industrial and agricultural education as a significant step to improve the socio-economic status of Black southerners. Armstrong's idea of extending education as an imperative step received support from the dominant White communities of both the North and the South. However, their support was driven by a hidden agenda to control Black labour: the idea was to provide enough education for their labour to be utilised and exploited, but to curtail opportunities so as to keep the Black working class at the bottom of the socio-economic ladder.

Before securing a proper education, Washington had worked as a house boy for a prominent man, where he was influenced by the Puritan ethic of hard labour, emphasis on hygiene and prudence, and the focus on acquiring an education. These later formed the crux of his social philosophy and shaped his life-long association with sympathisers from the White elite. At Hampton Institute, he received a liberal education and trade skills, and was exposed to more Christian influences; this experience shaped his personality and identity. Washington was not particularly impressed by the Baptist theological school in Washington, DC, and the one-year law course that he completed later. However, living in this northern city gave him insight into the gaps between urban and rural Black populations. He accepted Armstrong's offer to teach at Hampton, where he set up a night school programme for Black students who worked during the day. The programme was an instant success.³⁰ He sensed a lack of empathy towards the Black rural peasantry that reflected class, regional, and occupational divisions amongst the Black population.

THE RISE OF AN EDUCATOR

An ardent follower of Samuel C. Armstrong, Washington found in him a mentor for life who guided and assisted him in navigating biracial relations. His achievements with Hampton Institute prompted Armstrong to recommend his name for the head of the Tuskegee Institute in Alabama. He was appointed and began the institute's operations on 4 July 1881, and by 1900, this institute had become the most prominent post-secondary school for Black people in the US. It was here that Washington practised the art of 'interracial diplomacy', securing funds from the influential and wealthy White elite to build and run the school, while also spreading the word about the school amongst the Black community. Washington firmly believed that the Black community needed to be educated at least at a rudimentary level to acquire skills and secure employment that would allow for socio-economic improvement. He became an influential advocate of practical vocational education that included carpentry, blacksmith works, brick and wagon making, modern methods of agriculture, skilled artisanship, and training for women in housekeeping. These educational institutes became his social laboratory.³¹ Washington's ideals of Black education defined the pedagogy of the Tuskegee Institute, many land-grant colleges, and the Hampton Institute. He secured support for himself and financial assistance from some of the most powerful businesses in the US, to the extent that he was able to build many other Black institutions and colleges in the South. This only deepened Washington's conviction that a liberal arts education and advanced degrees were not meant for poor Black people. For his immense success, he was also called the 'Wizard of Tuskegee'.

FIG. 7.1: Booker T. Washington on his education tours, photo collage by Emmett J. Scott (1916)
Source: Wikimedia Commons.

THE ATLANTA COMPROMISE

Washington emerged as a national figure soon after his speech on 18 September 1895 at the Cotton States and International Exposition in Atlanta, where he addressed an interracial audience and exhorted Black people to devote their energies to the economic development of their community, arguing that racial equality, political rights, and an end to segregation would be achieved in the long term through a conciliatory relationship with White society. He reminded southern White Atlantans of the 'fidelity and love' that Black people had shown them, and asked in return only the assurance that they would continue to employ Black workers as the primary labour force of the South and that the economic progress of skilled and dedicated Black people would not be obstructed. The speech received a standing ovation by the dominant White community. The Atlanta speech won immediate acclaim nationwide, as Washington proposed a 'pragmatic compromise' to resolve the race problem. He wanted the White population to trust their Black counterparts. Washington's conciliatory and moderate approach led many to project him as a 'sensible and progressive' Black leader. Washington asserted that the generation of capital resources was the only way to earn the respect that Black people inherently deserved from the White establishment.[32] The speech came to be known as the 'Atlanta Compromise', particularly among prominent critics like Du Bois and other Black leaders who rejected the southern accommodationist approach. This framing reflects the criticism that Washington had surrendered any claim to voting and equal rights for African Americans. He accepted racial segregation, saying, 'In all things that are purely social, we can be as separate as the fingers, yet one as the hand in all things essential to mutual progress'.[33] He focused on Black land ownership, business development opportunities, and vocational training in the South. Black people had to develop their institutions, establish essential supplies stores, and create a separate economy. This pragmatic approach to maintaining segregation did attract the attention of Black small business operators, farmers, and educators in industrial training institutes.

Washington's educational, social, and political philosophies were intricately interlinked. His reading of Black history convinced him that slavery and Reconstruction had not prepared African Americans for freedom as they lacked essential training to achieve economic independence. Therefore, there was a need to teach them aspects related to the dignity of labour, to practice prudence, and to inculcate a faith that hard work would result in financial success. He stressed character-building and the inculcation of middle-class values. Through his autobiography *Up from Slavery* (1901), which narrated his journey from enslavement to freedom, Washington made it clear that he believed and accepted the standard nineteenth-century attitude that through self-help, one could rise from poverty to riches. The book traced his climb up to his position as an influential African American leader.[34]

Washington had a dual career as an educator and African American leader in the last 20 years of his life. In 1900, he founded the **National Negro Business League** in Boston, which assisted in the establishment of many Black-owned organisations like the National Banker's Association, National Association of Negro Insurance Companies, National Association of Funeral Directors, National Association of Real Estate Dealers, National Bar Association, and National Press Association. He aimed to promote Black entrepreneurship and advertise instances of economic success.[35] The League reflected his views on economic advancement and progress, and provided him with a cadre of loyal supporters in major northern cities. The existence of such organisations even encouraged Black women to start their businesses. For example, Maggie Lena Walker established the St Luke's Penny Savings Bank, in Richmond, Virginia, in 1903, and by 1924, it had branches in 22 states. Madam C. J. Walker established two beauty companies—the Walker Manufacturing Company and the Madam C. J. Walker Hair Culturist Union of America—distributing beauty products explicitly designed for Black women. She later became a staunch supporter of Marcus Garvey, and her daughter participated in the Harlem Renaissance. By 1904, Washington, at the height of his fame, was supported by Presidents Theodore Roosevelt, Wilson, and Taft.

Despite his immense fame and charisma, and his position as an early Black leader, Washington's influence and programme did little to lessen the racial conflicts, riots, and lynchings that marked postbellum USA, nor was there any decrease in racial bias. Black representatives were removed from public offices as segregation policies became prominent. During his lifetime, Washington himself faced racial slurs and degradation. He secretly sponsored many lawsuits against the exclusion of Black individuals from jury service, and to end segregationist laws. He provided funds to create public pressure on the state to secure the right to vote of African Americans and terminate the bonded labour system in the southern states. He also visited many European countries as a dignitary, although he never visited Africa, Asia, the West Indies, or even Haiti. Washington initially supported German colonisation of Africa, although later he rescinded support.[36]

Analysing the Great Leader

Looking at Washington's ideological stances and his 'survival' or 'accommodationist' policy, historians argue that he was a Black leader created by the White elite. It is ironic that despite being an advocate of racial self-help, some of the wealthiest among the White business class financed Washington's efforts. Contributors to Tuskegee included such multi-millionaires as J. P. Morgan, John D. Rockefeller, and Collis Huntington; big business corporations also gave him funds to publish newspapers where Washington advocated moderate viewpoints and a middle path that would answer the demands of Black people without threatening the status quo.

Some of Washington's earliest critics were Du Bois and John Hope, who both held the view that African Americans, like any other US citizens, should be allowed to pursue a more holistic education that included history, literature, languages, and the classics, and not be pushed only into vocational or industrial education. The latter, they argued, would stymie intellectual growth and the development of a distinct sense of personality.[37] In his book, *The Souls of Black Folk*, Du Bois emphasises acquiring knowledge through education, increasing one's intellect to become the centre of power and political protest. Du Bois's essays, such as 'Of Mr. Booker T. Washington and Others', were some of the sharpest critiques of the accommodationist position. Du Bois charged Washington with poor leadership that resulted in Black disenfranchisement, the creation of an inferior civil status for Black people, and the withdrawal of funds from institutions for the higher education of Black students. Du Bois pronounced Washington's vision as narrow, paradoxical, and reflective of empty materialism and spiritual pessimism.

John Hope considered Washington 'cowardly and dishonest', and Julius F. Taylor, the Black editor of the *Chicago Broad Axe*, termed him the 'Great Beggar of Tuskegee'.[38] William M. Trotter, the editor of the *Boston Guardian*, was another bitter critic of Washington. Opposition and criticism of Washington's ideas and his White-sanctioned position as a Black leader also came from a small group of mainly northern Black journalists, lawyers, clergymen, and educators.

James Weldon Johnson recalled that Du Bois's criticism provided a rallying point for Black people opposed to Washington, splitting the Black public into two contending camps. The Niagara Movement of 1905 and its successor, the NAACP, were to institutionalise this opposition to Washington.

Historians like August Meir and Allan Spear argue that supporters of Washington were the rising Black middle class who supported capitalist values and race solidarity at the cost of equal political participation. Eric Foner has contested the idea that for Washington, an important impulse was the desire for White 'acceptance' of the Black man. Based on the available evidence, he argued that Washington secretly fought for equal property rights and against literacy tests (which were a hurdle in Black enfranchisement). Foner also believes that Washington emerged as a Black leader during a period of rapid industrialisation and urbanisation; therefore, he advocated economic independence for Black people. Unfortunately, by the beginning of the twentieth century, America was already moving from industrialisation toward the information revolution. This point has also been highlighted by C. Vann Woodward, who pointed out that Washington's economic outlook was fast becoming obsolete at the turn of the century.[39] By the 1920s, America was giving importance to service sectors and the information technology industry, where higher education played an essential role, not just being a craftsman, skilled labourer, or farming hand.

During his lifetime, Washington formulated an elaborate plan and structure with a singular aim to create spaces for Black southerners to avail educational opportunities and participate in economic activities. He wanted to end Black dependence on plantations by upgrading farming and industrial skills to improve Black people's social and economic status. Scholars accept that he was a great strategist, coordinator of interracial relations and a paradigmatic emissary. According to Gunnar Myrdal, his final goal was racial equality. Had Washington advanced a radical and militant Black movement with insistence on education, the White elite would have killed it before it could become a viable political force in the South.[40] It was not only his immense popularity as a Black leader that assisted him in gradually carving out a space to end centuries of racial discrimination, by integration into American society. As Louis Harlan's biography of Booker T. Washington shows, he possessed 'multiple personalities' and covertly supported a more radical agenda. Washington secretly supported legal action against the Jim Crow laws even as he publicly advocated a policy of accommodation. His most significant contribution to the Black community was to initiate the post-Reconstruction African American movement by creating spaces dedicated to education and training for Black youth, using accommodative and non-confrontational methods that caught the attention of American politicians and the elite White establishment, as well as the Black middle and working classes.

Race Relations in Urban USA

After World War I ended in 1914, new kinds of identity formation emerged amongst Black communities, sparking a wave of new articulations against unequal citizenship rights, oppression, and discrimination based on the Jim Crow laws. The Great Migration, a marked surge in the movement of Black people from the South to the North and Midwest, mainly to New York, Chicago, Philadelphia, and Pittsburgh, took place in the early twentieth century. This shift was encouraged by Black print media, brought better jobs and wages, and offered an escape from southern discrimination, segregation, and lynching. This led to the upward mobility of educated and enterprising Black people and the establishment of the NUL in 1910, which allowed them to vote.

The Harlem neighbourhood in New York City, as we have discussed, began to flourish as a centre for Black thought, commerce, and creativity in 1904, resulting in the emergence of Black-owned businesses, renewed urbanisation, and distinct approaches to community living. The National Negro Business League had many prominent members like Philip A. Payton, Jr. (founder of the Afro-American Realty Company), Charles W. Anderson (Republican Party leader from New York), and T. Thomas Fortune (editor of the *New York Age*). This was a diverse neighbourhood as West Indians also settled down here, which created competition and rivalry for jobs and housing.

Black American soldiers serving in Europe during World War I got international exposure, despite the racial discrimination they still faced within the US Army. This was another influence on the protests and pressure groups that emerged in the 1920s for civil and political rights. Following the war, Africans and African diaspora began to migrate to the US, for example from the West Indies, as noted earlier. Black political action was also influenced by the general trends of the Progressive era (see Chapter 4), which played a role in the creation of the NUL. However, these gains were undercut by continued anti-Black mobilisation in the US. In 1919, many American cities witnessed a 'Red Summer': widespread anti-Black riots both in the North and South. These riots were partly caused by the resurgence of the Ku Klux Klan, which unleashed a new wave of terror, resistance to the entry of Black people into the US army, and extreme poverty and unemployment as the postwar economy began to shrink.

Despite systemic disadvantages, Black communities were now better educated, politically savvy and had come out of the oppressive environment of the South. Black leaders began to advocate for 'resistance' and the creation of a 'separate' nation within the US. The period also marked the emergence of a 'New Negro' who, rediscovering their African roots and American identity, began a new literary and artistic movement that came to be known as the Harlem Renaissance. This marked a new phase in anti-racist assertion and protest.

W. E. B. Du Bois: Intellectualism and Pragmatism

Du Bois was a contemporary of Booker T. Washington and, as we have established, had a fundamentally different ideological approach to the Black quest for social and economic justice. Washington had in 1900 refused to recommend Du Bois's name for the position of superintendent of Washington DC Black schools, creating friction between the two. Du Bois was an African American leader known for his fierce integrationist **Pan-Africanism**, his emphasis on the development of the Black economy, and belief in revolutionary socialism.

Born on 23 February 1868, in Great Barrington, Massachusetts, Du Bois was of mixed-race ancestry, due to which he experienced racial prejudice early in his life. He was educated at Fisk University in Nashville, Tennessee, where he acquired an understanding of African American culture, and a glimpse of the racist rural South. He worked on a research project, 'The Suppression of the African Slave Trade to the United States of America, 1638–1870' at Harvard University in 1895. He received a scholarship from the Slater Fund, went to the University of Berlin, and toured Europe from 1892–1894. He also undertook a sociological study of the Black community, particularly about housing, health, and educational facilities. Despite his brilliant

Fig. 7.2: A portrait of W. E. B. Du Bois, by James E. Purdy (1907)
Source: Wikimedia Commons.

academic background, he could not secure employment at any White institution. He first taught at Wilberforce University, a Black college in Ohio, and was then hired at the University of Pennsylvania (1896–1897) to research Philadelphia's Black community, which resulted in the publication of *The Philadelphia Negro*, the first social science project on the issue of race and racism in the urban milieu. At Atlanta University, where Du Bois was appointed professor of history and economics, his first task was to undertake extensive research on varied aspects of the African American people.[41]

At this time, Du Bois was also heavily involved in civic activities and the Pan-Africanist movement. He had organised the first Pan-African Conference in London in August 1900. In 1897 he, along with Alexander Crummel and other Black intellectuals, formed the **American Negro Academy**, America's first Black academic society, with a focus on expanding the cultural and intellectual revitalisation of the Black people. This philosophical movement was initiated at the time of rampant lynchings, racial segregation, and exclusion from universal franchise, political office, and public arenas.

Vincent Harding has stated that Du Bois emerged as a 'Black messiah'. Du Bois emphasised 'racial groups' as distinct cultural entities and believed in **cultural pluralism**, insisting that each group should enjoy equal rights and opportunities, and that each should maintain its unique identity, which cannot be homogenised in the 'melting pot' of the USA.[42] Du Bois is known for two outstanding contributions to the African American movement: (*i*) politically, the establishment of NAACP (which established him as a stalwart of the Civil Rights Movement); and (*ii*) his extensive research into Black history and the conditions of enslaved people and freedmen during and after Reconstruction. He was a literary giant and a liberal, pragmatic leader.

Instead of industrial education, as emphasised by Washington, Du Bois believed liberal higher education for Black people as an essential tool for creating intelligent Black leadership that would assist in the upliftment of Black people as a whole by helping them to modernise themselves and acquire a firm belief in their African identity. This ideology later evolved into the 'Talented Tenth' idea. This idea was based on the politics of modernisation whereby the educated elite would authoritatively and effectively control Black politics, generating a collective Black spirit, or racial unity, to combat racial prejudice and remove the backwardness of the Black people. To achieve this, Du Bois developed a vision of the 'Rational System' of Black Education through college education to enable Black people to take a broad view of life and create conditions to produce 'Black Captains of industry' and 'missionaries' of education in Black communities. Education was, therefore, a way for Du Bois to protest against the southern accommodationist policy. Over time, as Du Bois extensively researched Black lives, he sharpened his criticism of such policies. In the essay 'Of Booker T. Washington and Others', collected in *The Souls of Black Folk*, Du Bois posed the following questions:

  (i) Whether Booker T. Washington's policy was an assertion of the 'inferiority' of Black people;
  (ii) whether economic needs were more important than 'higher' aims of life;
  (iii) why Washington did not emphasise voting rights; and
  (iv) why, when Washington rose in social stature, Black people faced more racial segregation, no political equality, and no opportunities for university education.

According to Du Bois, Washington was more concerned about 'Black-White relations' than Black people themselves.[43] *The Souls of Black Folk* marked Du Bois's rise as a scholar-activist. Although he changed his thoughts over time, the book became a landmark for understanding Black history and literature.

Du Bois believed racial prejudice had isolated Black people; therefore, it was essential to develop group cooperation. In his article, 'The Philadelphia Negro' he stated that to overcome social injustice, it was important for Black people to participate in political and racial cooperation for economic development, reduce crimes in the Black community, and develop **self-respect** (rather than follow Booker T. Washington's policy of self-help), the dignity of labour and develop virtues of truth, honesty, and charity.[44] Multiple historians have noted that Du Bois combined racial solidarity with economic development, and middle-class virtues.

Through Du Bois's writings and related discourses, it is evident that two broad schools of thought were operating simultaneously within the broader ambit of Black activism. One of them was Washington's accommodationism, which emphasised reconciling with the southern White population and economic accumulation. Du Bois, on the other hand, advocated an approach that prioritised political rights and an end to racial prejudice through the weapon of higher education and civil rights. Washington believed that Black people needed to discipline their bodies and learn business skills to understand how to trade, which would assist them in defeating the Jim Crow laws and securing an equal space. In contrast, Du Bois held that the denial of civil rights to Black people would also undermine any attempts at self-help and would limit efforts to develop Black businesses. It was vital, therefore, to attack racial prejudice and backwardness directly and to educate each and every Black person in higher educational institutions.

UNDERSTANDING THE RACE PROBLEM

One of the most outstanding contributions of Du Bois to the Black movement was his extensive research to understand what he later began to identify as 'the race problem'. He studied this aspect from the perspective of philosophy, which fuelled a new academic foray into the philosophy of race. He understood race as a 'power tool' used by the White majority to establish structural relations of social domination. In the US, this established racial prejudice towards Black people, who themselves became culturally backwards due to their economic deprivation, lack of knowledge, and inability to organise their social life. After in-depth multidisciplinary research, Du Bois termed the 'Negro Problem' as one based on lived and felt Black experiences that he termed '**double consciousness**'.[45] In his study, *Strivings of the Negro People* (1897), which preceded *The Souls of Black Folk*, he concluded that Black people looked at themselves through the prejudiced White gaze.

According to Du Bois, what needs to be understood is that race is not based on physio-biological aspects but on spiritual distinctiveness, identified through social, historical factors like laws, religion, and thought processes. Race is a mentally inhabited state. Looking at the 'splendid failure' of the Reconstruction, it was clear that the reason for failure was the belief in Whiteness, which had legitimised the 'domination of the White'. Elaborating this further in the chapter 'The White World' of his book *Dusk of Dawn*, Du Bois concludes that for a long time, White society created a world based on habits, customs, folklore and folkways of White reasoning that accorded them self-importance, a sense of pride, racialised self-esteem, and a sense of superiority.

He also explains this in the context of the chapter 'The Black Propaganda' in his book *Black Reconstruction* (1935). Here, he takes on Charles and Mary Beard's colossal work *The Rise of American Civilization*, which interprets the Civil War as a conflict based on the moral 'impartiality' related to the American quest to secure their democratic right to self-govern. For Du Bois, this interpretation overlooks the fact that Americans secured their economic wealth through the enslavement of Black people and their labour, and that the settler state consistently denied them freedom and human dignity. What was needed was first to grant Black people their cultural identity, based on the fact that they were by now Americans—by birth, by language, and based on their political ideas and religion. Beyond this, Black people also had an African inheritance, so racial unity and recognition was essential to achieve cultural and economic independence. Du Bois, therefore, advocated separate education, business, and cultural institutions for Black people, so that they could realise their own 'Great Destiny'.

In 1905, Du Bois organised a meeting of Black intellectuals at Niagara Falls and launched the Niagara Movement. This movement demanded freedom of speech and expression, voting rights for Black people, an end to racial distinctions, universal school education for all, federal aid for education, equal employment opportunities, and protest as a strategy to secure rights. This movement in 1909 culminated in the formation of the NAACP, which received support from Progressives and intellectuals. The NAACP also started a magazine, *Crisis*, edited by Du Bois.[46] This movement aimed to free Black people from racial prejudice, bring them into mainstream society, secure political voting rights, and bring about social equality. NAACP leaders demanded corrective legislation, educated public opinion, and secured favourable court decisions to fulfil their aims and goals.

Historians note several paradoxes in Du Bois's ideological thought. His concept of economic nationalism was based on the creation of Black nation within the overarching boundaries of the USA. Though initially in favour of a group economy, Du Bois later advocated a cooperative movement. While he supported intermarriage, he also stated that due to inequalities, interracial marriage would result in social calamity. He maintained different views on race differences. In the early years, he reiterated stereotypes that Black people were backward, childlike, and undeveloped. After 1911, he revised his views and began to assert that Black people unambiguously deserved equal respect, and that they were responsible for many advancements in society—for example, in creating American music and the Egyptian civilisation. He strongly identified with other people of colour of the world, especially Africans, and created an ideology of Pan-Africanism.

Later, Du Bois became interested in the labour movement and socialism and joined the Socialist Party in 1911. He wanted exploited Black and White workers to unite and overcome exploitation, segregation, and subordination to create a society that ensured economic and social justice. For this reason, Du Bois came to oppose Garvey's goal of a Black economy, an idea that Garvey had borrowed from Washington. Still, Du Bois supported Garvey's concept of a movement 'Back to Africa'. Du Bois also supported American participation in World War I and the move for Black people to join the army. He sympathised with the Soviet Union in the Korean War and, in 1961, joined the Communist Party of America. In 1960, he went to Ghana to work on *Encyclopedia Africana* and remained there till his death in 1963.

Du Bois thus stood for the African American Movement for racial equality, cultural pluralism, political rights, and university education.[47] While he has been criticised for the changes and shifts in his ideology, with some seeing this as a lack of commitment to any one set of ideas, his continuous transformations were shaped by a rapidly changing political and economic environment. His fundamental beliefs, in racial equality and cultural pluralism, securing freedom, political rights, and a university education for Black people, remained unchanged.

Du Bois never became a successful mass leader or an efficient strategist who could lead the movement and remained aloof from the Black masses. However, he exerted a strong influence on Black intellectuals who were part of the Talented Tenth, and his ideology assisted the growth of a new Black consciousness, which later flowed into the Harlem Renaissance. Despite his intellectual prowess, he was never recognised or acknowledged by the dominant White community. He brought about essential aspects of Black economic and political rights and highlighted the need for racial integration in American culture. His role as leader of the Niagara Movement and NAACP was an important influence on the minds of educated Black people. However, he had to wage a constant battle against the control of elites, their conservative outlook and narrow perspective of political organisation.[48]

There were some similarities between Du Bois and Washington in the late 1890s: both believed in race solidarity based on economic development and middle-class virtues. Black business development was given great importance, with Du Bois terming it a mark of self-reliance, while Washington has been called the 'father of Black capitalism'. The two leaders also tended to place the onus of backwardness on Black people themselves, placing more emphasis on self-help and duties than securing rights. In 1901, Du Bois acknowledged the significance of the Tuskegee Institute's role in exposing the weaknesses of the sharecropping system for the Black community. These similarities reflect that both leaders, while ideologically different, were not wholly opposed to each other, as many scholars assumed. While both Frederick Douglass and Booker T. Washington were conventional and conservative in their philosophical outlook, Du Bois's activism was shaped by the deep influence of Marxism and socialism.

Unlike Washington, who wanted to see Black people become business entrepreneurs and economically independent, Du Bois wanted them to be educated to create a world where the working class as a whole—people of colour as well as White people—would get integrated to end the domination of White capital and thereby establish social justice under the aegis of socialism. However, he came into conflict with other members in both the organisations he was associated with: the NAACP, and the Talented Tenth. He believed the Talented Tenth had become elitist and conservative with a narrow vision. His conflict with the NAACP before he finally resigned was due to the rejection of his call for voluntary segregation and his idea of the Pan-African movement.[49] He firmly believed that the ultimate aim of the NAACP should be to secure full rights for Black people along with the emphasis on education, and building inter-racial organisations—ideas that would, in the long run, help in the growth and expansion of **Black Power**.

Du Bois remained rooted to the cause of African American rights till the end of his life, leading many scholars to term it his life's mission. One of his most enduring contributions to the community was restoring a sense of cultural pride and identity that enabled radical change, with Black people gradually gaining access to higher educational institutions and articulating new visions for their future. His intellectual insight gave the movement structure and dynamism.

Martin Luther King, Jr. stated in February 1968: 'Dr Du Bois's greatest virtue was his committed empathy with all the oppressed and his divine dissatisfaction with all forms of injustice.'[50] As a civil rights leader, Du Bois set up norms for modern Black America and emphasised the theory of human equality and the pursuit of justice. In the years that followed, Marcus Garvey took up the mantle of leadership and steered African Americans towards creating a mass movement with global outreach.

Marcus Garvey: Building a Mass Movement

Marcus Garvey was born in St Ann's Bay, Jamaica (which was then a British colony), in 1880. He was born to descendents of the Maroons—enslaved Africans who had launched an early anti-colonial resistance in Jamaica and managed to retain their independence by establishing communities in the mountains from the seventeenth to eighteenth centuries.⁵¹ Garvey's father was a skilled stonemason and deacon; he was literate and owned a private library. Garvey's account of his childhood revealed some formative experiences of racialisation. He developed a close friendship with a White girl, but her parents later sent her away from Jamaica to sever their interracial friendship. Such incidents left a deep mark on Garvey.

Garvey moved to Kingston and took up work at a printing shop. Here, he was elected leader when the Printer's Union went on strike, but the strike failed and he lost his job. This experience made him suspicious of the worker's movement and ideals of socialism. He began to work at the government printing office, where in 1910 he started a newspaper called *Garvey's Watchman* to highlight wrongful colonial policies in Jamaica, but this venture failed. Garvey then migrated to Costa Rica in 1910 to work at a banana plantation, where he witnessed the exploitation of West Indian immigrant labourers. This moved him to launch a second newspaper, *La Nacion*, which criticised the British Counsel for his indifference to the plight of West Indian migrants in the region. From Costa Rica, Garvey moved to Panama, where he produced another newspaper, *La Prensa*, to record the working conditions of Jamaican workers on the Panama Canal (see Chapter 10); he also travelled to Ecuador, Nicaragua, Honduras, Colombia, and Venezuela, where he encountered Black labourers suffering in similar working conditions. The idea of a Pan-African movement began to germinate in his mind at this point. Garvey conceptualised this in the form of a unified struggle to highlight the poverty, oppression, and exploitation of Black labour. He then stayed for some time in London, where he read the works of Booker T. Washington, mainly *Up from Slavery*, and worked with the Egyptian nationalist leader Duse Mohammad Ali, who acquainted him with Africa and urged him to learn more about African history.

On his return to Jamaica in 1914, Garvey established **UNIA— the Universal Negro Improvement Association and African Communities League**. However, mixed-race individuals and groups did not associate with the organisation, and Jamaicans did not appreciate the use of the term 'Negro'; instead, they wanted it to be replaced with 'coloured'. Thus, there were clear fissures and differences of opinion among the Black community in Jamaica.⁵² The motto of

UNIA was 'One God, One Aim, One Destiny!' Its primary goals were to unite Black people and build a Black political consciousness, develop Black nations, and establish Black embassies and educational institutions (including universities and schools). During this period, Garvey was significantly influenced by Washington's goals of self-help, racial pride, and opposition to social equality,[53] and considered him his guide and mentor.

Arrival in the United States

Marcus Garvey arrived in the USA in 1916 on a lecture tour to raise funds for a Jamaican industrial institution. After spending extensive time in various states, he decided to migrate to Harlem, where he set up a unit of UNIA. In 1919, Garvey established the weekly newspaper *The Negro World* that aimed to address the concerns of Black people. As the newspaper grew in popularity, Spanish and French editions began to appear, apart from the English. It became popular in the US, Latin America, the Caribbean, and Africa.[54] It was in *The Negro World* that Marcus Garvey presented the eight-point aim of UNIA:

(i) The decolonisation of Africa;
(ii) self-awareness;
(iii) self-belief;
(iv) self-determination;
(v) self-consciousness;
(vi) development of Black media;
(vii) self-help; and
(viii) respect and appreciation for the Black race.

Garvey then set out to create institutions to support the UNIA. He established libraries and meeting halls, and in 1926, the UNIA established **The Negro Factories Corporations** to build industrial centres in the US, Central America, West Indies, and Africa. It developed a chain of grocery stores, a restaurant, a steam laundry service, tailoring, a hotel, a doll factory, and a printing press in Harlem.[55]

In 1919, Garvey organised the Black Star Line, a steamship company, which was developed as a challenge to White dominance in the maritime industry and to promote racial pride and business skills among the Black community. In the 1920s, Garvey began to emphasise the idea of self-determination and urged Black communities to develop economic self-interest.

The UNIA was the most significant Black mass organisation established in Jamaica in 1914, and it was incorporated in the US in 1918. It was a mixture of militant Black nationalism and Booker T. Washington's ideals of self-reliance. Over time, the UNIA established a presence across 41 countries.[56] In 1920, Garvey and UNIA organised the **First International Convention of Negro Peoples of the World** in New York to promote Black pride. To attract media and public attention, Garvey organised a spectacular parade on the streets of Harlem where he showcased other units of UNIA—the uniformed African Legion, the Black Cross Nurses, the Black Flying Eagles and the Universal African Motor Corps. The parade hoisted the flag of the UNIA and its anthem was played to represent the pride and nationalistic spirit of Black peoples rooted in African tradition. The convention announced various honours

FIG. 7.3: UNIA march, Harlem, New York City, by James Van Der Zee (2 August 1920)

Source: Wikimedia Commons.

and citations, and a draft of the 'Declaration of the Rights of the Negro Peoples of the World' was passed; the convention also called for an end to European imperialism in Africa and lynchings in the United States.

However, most of UNIA's economic ventures reported huge losses, mismanagement, and financial bungling. Garvey also began to interact with the KKK. In an interaction in Atlanta, Georgia, he stated that while the Klan was working to build a 'White nation', he was working to make Africa a 'Black man's continent'. He did not believe in the social equality of the two races and advocated racial purity and separation.[57] Amidst these controversial ventures, in 1922, Garvey was arrested on a mail fraud conviction and in 1925 he was sent to jail. President Calvin Coolidge ordered his deportation to Jamaica. There, he continued his activities with UNIA and worked to open branches in Paris and London, but his popularity had already waned considerably.[58]

EVALUATION OF GARVEY'S ROLE AS A BLACK LEADER

Marcus Garvey's ideology was based on notions of Black nationalism. According to Jeffrey O.G. Oghar, Garvey believed that the Black communities were a 'troubled' people with a dependence on a hostile White population for food, clothing, employment, education, governance and healthcare. Black people could only redeem themselves by becoming independent and experiencing cultural rebirth.[59] His religious views, too, foregrounded a Black God and Black Christ. He encouraged economic independence without the influence of either capitalism or socialism.

Garvey believed in the liberation of Africa from colonial rule and argued that strengthening African nations would enhance the prestige of Black people globally. It would also encourage Black people in the West to migrate to Africa. Some scholars have asserted that while Washington was not a mass leader and Du Bois was 'too intellectual', Marcus Garvey's assertive leadership, natural charisma, and belief in racial pride made him a popular mass leader who began a 'crowd movement' that drew in the Black working class, who were greatly influenced by his use of cultural symbolism, African ritualism, and conviction in race pride.[60]

J. W. Johnson wrote that Marcus Garvey possessed 'a Napoleonic personality', displayed remarkable daring, and had formidable fundraising abilities, but that in reality he was self-serving.[61] Others have rejected his idea of racial separation and non-engagement in civil rights protests. Garvey had revolutionary zeal but not revolutionary consciousness as he was more of a propagandist. His knowledge of Africa was inadequate, his notion of Black capitalism was not based on any conceptual foundations, and his over-emphasis on the 'purity' of race alienated multiracial people.

Leftist Black leaders opposed Garvey's economic and political views and his strand of Black nationalism. Garvey and Du Bois, for instance, had very different views on education, and their ideas of Black nationalism and Pan-Africanism were irreconcilable. While the two leaders were at times harsh in their criticism of each other, in later years, Du Bois became less critical of Garvey.

Marcus Garvey had a mass following, and in a short period, he endeared himself to the public. His emergence as a prominent Black nationalist leader coincided with the period when the US was about to enter World War I. He brought a new dimension into the African American movement by taking the pledge to decolonise Africa, advancing a programme of African pride, and by calling for Black separatism.[62] He established a racial philosophy that attracted the attention of the working classes, especially in Harlem, where he remained a dominant figure for a reasonably long period. Marcus Garvey became a precursor to militant and radical forms of African American nationalism, such as the 'Black Power' movement.[63]

However, Garvey's idealistic notion of a 'return to Africa' failed to get much attention. Many other Black leaders and intellectuals considered him a 'demagogue', a 'reactionary' and a 'racial fantasist'. Still, they all acknowledge that it was Garvey who inculcated a fierce sense of pride and identity in the Black people, and who built their confidence and courage to articulate their thoughts, rights, and aspirations in an open arena.

Notes

1. John White, *Black Leadership in America, 1895–1968* (New York, 1985), p. 13.
2. Ibid., p. 14.
3. Ibid., p. 15.
4. Ibid., pp. 15–17.
5. Ibid., p. 16.
6. Ibid., pp. 16–17.
7. Todd Vogel, ed., *The Black Press: New Literary and Historical Essays* (New Brunswick, New Jersey, and London, 2001). See also Thomas Cripps, *Slow Fade to Black: The Negro in American Film, 1900–1942* (New York, 1993).
8. Ibid., pp. 1–2.
9. See D. A. Gerber, 'A Politics of Limited Options: Northern Black Politics and the Problem of Change and Continuity in Race Relations Historiography', *Journal of Social History* 14, 1980–1981, pp. 235–255.
10. Eric Foner, *Give Me Liberty! An American History*, 3rd ed. (New York, 2011), p. 312.
11. Joseph F. Healey, *Diversity and Society: Race, Ethnicity, and Gender* (California, 2007), p. 82.
12. Ibid., p. 83.
13. Alferdteen Harrison, *Black Exodus: The Great Migration from the American South* (Mississippi, 1991). This migration completely changed the USA's socio-economic structure, and the South lost the bulk of its labour force to northern cities like Philadelphia, Chicago, and New York. For Black migrants, this was an attempt to escape a world of racism, poverty, and degradation. They also transported their cultures to northern cities through music, art, church, and new social institutions.
14. Healey, *Diversity and Society*, pp. 83–84.
15. The term ghetto generally refers to areas or neighbourhoods occupied by marginalised social groups. Historically, ghettos usually form due to patterns of spatial exclusion (where social segregation is widespread, or where minority groups are displaced from areas where they had earlier lived), and this process is often termed ghettoisation. In the context of the US, the word has sometimes been used in racist or derogatory ways, due to stereotypes of Black and Hispanic neighbourhoods as prone to violence and criminality.
16. Robert A. Bone, 'The Background of the Negro Renaissance', in *The Negro Novel in America* (New Haven, 1965), p. 375.
17. Ibid., pp. 376–377.
18. Ibid., p. 378.
19. Ibid., p. 383.
20. Healey, *Diversity and Society*, pp. 81–83.
21. White, *Black Leadership in America*, p. 379.
22. Ibid., pp. 381–383.
23. Ibid., p. 381.

24. Ibid., pp. 384–385.
25. Ibid., pp. 385–387.
26. Ibid., p. 388.
27. Ibid., p. 390.
28. Ibid., p. 414.
29. Ibid., pp. 28–29.
30. Ibid.
31. Ibid., pp. 30–31.
32. Ibid., pp. 33–34.
33. Francis L. Broderick, *W. E. B. Du Bois: Negro Leader in a Time of Crisis* (Stanford, 1959), p. 18.
34. White, *Black Leadership in America*, p. 34.
35. Ibid., p. 37.
36. Ibid., pp. 35–39.
37. Hugh Hawkins, *Booker T. Washington and His Critics: The Problem of Negro Leadership* (Boston, 1962).
38. White, *Black Leadership in America*, p. 39.
39. C. Vann Woodward, *The Strange Career of Jim Crow*, third revised ed. (New York, 1974).
40. Gunnar Myrdal, *An American Dilemma: The Negro Problem and Modern Democracy* (New York, 1962).
41. Manning Marable, Charles Lemert, and Cheryl Townsend Gilkes, *The Souls of Black Folk: W.E.B Du Bois*, 100th anniversary ed. (New York, 2016).
42. Vincent Harding, *There is a River: The Black Stuggle for Freedom in America* (New York, 1981).
43. White, *Black Leadership in America*, p. 52.
44. Ibid., p. 51.
45. In a penetrating study, Richard L. Allen has explored the idea of double consciousness as established by Du Bois and situated it in African-centred consciousness based on a study of polity, society, and psychology. The aim was to develop a model of self that could potentially evolve an African worldview, offering a promising path for Africans in the diaspora. Richard L. Allen, *The Concept of Self: A Study of Black Identity and Self-Esteem* (Detroit, 2001).
46. White, *Black Leadership in America*, pp. 45–57.
47. Ibid., pp. 61–65.
48. Ibid., p. 159.
49. August Meier, *Negro Thought in America, 1880–1915* (Ann Arbor, 1963).
50. Barbara Harris Combs and Obie Clayton, 'An Introductory Essay to the Special Volume of *Phylon*', *Phylon*, 2018, pp. 3–8.
51. White, *Black Leadership in America*, pp. 68–69.
52. Ibid., p. 75.
53. Ibid., pp. 73–74.
54. Ibid., pp. 75–76.
55. Ibid., pp. 76–77.

56. Jeffrey O. G. Oghar, *Black Power: Radical Politics and African American Identity*, revised ed. (Baltimore, 2019).
57. White, *Black Leadership in America*, p. 79.
58. Ibid.
59. Oghar, *Black Power*, p. 7.
60. White, *Black Leadership in America*, p. 84.
61. Ibid.
62. Theodore G. Vincent, *Black Power and the Garvey Movement* (San Francisco, 1976).
63. E. U. Essien-Udom, *Black Nationalism* (Chicago, 1962).

Chapter 8

The Civil Rights and Black Power Movements
Martin Luther King, Jr., and Malcolm X

Introduction

The Great Depression of 1929 had the worst impact on Black people, due to pre-existing systemic disadvantages that placed them at the bottom of the economic hierarchy. Government data shows that a substantial share of the Black population depended on government relief for survival. Most southern tenant farmers and sharecroppers were falling into a cycle of debt. Neither the National Association for the Advancement of Colored People (NAACP) nor the National Urban League (NUL) could relieve this suffering.

Roosevelt's electoral victory in 1932 and his unveiling of the New Deal (see Chapter 5) generated hope and optimism, even though racial bias was evident in many New Deal policies. Despite its drawbacks, the New Deal gave the NAACP and NUL renewed momentum in the fight to secure more rights and economy security for African Americans. Economic reforms bolstered the Black middle class and the NAACP grew in size and influence.

The Progressive era had seen the rise of W. E. B. Du Bois, who advocated for 'racial separatism' through developing a Black collective economy (see Chapter 7). The NAACP opposed this. The **American Communist Party**, established in 1919, had Black party members and supported political and civil rights for Black Americans. Many among the party began to advocate for 'self-determination' rights for African Americans. They went so far as to call for the establishment of a '49th state' in the South where majority of the population would be Black. The Communist Party later shifted its stance and began to focus on advocating for equal rights. Black religious nationalism emerged in the same period, with Noble Drew Ali's **Moorish-American Science Temple in 1913**, which brought together many of Marcus Garvey's former supporters after his deportation in 1927. Separate strands within Black religious nationalism can be seen in **Father Divine's Peace Movement**, established in 1919 at Long Island. With the cooperation of its followers, the organisation provided jobs, food, and housing for its members in New Jersey and New York, thereby providing sustenance to many Black individuals who were excluded from the programmes of the New Deal.

It was the persistence of civil rights organisations that paved the way for the formation of the **Joint Committee on National Recovery to Fight Discriminatory Practices**, one among several federal relief agencies. However, the real push in activism came from the strategic alliances formed by Black organisations. The newly established **Congress of Industrial Organizations (CIO)**, a federation of unions headed by John L. Lewis, a popular leader of the United Mine Workers, aimed to bring together both skilled and unskilled Black workers into industrial unions. The CIO's move to encourage union membership for Black workers prompted the NAACP to seek an alliance with it, thereby linking together the struggles for labour and Black rights. Franklin D. Roosevelt secured the support of Black voters in 1940 due to this alliance, paving the way for his third consecutive term as US president. In March 1941, A. Philip Randolph, president of the **Brotherhood of Sleeping Car Porters (BSCP)**, the first Black-led union to be chartered by the **American Federation of Labour (AFL)**, announced plans for a non-violent mass agitation based on Gandhian philosophy to demand an end to racial discrimination in the US armed forces, government offices and defence industries. Faced with the prospect of immense public mobilisation, President Roosevelt was forced to come out with **Executive Order 8802 on 25 June 1941**, which banned employment discrimination in the defence industry and the government (including the armed forces).[1]

In the **postwar period**, more African Americans continued migrating to urban centres in the North and West. A rising rate of voter registration among Black citizens encouraged the development of a new political consciousness, leading to active participation in action to support civil rights. President Harry S. Truman in 1948 passed an executive order that provided for 'equality of opportunity for all persons in the armed forces, without regard to race, color, or national origin', which resulted in the **desegregation** of the armed forces. It also led to the establishment of the **Federal Civil Rights Commission**, a milestone for civil rights activists as it ultimately compelled Congress to pass important legislation guaranteeing racial equality.

Emergence of Major Civil Rights Organisations

The **Congress of Racial Equality (CORE)**, a civil rights organisation, was established in 1942 by James Farmer along with members of the **Fellowship of Reconciliation (FOR)**. The organisation believed in the application of non-violent methods of resistance and opposition to racial bias and violence, and sought to contribute to the civil rights struggle through negotiation, mediation, demonstration and picketing. CORE put this into practice in 1943 in their opposition to a Chicago eatery that had refused to serve Black customers. At the end of World War II, a new wave of protest for Black rights emerged, motivated in part by international experiences and the service of Black soldiers on the warfront. They began to exert increasing pressure on the federal government, realising the growing significance of their vote, and of becoming politically organised themselves. Within this context, CORE persisted with its goals through the 1950s to 1960s, aggressively pursuing higher voter registration for Black citizens in the South. Their work brought the group in direct conflict with White supremacist and racist groups. In 1964, three CORE members were murdered by the Ku Klux Klan (KKK) in Philadelphia, Mississippi. The NAACP, too, continued to work towards securing rights for African Americans, as outlined in the 14th and 15th Constitutional Amendments. The persistent efforts of NAACP bore fruit when the

Supreme Court, in **Brown v. Board of Education (1954)**, ended educational segregation, stating that 'in the field of public education the doctrine of "separate but equal" has no place'.

Nevertheless, most southern states defied the court ruling, and this forced Black organisations to pursue direct action through boycotts of stores and restaurants that practised segregation and racial discrimination, including bus boycotts in the southern states where the 'separate but equal' racial policy still applied in the public transport system. In 1957, CORE, along with FOR, organised the 'Journey of Reconciliation', eventually termed the **'Freedom Rides'**, in the Upper South to push for implementation of a Supreme Court ruling that segregation in interstate transportation was unconstitutional.[2] Martin Luther King, Jr. emerged as one of the most prominent African American leaders in this environment.

Life History of Martin Luther King, Jr.

King was born in 1929 in Atlanta, Georgia, and was brought up in the Southern Baptist tradition. His father was deeply rooted in and influenced by the German Protestant religious leader Martin Luther, and therefore adopted the name for himself and his son. King was educated and brought up in a relatively secure middle-class environment, and grew up with the conviction that racism and segregation were against the will of God. He received his schooling at Booker T. Washington High School and then went to Morehouse College in Atlanta to study sociology. It was in college that he came under the influence of Benjamin E. Mays, who was known for advocating racial equality and using Christianity as an avenue for social transformation. King subsequently joined Crozer Theological Seminary at Chester, Pennsylvania and completed his doctoral degree in systematic theology at Boston University in 1955.

KING'S ENTRY INTO THE MOVEMENT

The South was still steeped in racial discrimination, with African Americans experiencing continued social, economic, and political inequalities. This internal situation was in contrast to what was happening outside the US. After World War II, a wave of decolonisation movements had emerged across the world. The **United Nations (UN)**, founded in 1945, emerged as a forum promoting international cooperation and mediation, providing a platform to nations that had been oppressed within the prevailing world order. The impact of external changes started to be felt inside the US, too, when on 1 December 1955, civil rights activist and seamstress Rosa Parks refused a White bus driver's order to vacate her seat for a White passenger. The segregation in buses was a common practice and legal in Montgomery as per the city's municipal codes. Parks had made similar refusals in the past, but was taken into custody and fined on this occasion. Understanding the importance of her arrest, E. D. Nixon, who was heading the local unit of NAACP as well as a member of the BSCP in Montgomery, decided that civil rights groups should confront Jim Crow laws directly in the city. Nixon and others formed the **Montgomery Improvement Association (MIA),** which initiated a 381-day boycott of the Montgomery Bus Company till their demands were met: for 'civilised behaviour' from White bus drivers; employment for Black drivers on routes for historically Black neighbourhoods; a seating arrangement on first-come, first-served basis, where Black passengers would be seated in the back half of the bus and White passengers in the front half. These demands were seen as a compromise, as boycott leaders felt that city authorities would reject a demand for integration.

Martin Luther King, Jr., was elected president of the MIA and his main task was to push through these demands. The MIA implemented the boycott methodically by creating a car pooling system. Since car ownership was restricted to the wealthy, upper-class Black people also joined the agitation, thereby widening its social base. The White-dominated city authorities and White organisations adopted several tactics to break the momentum of the boycott:

(i) Black car owners' insurance was cancelled by the state (the Lloyd's Insurance Company of London was requested to fill this void).

(ii) The city's mayor arrested Martin Luther King. Jr., on a flimsy speeding charge and he was put behind bars.

(iii) On 30 January 1956, King's house was attacked.
(iv) On 22 February, 115 Black individuals were accused of breaking a 1921 anti-labour law that stated that no business can be hampered without 'just cause or legal excuse'.
(v) The intensity of violence increased against the Black people, and many Black churches were targeted with fire-bombs in an attempt to terrorise protesters.[3]

INTEGRATION OF CHRISTIAN AND GANDHIAN CONCEPTS

At this crucial juncture, when the city authorities were exerting pressure on the King to withdraw the boycott, King met Ranganath Diwakar, former Indian minister of Information and Broadcasting, who urged him to become an example of individual suffering, arguing that this would increase the momentum to the boycott and allow the movement to capture media attention. The boycott began to be reported in the national press, and the civil rights groups carried on a dignified civil disobedience movement based on non-violence. The campaign garnered support, both personal and financial, from the NAACP, the United Auto Workers, and even sources outside the USA. King also received support from Ralph Abernathy, a Black pastor and social activist associated with the Baptist Church, and Bayard Rustin, a civil rights proponent and member of FOR. King was now beginning to understand the power of non-violence and strategies to lead the public in a disciplined and well-rehearsed manner even in the face of grave provocation by the city authorities. His oratory skills and magnetism drew more people to the movement, and he avoided letting the movement go out of hand by urging protestors to remain disciplined. King invoked the words of Booker T. Washington: 'Let no man pull you so low as to make you hate him.' The Montgomery bus boycott became a prelude to the civil rights movement in the 1960s.

King's astonishing leadership qualities became evident before a larger audience when, in 1957, he took a 'Prayer Pilgrimage' to Washington, DC, and delivered a powerful speech that demanded

African Americans be given the ballot to exercise their legal rights as mandated in the US Constitution. In the same year, he, along with a set of fellow clergy members, established the **Southern Christian Leadership Conference (SCLC)**, aiming to expand and integrate the idea of non-violent civil rights protest across the South, using strategies rooted in both Christianity and the Gandhian concept of satyagraha. The SCLC had a direct grassroots connection with Black southerners. They used words couched in religious phraseology to propagate their political ideology, imbuing it with the power of a divine mandate. The SCLC formulated a plan to desegregate the downtown business district in Birmingham, Alabama. It organised demonstrations, leading to King's arrest and imprisonment, where he wrote the 'Letter from Birmingham Jail', which instantly became a popular text and further established his credibility as an influential leader.[4]

King visited Ghana, Nigeria, and several European countries, including the land of Mahatma Gandhi, India. His visit to India affirmed his deep faith in the use of non-violent resistance to end all forms of oppression. He also learnt about clauses in the Indian Constitution that outlawed discrimination based on caste and made acts like untouchability legally punishable. He believed such clauses provided more protection and social equality than efforts to eradicate racial discrimination in the US.

Beginning of the Freedom Struggle: Direct-Action Sit-in Protests

In 1959, King moved to Atlanta, Georgia, to give his full attention to SCLC activities, including strategies of direct confrontation against racial segregation and to get as many Black voters registered on the rolls as possible. In Atlanta, King joined the **Student Non-Violent Coordinating Committee (SNCC)** and began to initiate steps towards a unified student opposition movement against segregation. He educated protestors and participants about the value of non-violent protest. To attract attention of the federal government as well as the public, King began to consistently refer to civil rights activism as a 'freedom struggle' initiated by student volunteers who were willing to go to prison for a just cause. He also urged students to establish permanent organisations and initiate sit-in protests against the segregated lunch system in the South.

King also established a good rapport with President John F. Kennedy, who intervened to arrange his release from jail after he was taken into custody on a trumped-up driving offence in Georgia. Black voters therefore overwhelmingly supported Kennedy in the 1960 presidential elections, which raised hope for more proactive action from the federal government to end segregation in the South.

FIG. 8.1: US Marshals with young Ruby Bridges on school steps, New Orleans (1960)

Source: Wikimedia Commons.

Note: This iconic photograph captures the difficulties of desegregation in schooling. After a federal court ruling ordered desegregation in Louisiana, White segregationists launched protests in front of schools. Students like Ruby Bridges had to be escorted to and from school by federal personnel.

FREEDOM RIDES

In the meantime, King continued with his direct-action protest programme to add momentum to the civil rights movement. He supported the CORE-initiated Freedom Riders on interstate transportation. White southerners' attacks on the Freedom Rides were extensively reported in the media. By directly challenging this practice, protesters and the media exposed the brazen defiance of the southern state governments, which had refused to comply either with verdicts of the Alabama and Mississippi Courts, or with the Interstate Commerce Commission that had nullified segregation in interstate travel.

DEMAND FOR DESEGREGATED FACILITIES AND EMPLOYMENT

From 1961 to 1962, King and SCLC organised a mass direct-action movement in Albany, Georgia, with a specific demand for interracial facilities and job avenues to be developed by recruiting Black people in the city's police force and municipal offices. This movement failed due to a lack of planning and coherent strategy, leading to King's arrest. King learnt from this failure, and for his next move, he planned out every aspect of the protest strategy to be deployed.

In Birmingham, Alabama, there were 17 'unsolved' attacks on Black churches and the residences of African American leaders between 1957 and 1963. King was invited to Birmingham by the Reverend Fred Shuttlesworth, pastor of Baptist Bethel Church, after students from his organisation, the Alabama Christian Movement, picketed shops that practised racial segregation at the lunch counters and in jobs. The protest had led to Shuttlesworth being arrested eight times, and his home and church had both been attacked. At this juncture, Shuttlesworth invited King to lead a movement against this racial attack as well as against segregation.

In the first step, King recruited new members to the SCLC who had ample experience generating awareness about voter registration and working at the ground level. King was now convinced that any resistance movement needed to establish 'creative tension' to generate a response from the opposition. He first understood the complexity of the problem in Birmingham, Alabama, where not only were racial problems multiplying in terms of aggressive segregation, but also the threat of violence against Black people had increased to unprecedented levels. King formulated and presented three demands before the city authorities:

> (i) An end to segregation at lunch counters, stores, restrooms, and water drinking stations.
> (ii) To enhance the skills of Black residents and generate job opportunities on an interracial basis both in industry and business activities.
> (iii) To establish a biracial committee to plan, strategise, and evolve a timetable for complete desegregation in the city.

With these demands in place, King planned the timing of the protest, initiating it at a time when the racist police commissioner Eugene Bull Connor had secured a court order prohibiting public demonstration. In defiance of this order, King and his supporters marched to the city hall and were immediately arrested, only to be released after President Kennedy's intervention. In jail, King wrote a statement that clearly reflected his understanding of the American political landscape. King saw himself standing between two polarising forces—the racist White establishment in one direction, and Black Muslim supporters (who had lost faith in the USA altogether and denounced Christianity as representative of the 'evils' of White people) in the other.

After his release, King continued with his action plan, and this time he moved to generate mass opposition: thousands of protestors, including women and children, stood before water cannons, police clubs, and dogs, which eventually led to the arrest of 2,500 demonstrators. The intensity of protest led to extensive media coverage both in the US and in the rest of the world. The Birmingham administration was forced to enter negotiations and agreed to establish a biracial commission within two weeks, promising to implement some demands within a window of 90 days. This narrow victory raised King's popularity to an unprecedented level, and even President Kennedy was forced to put pressure on Congress.

On 19 June 1963, the President presented a more powerful Civil Rights Bill that included the clause of fair job practices to protect the political rights of African Americans in the South and resolve the issue of public accommodation.[5] President Lyndon Johnson finally enacted this in the form of the **Civil Rights Act of 1964**, which also gave power to the executive authority to withdraw federal funds from the states and local governments found practicing discriminatory racial policies.[6]

Introduction of Confrontational Policy Based on a Radical Approach

On 28 August 1963, King indicated an ideological shift when he introduced a 'confrontational policy' in the form of a march on Washington, DC, for 'Jobs and Freedom'. In this mass demonstration, a crowd of about 200,000 people, of varying racial and ethnic backgrounds, assembled under the shadow of the Lincoln Memorial. It was here that he delivered his most famous speech: 'I have a dream that my four children will one day live in a nation where they will not be judged by the colour of their skin but by the content of their character.'

These successes raised King's stature. However, the issue of racial equality remained polarising. A Gallup poll in 1966 claimed that two-thirds of Americans had an 'unfavourable opinion' about King, and his popularity decreased when he spoke out against the Vietnam War. At the same time, in July 1964, he appeared on the cover of *Time* Magazine as the 'most compassionate' Black leader in the US, and in the same year, he was awarded the Nobel Peace Prize. His prize acceptance speech linked civil rights with world peace and human rights.

In the following action plan, King, the SNCC, and CORE participated in the **Selma Voting Rights Campaign** in Selma, Alabama, in 1965. This movement had internal fissures, with the SNCC unwilling to accept King's attitude of 'compromise' or the use of religion in his rhetoric. Nevertheless, they still lent their organisational support. This support came in spite of the fact that

FIG. 8.2: Civil rights march on Washington, DC (28 August 1963)
Source: Wikimedia Commons.

King, even in this demonstration from Selma to Montgomery, turned back instead of breaking through the police barricade, defying the expectations of protestors. This was part of King's carefully crafted strategy to highlight the problems in Selma. The city was already on the boil due to the killing of a White Unitarian minister sympathetic to the Black cause, and also due to the events of **Bloody Sunday (7 March 1965)**, where authorities used tear gas and baton-charges at an earlier demonstration. The events as Selma prompted President Johnson to call for a special session of the Congress in order to implement the Civil Rights Act, and in the meantime, a federal court in 1965 gave sanction for the **Selma–Montgomery March**. President Johnson provided protection for this march, which took place on 25 March 1965, and in another powerful speech, King termed this march the fulfilment of the American dream, and a power call to end poverty, racial discrimination, and segregation. The march brought the issue of Black rights in the southern states onto the national platform, establishing King as one of the most powerful leaders of the African American movement.[7]

To retain national attention and ensure that the movement was not reduced simply to a 'regional' issue, King turned his attention to the problems faced by urban, poor African Americans living in northern cities. He also criticised American involvement in Vietnam as war clouds loomed on the horizon. In this period, King's ideological stances palpably changed, and he was becoming more radical in his thoughts and approach, taking the Black rights movement from the national to the international arena. His critical insight on Vietnam earned him support from CORE and SNCC, but the NAACP and NUL opposed his view. However, King was still opposed to the perceived radicalisation of the **Black Power Movement** under Malcolm X.

In 1966, King moved to Chicago to take charge of a non-violent action campaign to end racial segregation in slum housing and segregation in schools and employment. However, here King faced a powerful foe, Richard J. Daley, mayor of the city, who had previously defeated all efforts at racial integration with his cleverly crafted delaying tactics. From 1966 to 1967, there appeared to be growing differences between King and the SNCC. CORE wanted a more radical approach based on Black Power. By this time, King's position on the Civil Rights Movement had also been criticised by Stokely Carmichael and many others, who wanted to initiate a more militant form of Black protest.[8] On the other hand, King's critical approach towards US militarism and imperialism in Vietnam angered President Johnson.

At this crossroads, in 1967, King planned a People's March on Washington, where he formulated a new strategy to highlight the uneven distribution of wealth and economic power and resources in the US. He identified this unevenness as the cause of rising disparity between different races and economic classes and as the core reason for rising social conflict in American society. In February 1968, he went to Memphis, Tennessee, to lead a protest march for union recognition and improvements in salaries and working environment—this was meant as a prelude to his People's March. The demonstration ended in clashes that caused the death of many Black youth, and King faced media accusations of resorting to violence despite his commitment to non-violent methods. King returned to

Memphis soon after to address a gathering of Black people, where he publicly acknowledged threats to his life. On 4 April 1968, Martin Luther King, Jr., was assassinated outside his motel room in Memphis, Tennessee. His death shocked the American public and sparked a wave of race riots throughout the US.[9]

Legacy of a Great Leader

The Civil Rights Movement, and Martin Luther King's leadership, drew from a history of African American activism. This was acknowledged by King. He had a special respect for Booker T. Washington's philosophy of self-help, personal cleanliness, and morality. He also respected W. E. B. Du Bois's notion of the 'Talented Tenth' even as he critiqued the elitism of such an approach. King recognised Du Bois's scholarly prowess, his commitment to people's movements, and his ability to comprehend social truths. King also highlighted the contributions of Marcus Garvey in organising mass movements and instilling a sense of dignity, identity, and positive destiny among African Americans.

King rejected some of the fundamental assertions of the Black Power Movement taken up by Malcolm X, who propagated violence to achieve political goals and combat injustice. At the same time, King praised Malcolm X's autobiography, his attempts at eradicating the problems faced by Black people in the USA, his spiritual approach, and his unquestioned love for the Black community.[10]

It is well known that King, right from the time of the Montgomery bus boycott, initiated steps to propagate non-violent direct action. His tone and speeches were interspersed with Christian terminology, symbols of love and compassion, as well as non-violence ideologies drawn from Christ, Hegel, Mahatma Gandhi, and others. This messaging helped him gain a wide support base, and to White society he initially appeared as more of an intellectual than a preacher. He represented a middle path between the conservatism of NAACP and the NUL, and the radicalism of SNCC and CORE. Towards the end of his life, there was a clear shift in his ideological position, based on his realisation that economic poverty affected all

Americans. However, before this new position could be developed, King lost his life to the cause that he had so strongly advocated.

FIG. 8.3: Civil rights march on Washington, DC (28 August 1963)
Source: Wikimedia Commons.

Note: From publicly available sources, this appears to be the only time that Martin Luther King, Jr. (left) and Malcolm X (right) met, for about one minute.

While the Civil Rights Act and Voting Rights Act were extremely important, economic and social segregation persisted in jobs and education. The prevalence of systemic racism in the US fuelled extreme poverty among Black people, who continued to be ghettoised within the city space, sparked race riots in Harlem (1964), Watts, Los Angeles (1965), Newark, New Jersey, Detroit, and other urban centres (1967–1968).

Emergence of Black Organisations

In this environment of extreme racism emerged the concept of Black Power, a term made famous by Stokely Carmichael, head of the Student Non-Violent Coordinating Committee (SNCC). The SNCC advocated Black political activism without the support of any political party and pursued the idea of initiating guerrilla warfare against racist and White supremacist groups.[11]

Their work influenced the **Black Panther Party**, established in Oakland, California, under the leadership of Huey P. Newton and Bobby Seale in 1966. The core aim of the Black Panthers was to acquire greater agency over their destiny, raise demands for land, affordable food, gainful employment, housing, education, and basic amenities. This was part of a broader set of demands to ensure justice, peace, and egalitarianism. The Panthers also demanded freedom for those jailed on segregation laws; they advocated exemption from military service for Black people, and raised the issue of rampant police brutality against Black people. In later years, the party adopted Marxist-Leninist ideology and began to argue that only a socialist revolution would provide substantial freedoms to those suffering under the yoke of racial discrimination.

The other organisation was led by Floyd McKissick of CORE, which allied with different groups that worked closely with the Democratic Party. They advocated the use of violence for self-defence and the establishment of all-Black businesses and financial institutions by boycotting White economic avenues.[12] The organisation went on to mould many future leaders of the Nation of Islam, which expanded rapidly in the decades from the 1950s to 1960s under the leadership of Malcolm X.

The Multiple Lives of Malcolm X

Malcolm Little was born on 19 May 1925 in Omaha, Nebraska, to a West Indian mother and a Black American father. His father, Earl Little, was a Baptist minister and a follower of Marcus Garvey. Earl was forced to leave Omaha and move with his family to Lansing,

Michigan, after receiving threats from the KKK. Malcolm's father accused the White supremacist group Black Legion of burning down the family home in 1929—they had previously harassed him for his work with UNIA. Earl Little died when Malcolm was just six. Although his death was officially ruled a streetcar accident, Malcolm's mother, along with many Black residents, alleged that the Black League had murdered him. These acts profoundly impacted Malcolm Little. His mother suffered a psychological breakdown and was sent to a state hospital; Malcolm and his siblings were separated and sent to foster homes. Despite showing great academic promise and his aspiration to become a lawyer, he faced persistent discrimination in his Midwestern school. These adverse events, encounters, and experiences left Malcolm Little with a sense of isolation, alienation, and resentment towards White society.

In 1941, Malcolm shifted to Roxbury, Massachusetts, an impoverished Black ghetto, to stay with his half-sister. He dropped out of school to become a teenage delinquent, and entered the workforce early as an unskilled worker: initially a shoeshine boy, Malcolm later worked as a dining car porter on the Boston–New York route. He then decided to find 'the easy way' out of poverty by becoming a petty criminal, adopting the nickname 'Detroit Red' (due to his reddish hair). In 1945 he returned to Boston, where he became a small-time swindler. He was convicted on charges of theft at the age of 21 and sentenced to seven years in prison. While still in prison, Malcolm was introduced to the Black Muslim community and to **Nation of Islam (NOI)** leader Elijah Muhammad. Malcolm converted to Islam and became its ardent propagator.[13]

Association with the Nation of Islam

The NOI, according to Jeffrey O. G. Oghar, developed out of a matrix of political, cultural, and social tumult at a time when the USA was primarily an anti-Black society.[14] The organisation had emerged from the shadows of the Moorish-American Science Temple established in Detroit in 1930 by Wallace Fard Muhammad, who believed that he was a 'Muslim Prophet' and spread the message of Black vindication by embracing Islam. He established the Temple of Islam, which revolved around rituals and the art of specific worship, which became the base for his religious ideology. Fard set up the University of Islam, which imparted school education based on a curriculum he had devised himself. He also established a Muslim Girls' Training Class to train young women in the 'science of homemaking'. To deal with the White racist police force, he founded the Fruit of Islam, a military-style organisation where ex-army men trained Black soldiers in war tactics and firearm use. Fard appointed a Minister of Islam under whom he placed a staff of assistant ministers to administer the organisation.

The NOI was a **Black nationalist organisation** that insisted on the acquisition of land either in North America or Africa for the development of a Black nation-state. It set up a virtual nation with business linkages, farms, a cannery, apartments, supermarkets, and schools to show that they were true representatives of the African American masses. Its supporters were poor Black people, particularly men. NOI was the first organisation to use the term 'Black' or 'Afro-American' when 'Negro' was the terminology in use, insisting that the latter term was derogatory.[15]

In 1933, Elijah Poole joined the NOI, changed his name to Elijah Muhammad, and became a self-proclaimed 'Allah's Prophet'. He established temples in Chicago, Milwaukee, and Washington DC, where a large share of the working-class Black community joined the organisation. The organisation had its newspaper, *Muhammad Speaks*, and it published its history textbooks that presented African history from the perspective of Black people. Muhammad insisted that his followers stop using their surnames and instead use the suffix 'X' and adhere to a strict code of personal conduct that included adherence to conjugal fidelity and non-consumption of pork, tobacco, alcohol, and narcotics. An advocate of **Black separatism**, he even banned interracial marriages and intermingling. Muhammad's followers could not join the army or vote in the elections; they had to reject government welfare or relief programmes, including the assignation of social security numbers; they could not be involved in any political engagements; and they were expected to have minimum contact with White people.

Scholars have observed commonalities between Garveyism and the NOI. Both focused on the development of Black individual and group identity, an independent Black economic structure, and an armed force to protect African Americans. Elijah Muhammad preached militant as well as assertive separatism.[16] The NOI preached cautious and pragmatic resistance, simplicity, and cultural regeneration—these became hallmarks of Black nationalism. The NOI, from this perspective, represents attempts to rebuild, redeem, and rejuvenate Black people.[17]

Influenced by these ideas, Malcolm escaped prison in 1952 and reached Detroit. He dropped 'Little' from his surname and became known as Malcolm 'X', and was ordained as a minister of the Islamic temple in Boston (he later held the same position in Harlem in New York and in 1955 in Philadelphia). In his speeches, Malcolm began to speak out against Martin Luther King, Jr.'s non-violent civil rights movement. He termed King's supporters 'Uncle Tom', characterising them as self-serving, peaceful, and accommodative. Malcolm projected himself, in contrast, as someone who took pride in the colour black and believed in racial separatism. Malcolm's popularity increased after he picketed a police station along with his supporters in response to the police wrongly beating up a Black man.

By 1964, Malcolm X had gained popularity as a speaker and leader. However, he also began to question the tactics and ideology of Elijah Muhammad, and this relationship became destructive as there were generational and ideological differences between the two figures. In 1963, when Malcolm X spoke on the murder of President John F. Kennedy in spite of a directive from Elijah not to comment on it, he was suspended from the NOI for 90 days. Malcolm was forbidden to speak at any forum.[18]

An Independent Black Leader

Malcolm resigned from the Nation of Islam in 1964, and in his statement, which he called the 'Declaration of Independence', he set up an independent organisation called 'Muslim Mosque Incorporated' in New York. He extensively toured West Asia and

Africa in 1964. The turning point came when he visited Mecca, where he was influenced by a sense of Islamic brotherhood to launch a united fight for Black people to secure fundamental human rights. Malcolm X was now El-Hajj Malik El-Shabazz. And from then on, ideas began to germinate about Pan-Africanism.[19]

In the same year, Malcolm established the **Organization of Afro-American Unity (OAAU)** based on the idea of Pan-Africanism, self-defence, and an end of all forms of racial exploitation and violence. This would be achieved by advocating complete independence of the Black peoples to establish world peace. He wanted OAAU to become an umbrella organisation uniting Black nationalist groups and ideas for a unified, coordinated movement. Malcolm wanted to reconstruct and reconstitute African culture to assert a new sense of African identity and make it a tool of resistance and racial pride. Another goal was to present the problems of Black people at the United Nations Human Rights Commission. The OAAU was also meant to provide better educational and welfare facilities and support Black politicians who wished to run for office. Malcolm identified the need for aggressive voter registration drives to enhance the collective power of African Americans.

Malcolm X advocated the 'psychological' return of Black people to Africa, but not a 'physical return'. After his second visit to various African capital cities in 1964, he began to look for support from non-racist White people. Inspired by socialism, he became an inspired agitator, emerging as a Black nationalist deeply committed to African Americans' spiritual and material upliftment. At this juncture, he began writing his autobiography, which was completed and published posthumously by his collaborator Alex Haley. This autobiography focused on Malcolm's transformative experiences at Mecca that changed him spiritually and metaphysically and propelled him onto his chosen path as an independent Black leader. It focused on three goals for African Americans: self-respect, self-reliance, and economic empowerment. All three were critical to effectively challenge the dominant White culture and launch a critique of racial hierarchy.

Malcolm gave power and strength to those in the Black community who were deeply unhappy about their subjugation. He gave political expression to their anger, thus challenging the complacency of White

America and calling for a definitive end to racial discrimination. If necessary, force could be used to bring about much-needed social transformation. Malcolm openly addressed the problems faced by African Americans, whose experiences of oppression were rooted in racial hierarchy, restrictions, and White conservatism. His ideas and policies underwent significant shifts over time, and he re-invented himself at multiple points in his life. Despite being a controversial figure, Malcolm X was a powerful orator and leader of the poor Black masses.[20]

Conclusion

Malcolm X was an influential leader who espoused the cause of Black rights and dedicated his life to the spiritual awakening of his people. In his public speeches, he extensively used language and rhetoric that carried images, slogans, and influences of African American history, musical traditions, and folklore. In doing so, Malcolm borrowed the rhetorical style of Black Christian preachers in their churches. Although he was unable to establish a solid institutional foundation for his organisation, his reach went beyond the boundaries of North America due to the media coverage he received, which helped propel the issue of equality and racism to the international stage. Malcolm's followers were not only Black Americans, but also oppressed people across the globe drawn to his 'geographical imagination'.[21]

Another revealing facet of Malcolm's personality was his ability to continuously expand his intellectual capabilities through new experiences. This is reflected in his decision to adopt the Islamic faith, and later in his advocacy of a socialist worldview. He was especially popular among the Black youth, who wanted a radical movement that could bring about a significant change in American society. Civil and human rights goals, for him, were to be extended to all the people of colour in the world. Malcolm also understood and emphasised the importance of education as a stepping stone to economic upliftment. This ideological focus drew members of the SNCC and CORE to Malcolm X. He brought a ray of hope and aspiration to urban, working-class Black communities in the 1960s, and transformed ghettos into sites of growing political consciousness, enterprise, and liberation. The Black Rights movement emphasised confidence, a distinct identity and status, and a belief that African Americans too could rise with a committed purpose, in defiance of a system that condemned them to poverty, broken families, and violence. Malcolm X empowered his people to comprehend and critique the 'oppressive landscape' of everyday reality.

Notes

1. John White, *Black Leadership in America, 1885–1968* (New York, 1985), pp. 121–122.
2. Ibid., pp. 122–125.
3. Ibid., pp. 126–134.
4. Sheila Hardy and Stephen P. Hardy, *Extraordinary People of the Civil Rights Movement* (Washington, DC, 2007), p. 145.
5. Ibid., p. 146.
6. White, *Black Leadership in America*, pp. 134–138.
7. Ibid.
8. Hardy and Hardy, *Extraordinary People of the Civil Rights Movement*, p. 146.
9. White, *Black Leadership in America*, pp. 139–143.
10. Ibid., pp. 143–146.
11. Ibid., pp. 101–102.
12. Ibid.
13. Robert Terrill, *The Cambridge Companion to Malcolm X*, reprint ed. (New York, 2010).
14. Jeffrey O. G. Oghar, *Black Power: Radical Politics and African American Identity*, revised ed. (Baltimore, 2019), pp. 7–8.
15. Ibid., pp. 4–5.
16. White, *Black Leadership in America*, pp. 104–106.
17. Oghar, *Black Power*, p. 9.
18. White, *Black Leadership in America*, pp. 107–110.
19. Ibid.
20. Ibid., pp. 114–118.
21. Terrill, *Cambridge Companion to Malcolm X*, p. 7.

Chapter 9

Women in American History

Introduction

Historians studying gender roles and the perspectives and experiences of American women have had a complex task ahead of them. With men typically being seen as the 'doers' of history, women were often relegated to the margins in politics and society at large. Further, since the academy is also a social institution impacted by patriarchal norms, history-writing often privileges men's voices and male-centric historical sources. In the process, women's role in historical events was ignored.

Uncovering 'women's histories' was only possible once historians began to take note of women's distinct subcultures, patterns of work, social attitudes, and self-fashioning. Feminist scholars also began to interrogate the historical development of masculinity and patriarchal culture in the US. Equally importantly, there was a growing focus on women's experiences across class, racial, and ethnic lines, mainly Indigenous, African American, Irish, Hispanic, and Asian women, many of whom were working class and were immigrants. These women had been rendered invisible in conventional histories of the USA. This new historical lens uncovered conclusive evidence of the political and economic marginalisation of women in the USA's modern history.

This research led to the rise of a new wave of women's history. Barbara Welter came out with an influential study of the nineteenth-century ideal of femininity, or **'the cult of true womanhood'**.[1]

She traced how Christian ministers and male moralists successfully imposed an ideology of 'true womanhood' based on the prescription of four virtues: piety, purity, domesticity, and submissiveness. Welter's study proved that patriarchal authority forced women to accept their subordination to maintain men's hold, power, and superior social status. Any deviation from the norm was deemed 'unfeminine'. The study opened up pathways for other women historians to explore areas of research that had earlier been neglected.

Carroll Smith-Rosenberg's article, 'The Female World of Love and Ritual', published in 1975, emphasised that the 'woman's world' of domesticity allowed for relatively independent spaces in which women could form friendships with other women and exercise control over family rituals, relationships, and traditions.[2] Similarly, Linda Gordon's writings on women's birth control techniques showed how they resisted male-centric sexual norms to assert their political power and develop reproductive control mechanisms. Nancy Cott, in 'Passionlessness: An Interpretation of Victorian Sexual Ideology, 1790–1850', argued that women deliberately promoted the notion of female purity as it granted them moral superiority over men. Estelle Freedman similarly suggested that women became empowered when they established separate women-centric organisations and institutions, since these gave them the power of self-development and provided a space where they were not subsumed by the power of men. It was when women attempted integration with men's institutions that they lost out. These debates demonstrate the multifaceted perspectives in studies of women's oppression, and, significantly, represent women's struggles for power, authority, and dignity. These studies also brought attention to issues of sexuality and patriarchal morality. For example, through these studies scholars also asserted that women's right of sexual autonomy and pleasure had to be decoupled from masculine expectations or the social expectations around reproduction.

Labour historians, too, began to acknowledge that women performed essential work that had been undervalued because it was unpaid, including farm labour, domestic work (including cooking), stitching and needlework, and childcare. When they entered the formal labour force, women were paid lower wages than men for similar work. For instance, 'mill girls' were hired in the textile mills, working 14–16 hours a day on low salaries—these were generally young girls who wanted to augment their family's income (see Chapter 4). They were accommodated in company boarding-houses, where they experienced a degree of personal freedom. The development of labour consciousness among women workers led to demands for better wages and conditions of work, assertions against unreasonable targets and exploitative foremen, and even led women to establish labour union and conduct strikes.[3]

Women's Changing Role in the Nineteenth-Century American Economy

From 1800 onwards, when the US was taking tentative steps towards urban crafts production under mercantile capitalism, merchants tended to distribute raw material to a cross-section of women. This brought them within the fold of the market economy and made them wage earners. Extensive research has been conducted on female agricultural workers and farmers, who played a crucial role not only in the early phases of US history, when subsistence agriculture was the primary mode of production, but also in later stages when large-scale and commercial agriculture became the dominant form. However, with the onset of the commercial economy, women began to be sidelined due to their inability to get credit and travel for work.[4]

From 1830 to 1865, the United States was on the path of industrialisation and urbanisation, even as the agricultural economy expanded. Rapid immigration from non-Anglophone Europe brought a range of new social groups to the US.[5] Even before the transportation revolution took place in the US, women were making and marketing a wide range of agricultural products, as Joan Jensen attests in her account of the 'Butter Belts' that developed in the mid-Atlantic region.[6] Women in the dairy business employed other women to do household work. They even bought clothes from the market from the money they made by selling dairy products, and this played a significant role in marking the shift from women as primarily producers to their new roles in a consumerist economic structure.[7]

Paid domestic work was, in fact, an important category of work for women. By 1850, as women were excluded from the marketing economy, domestic service emerged as the primary means of earning one's income—about three-fifths of American women worked as domestic servants in affluent families, which promised them safety, protection, and respect.[8] Interestingly, between 1820 and 1845, an influx of Irish immigrants escaping extreme poverty and massive crop failures that preceded the Great Famine (1845–1852) led to increased competition for domestic work in the northern states.[9] Since the Irish were ethnic outsiders and willing to work for meagre wages, they were employed but treated as 'inferiors', marking a shift from being considered 'help' to being identified as 'servants'.[10] A growing demand for sewing after 1816, when Congress raised tariff duties on imported manufactured clothes, led to the emergence of 'slop work' that women carried out at home to supplement the family income.

With gradual westward expansion, the US transitioned from subsistence farming to a system of commercial agriculture that used an enslaved labour force. The rural economy became linked to market forces. From the 1830s onward, the development of transportation systems that provided easy access to ship agricultural products marked the beginning of a boom period for the agricultural economy. This can also be attributed to the **Louisiana Purchase** three decades earlier, in 1803, which brought in fertile lands. In addition, the Purchase popularised Jeffersonian principles, providing the ideological ground for the expansion of the rural economy and assisting in the movement and development of White settlers and enslaved people into new territories. These territories were carved out by displacing, marginalising, and exploiting the original or Indigenous peoples of the USA.[11] However, these changes also marginalised White women, as two different forms of farming economies emerged: (*i*) subsistence farming, which was dependent on family labour, and (*ii*) the plantation system, where only slave labour was used. In the plantation-based, slave-dependent economy, all physical work was done by the enslaved people, so the White woman was further confined to the home and domestic responsibility.[12] Thus, even as White women were complicit in and benefited from the enslavement and exploitation of non-White women, whether Black or Indigenous, they also found themselves pushed into increasingly narrow definitions of genteel White femininity.

Similarly, in the family farms of the Northeast and the Midwest, with greater mechanisation, women were no longer required to work in the fields. With the growth of commercial agriculture, male dominance increased, while women were limited in looking after their families and homes. A similar situation could be seen among urban women, where only a tiny percentage of women were involved in domestic manufacture and food production. In the emerging culture of the USA, women were projected as domestic figures taking care of the home economy, while men became the 'breadwinners', dividing the workspace based on gender.[13]

The Impact of White Settlements on Indigenous Women

As White settlements and processes of state-formation expanded, colonisation affected gender relations in Indigenous societies as well. Anthropological and archaeological evidence suggests that in the traditions of Turtle Island,[14] the conception of gender and sexual division of labour were very different from Western normative understanding. As evident from the creation stories of many Indigenous societies, women were engaged in the agricultural economy, served other sacred functions, and possessed extraordinary power, reflecting their importance in the economic and political life of the tribe. In many of these sources, women appear as equals of men.[15]

However, with the gradual penetration of European settlers, not only did Indigenous peoples lose their sacred lands, their societies were also decimated by war, the impact of European diseases, and the policy of deliberate marginalisation by pushing them behind reserves and forcing them to assimilate into White settler society. All of this eroded the societal structures of Indigenous communities.[16] In general, the development of the cult of womanhood had little bearing on Indigenous women, since many Indigenous communities followed their family norms and traditions (which varied from place to place) in spite of being uprooted from their traditional environments. However, over time the impact of Western gender norms became more visible. It was when reserves developed that Indigenous women's traditional lifestyles began to be disrupted and destroyed.[17]

The Enslavement of Black Women

The expansion of agriculture to the Lower South was sustained by an expansion of slavery as a source of labour. When slavery became entrenched as a labour system in the American colonies, enslaved women and men became economically 'essential', even though they were systematically deprived of any benefits accruing from their labour. Enslaved women were encouraged to bear more children by their enslavers, especially since American law had determined that the status of 'slave' would be inherited from mother to child, ensuring the continuation of the system of slavery. Enslaved women were, thus, exploited for their reproductive and productive labour on the plantations. C. L. R. James, W. E. B. Du Bois, and Eric Williams were among the first scholars to research slavery within the broad spectrum of class struggle and capitalism.[18] These arguments were further developed by Cedric Robinson, who argued that capitalism was a racialised system. Marxist historians, in a similar vein, concluded that the history of American slavery was interlinked with the rise of American capitalism. In the New Histories of American Capitalism, cotton slavery was termed 'slavery capitalism'. Scholars have therefore suggested that after the American Revolution, with the expansion of settler colonialism and gradual integration with the industrial economy that ushered in the age of machinery, there was also a corresponding expansion of the institution of slavery.

Walter Johnson argued that the expansion of enslavement in the Deep South coincided with the development of a practice where enslavers would purchase enslaved women as sexual partners for enslaved men; as children of enslaved women were automatically given the same status, this was a way of adding to the workforce.[19]

Only in the 1980s did women scholars begin to work on women's experience of enslavement, with particular importance given to the dual exploitation of enslaved women in terms of demands to perform both reproductive and productive labour. The differential experiences of enslaved men and women were thus delineated in scholarship, taking into account the patriarchal structure of the plantation. The scope of scholarship broadened to include aspects of enslaved women's lives—pregnancy, birth, and childcare— and to analyse how the growing exploitation of enslaved women assisted in the further entrenchment and expansion of slavery as an institution. Researchers also carried out analyses of slave families to better comprehend aspects of gender relations and power. According to Sebastian Conrad, this contributed to academic understandings of the 'Black Atlantic',[20] placing the growth of slavery in a broader framework that also incorporated diverse histories of family, sexuality, and masculinity. Conrad suggests that the 'Black Atlantic', as a category of global study, should be understood from a gendered perspective. In a path-breaking work, Deborah Gray White studied how enslaved Black women developed group cooperation to endure the exploitative nature of enslavement. Over a period of time, this assisted in the development of 'self-reliant' and 'self-sufficient' socio-economic groups of formerly enslaved women.[21]

Claudia Jones and Angela Y. Davis, working within the Black feminist tradition, have emphasised the importance of women's reproductive labour on the plantation system; their work coincided with studies by Silvia Frederici, Maria Mies, and Selma James that linked women's labour with the rise of a slave-based capitalist system that eventually developed and later expanded in the British American colonies.[22] After the transatlantic slave trade was banned in 1808, there began in America a new regime of both social and economic control mechanisms under which enslaved women's reproductive health was carefully supervised. This was the case especially when the demand for Black labour was rising in the Lower South, which led to the further subordination of enslaved women to White people as well as Black men, resulting in their sexual and racial exploitation.

To perpetuate the subordination of enslaved women, the Eurocentric patriarchal system functioned through a logic of morality. There were two categories of women—virtuous and non-virtuous—and Black women were condemned to be part of the latter category since the Western norm of femininity was designed to exclude them. The children born of such 'non-virtuous' women remained enslaved for life, since in the US the status of a slave had matrilineal heritability of slavery. Racial hierarchy could thus be institutionalised by arguing that Black women were unvirtuous and could not be trusted with freedom. According to Thomas Morris and Christopher Tomlins, since White society systematically refused to recognise marriages between enslaved persons or their structures of family and kinship, their parental lineages were never acknowledged. By this logic, all Black persons—women, men, and children—were automatically seen as 'illegitimate', and therefore, enslaved people became chattel property. The children born to them also became enslaved as they were illegitimate. The entire Black family had to follow the command of their enslaver.

This also meant, according to Deborah G. White, that the social construction of enslaved womanhood was built on 'de-feminisation'. Much like Black men, enslaved women were involved in hard labour, from clearing land for agricultural expansion, to moving heavy logs, ploughing fields, and even digging up soil with heavy metal tools, as well as digging ditches, spreading fertiliser, and collecting fodder. Women were also engaged in the construction of roads and railroads and picked cotton just like men did. White writes that many scholars have taken this as evidence that over a period of time, Black women lost their 'female identity'.[23] She contests such a claim. White contends that a careful reading of historical sources points to the development of distinct female identities and cultures and forms of gender differentiation. What remains consistent across women's and men's experience of enslavement is persistent dehumanisation. The enslavers, White shows, categorised pregnant Black women as 'half' or 'quarter hands', while young, healthy women who were not pregnant were categorised as 'three-quarter hands' and made to work harder. Apart from utilisation of their labour, all Black women performed a double duty—working in the agricultural fields and also spinning, weaving, sewing, washing clothes, and making quilts.

Even within these systems, women socialised by singing and praying together and forged a sense of togetherness, cooperation, and interdependence, without which it would have been difficult for them carry out their work. Midwives played an important role as medical providers, often assisting in enslaved women's resistance against their enslavers. They would tend to pregnant women if they were hired by neighbouring plantations, and even aborted babies if requested, to prevent the child from entering a life of enslavement. Elderly women looked after young children, giving them a sense of belonging and dignity. Skilled women like seamstresses and cooks were granted spatial independence. Deborah White provides a picture of close-knit communities of Black women, suggesting that these community bonds were a crucial factor that helped women cope with the dehumanising nature of enslavement.[24]

The plantations were organised to maximize profits for the enslavers, and no gender division was permissible here, unlike in the White community. According to S. J. Kleinberg, 'enslavers regarded both sexes as units of production from whom they extracted maximum labour contributions'.[25] In the slave world of the South, slave women were shown some 'leniency' only if they were pregnant or had a child. Enslavers used different strategies of organising labour. Enslaved people generally worked in a family group system where men undertook heavy work. This system also protected those who were sick or too weak for labour. In the cotton plantation, the gang labour system was deployed and supervised by White overseers and Black slave drivers. Sexual exploitation, particularly by the enslaver, was a pervasive issue. In the aftermath of sexual violence, enslaved women were often blamed by White women for the sexual transgressions of White men. These women were often forcibly separated from their children, particularly in the case of biracial children fathered by the White enslaver.[26] Enslaved women and men both faced harsh punishments meted out by slave patrols, such as 'paddy rollers'. Apart from working in the fields, enslaved women worked as cooks, seamstresses, laundresses, midwives and house servants. In some cases, they were even given a dowry and hired out to work in urban centres.[27]

The construction of a racialised, patriarchal hierarchy thus rendered enslaved women vulnerable to sexual violence and exploitation. At the same time, to maintain White dominance over landholdings, marriage was made into a legal contract between White women and men, with the singular purpose of establishing a gendered and racial inheritance system. The fact that enslaved women were branded as inherently lacking 'virtue' added to their dehumanisation and made it legally impossible for them to resist sexual exploitation.

The cult of true womanhood, for this reason, did not apply to enslaved women, who were assumed to be of 'loose' character. Constantly faced with the 'sexual terrorism' of the enslaver, they had no legal protections—for instance, the southern courts did not recognise rape as a punishable offence in the case of enslaved women. Every aspect of life, personal, physical, social, and economic, was dominated by the rules and parameters of White society. Therefore, Black women's experiences of gender roles and differentiation were very different from those of White women.[28]

Despite the obvious rigidities of this oppressive social system, Joseph C. Miller argues that enslavers' control over enslaved people was extraordinarily fragile, and that enslaved people never lost an opportunity to rebel against their circumstances. However, while Miller attributes conflicts to a high population of enslaved men, the fact is that women often played a significant role in armed rebellions. From the 1780s, the movement to abolish slavery gained momentum in Britain after the Haitian Revolution, bringing the entire slave trade into question. Nevertheless, this coincided with the expansion of land, and so slavery persisted and even grew from Maryland and Virginia, particularly to the cotton-growing lands of Alabama, Mississippi, Texas, and Louisiana. The ban on the transatlantic slave trade in 1808 placed new pressures on enslaved women.

Racism continued to define Black women's experiences even after Emancipation. In the southern states, racial hierarchy was reinstated after the failure of Reconstruction, and this was enforced by unleashing racialised violence against Black men and women. After the Civil War, the US saw an increase in demand for the export of various commodities, and this demand was met through the evolution of systems like sharecropping, which pushed free Black women towards household work. However, when Black men moved out of the South in the early twentieth century, Black women found a space to take on new social roles.

Women's Activism in the Early Nineteenth Century

As we have noted, westward expansion brought about transformational changes in the economic role of middle-class White women. They were shunted from domestic manufacturing and into domesticity, away from the rapidly changing urbanised and industrialised world, in a process that eventually gave rise to the mid-nineteenth century cult of domesticity. At the same time, men were made responsible for providing economic sustenance to the family. The burgeoning culture of women's magazines also propagated this ideal of domesticity, which carried articles about women's responsibilities, physical weaknesses, and reliance on Protestant Christian values.[29] Linda Kerber finds that after the American Revolution, as a means to inculcate loyalty towards the new Union, 'Republican motherhood' was projected as a cardinal function to maintain the family's (and the nation's) emotional well-being.[30] The centrality of motherhood and domesticity relegated the women to the family sphere and removed them from the sphere of economic and political activity. In spite of these restrctions, women drew on their education and family experience and began to question, in the words of S. J. Kleinberg, intemperance, immorality, poverty, and slavery, and began to undertake reform measures in both cultural and social spheres.[31] In the period before the Civil War, particularly from 1815 onwards, the entry of a large number of immigrants from Ireland, Germany, and Scandinavia pushed women out of the labour market. During this period, the birth rate began to decline as women began to practise various methods of birth control, including the use of condoms, especially among the middle and affluent classes.[32]

Nevertheless, the cult of true womanhood was not a universal form of patriarchal control. It remained confined to the upper classes, since women with fewer means were forced to work to sustain themselves and their families. Rural and working-class White women, who remained deprived of new technologies and landholdings, continued to live in poor conditions: overcrowding and lack of nutrition, fresh water, and sanitation allowed diseases to spread quickly. These women continued to work as domestic servants and labourers to feed their families. Further, since the cult of true womanhood was tied to notions of White Christian morality, Indigenous and Black women were automatically excluded from the fold of 'virtuous femininity'. The multifold marginalisation they faced in a patriarchal and deeply racist society, which deprived them of resources, civil and political rights, and blatantly subordinated them to both White men and women, manifested in different ways.[33]

The period just before the Civil War, when more and more White, middle- and upper-class women were acquiring a modern education, saw the rise of **maternal associations** and women-centric magazines like *Mother's Magazine*,[34] which was started in 1833 by Abigail Whittlesey. Women also began to publish prose and poetry that, according to historian Barbara Walter, further perpetuated the cult of true womanhood by idealising women's traditional roles. All women-centric magazines idealised maternity and family life. As women began to interact with new technologies, like piped gas for cooking, running water, electric bulbs, and heating systems inside homes, new types of books and magazines emerged that had writings about new cooking styles and recipes. The science of home care began to evolve. Increasingly elaborate processes of cooking became another symbol of one's maternal instinct. Additionally, the invention of refrigeration technology and the mass production of meat and cloth transformed women from producers to consumers.

Simultaneously, a section of women began to question why they were relegated to domestic and care work, and instead sought to bring attention to social ills. From the 1820s onwards, these women began to participate in public activities, from religious movements to antislavery mobilisation and politics. These women demonstrated a profound understanding of the issue of gender, or the 'woman question'.[35] One example is the abolitionist Sarah Grimke and her antislavery crusade (see Chapter 4 for Grimke's involvement in the

Lowell women's strike). Thus, in the pre-Civil War era, some women did break away from the cult of domesticity to make their mark through social activism and reform activity.

Public forums to discuss women's issues had emerged from the late eighteenth century and gradually grew in influence. These reform efforts were organised by women from different racial, ethnic, and religious backgrounds. A group of African American women established the Female Benevolent Society of St. Thomas (Philadelphia) in 1793; the Moravian Brethren Church founded in 1770 was a widow home; in 1803, the Mariner's Family Asylum was set up for wives, widows, and daughters of seamen on Staten Island, New York. Many children's orphanages were set up between the 1830s and 1840s by the Roman Catholic Church. The Church also developed the New York Female Moral Reform Society and established Magdalene Home in 1838 for sex workers and unwed mothers.[36] The wide-ranging nature of women's societies and work indicates both awareness and methods evolved to deal with the situations.

Views on the Temperance Movement

With the beginning of industrialisation and immigration, along with rapid urbanisation in the 1820s and 1830s, excessive alcohol consumption became a widespread issue.[37] The emergence of saloons and a pub culture, brought into America by Irish and German workers, sparked a counter-current against alcohol consumption, leading to the formation of the **American Temperance Society**, which had 5,000 branches that advocated abstinence. The movement was inspired by religious practitioners who believed that alcohol consumption threatened family values and obligations. The aim of this movement, as explained in the reform newspaper *The Lily*, was to prevent men from drinking and protect wives from physical abuse and children from starvation. As the movement's push for abstinence was guided by the belief that men should earn their living and provide for their families, it remained rooted in a patriarchal logic.

Women's Entry in Public Spaces

The period from the 1820s to 1850s also saw a significant change in the women's movement, moving away from private affairs of the home—such as questions of social purity or the Temperance Movement—and instead training their gaze onto the public sphere by actively participating in the civil reform movement. Amid rapid economic transformation, women found new avenues to become politically active. Women's participation increased during the **Second Great Awakening** in the late eighteenth and early nineteenth centuries, which also saw the rise of new religious orders.[38] There was a massive increase in the membership of Protestant denominations, which emphasised a more emotional and tangible connection to the spiritual realm. Despite the propagation of the cult of true womanhood, women formed evangelical societies, made clothes for the poor, and even raised funds to improve the material condition of impoverished people. They began to teach at Sunday Schools to spread the light of education and also established missions for people experiencing poverty, especially women and children.

Some women came to the forefront to secure the right to dress as they wanted and secure jobs, property rights, and inheritance rights, including legal custody of their children. They wanted the abolishment of a feudal system of legally confining women to the bondage of family status, rather than accepting them as independent individuals with constitutional rights.[39]

The **Whig Party** emerged at this vital juncture and found a ready support base among evangelical Protestant churches. The party's main planks were abolitionism, temperance, and women-centric affairs, which allowed them to attract new members and broaden their support base. The Whig Party encouraged women to participate actively in public rallies, party-related activities, and meetings.

These significant shifts were particularly visible in the northeastern and midwestern regions, where women were already active participants in the Temperance and abolitionist movements. Historical scholarship suggests that abolitionism, in particular, made women activists aware of their political power. However, their vision remained narrow at this stage as they were influenced by social reasons to bring about change, rather than launching broader critiques of the system of slavery or on the lack of equal rights. Discourses about the condition of enslaved women, or the need to build support systems for working women, were still lacking.[40] There was no

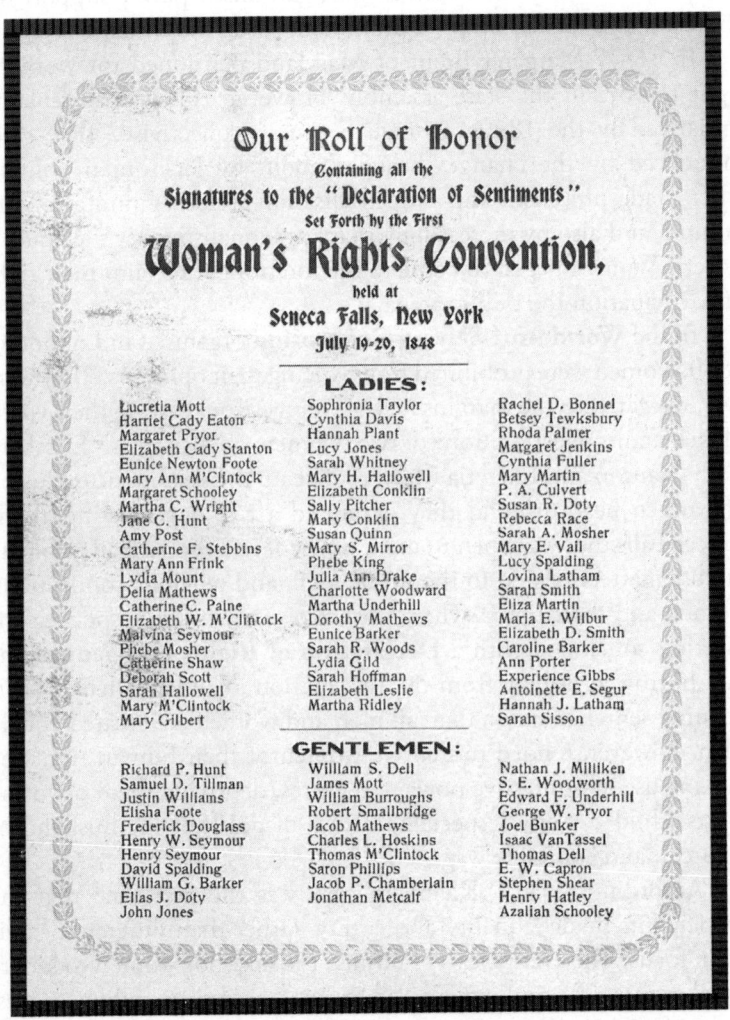

FIG. 9.1: Signatories of the Declaration of Rights and Sentiments (19–20 July 1848)

Source: Wikimedia Commons.

feminist, rights-based discourse at the time. This phase, thus, can be understood as a transitional period where women were still testing old and new ideas. It is now accepted that the abolitionist movement eventually made American women more radical in their thought and political demands, which in turn galvanised public support for abolition and turned it into a prominent social movement.

In 1847, Margaret Brent of Maryland petitioned for women's right to vote in the state assembly. However, this was an isolated initiative. By the 1840s, women began to collectivise. They were influenced by the changes brought about by Jacksonian politics, when trade unionism and industrialisation were beginning to gain ground, and also by increasingly sharp sectionalism over the issue of slavery. Women began to come to the forefront and claim their right of participation the public arena.

In the **World Anti-Slavery Convention** organised in London in 1840, women were prohibited from voicing their opinions. They were even relegated to the margins and prevented from casting their votes. This blatant rejection forced two women abolitionists, Elizabeth Cady Stanton and Lucretia Mott, to take up the systematic exclusion of women head-on, and they organised a two-day meeting at the Seneca Falls that was open to men, women, and the general public to discuss matters related to the social, civil, and religious condition of women and their rights. There was an overwhelming response. The meeting concluded with a **Declaration of Rights and Sentiments** that borrowed heavily from the Declaration of Independence, as its opening sentence stated that 'all men and women are created equal'. Men, however, tended to deprive women of their human rights by making use of oppressive power structures, depriving them of voting rights, child custody (especially in case of death of the husband or divorce), and equitable wages.

According to S. J. Kleinberg, this was the first time that the participants made 'equality and equity, rather than difference' their main focus. The event clearly outlined the need for women to secure equal rights of employment, education, access to public spaces, and citizenship. This also meant that women should only be held to the standards of virtuous social behaviour that applied to men, rather than being subjected to unattainable and restrictive notions of feminine virtue.⁴¹ Although there were disagreements over many issues, the Declaration of Sentiments was a milestone. It was later adopted by women seamstresses who conducted a strike demanding better wages for their work. The media opposed this declaration, but found support in Frederick Douglass, who fully supported women's rights in his publication, the *North Star*. Douglass felt that the anti-slavery and women's struggles should be kept separate, as they were different issues. However, the intersections of these two movements were already visible at this point. As there were no African American women representatives at Seneca Falls, in 1848, at the **National Convention of Colored Freedmen** organised in Cleveland, Black women put forward their right to vote and speak in public. Till the 1850s, women reformers continued to send petitions to various legislatures demanding their inherent right to property, vote, and end legal discrimination against women.

Women and Abolitionism

Women who wanted equal rights traversed through a mélange of pre-Civil War reform movements and finally found their voice and strength by supporting abolitionism. Early women activists emerged across race lines: Sarah and Angelina Grimke found support among evangelical and Quaker women like Lucretia Mott and Lucy Stone; Sojourner Truth, Margaretta Charlotte, Sarah Forten, and Maria W. Stewart, who openly raised their voices against the institution of slavery, also foregrounded issues unique to Black women.⁴²

Right from 1832, Maria W. Stewart, a prominent woman activist, began to implore African Americans to get educated and overthrow the shackles of slavery. Some activists sought to build commonalities between enslaved persons and White women, pointing out that in different ways, they were both considered the property of White men. However, many disagreed.⁴³ Many male abolitionists wanted women's participation but not their active role in the movement. This, perhaps, explains why, when Sarah and Angelina Grimke began to give public lectures, it was not appreciated either by the clergy or by many White women reformers like Catherine Beecher. In an influential text titled 'Essay on Slavery and Abolitionism', Beecher had advocated for community participation without relinquishing the cult of true womanhood, letting the primary struggle be carried out by men. The Grimke sisters rejected such a passive role. Angelina Grimke became the first woman in Massachusetts State Legislature to present an anti-slavery petition.

Women abolitionists also began to establish all-female societies, and some of the prominent ones were:

(i) Anti-slavery societies in Salem and Rochester, established in 1832;
(ii) Boston Female Anti-Slavery Society, set up by Maria Weston Chapman and her sisters;
(iii) Female Anti-Slavery Society, established by Charlotte, Margaretta, Sarah Forten, Sarah and Grace Douglass, and Lucretia Mott.

By 1837, the United States had more than 1,000 abolitionist societies, of which 77 were exclusively set up and run by women. In 1837, women abolitionists organised the first National Female Anti-Slavery Convention that saw a congregation of 81 women delegates who represented 12 states.[44] Black women actively participated in these societies but faced opposition from White women. Despite significant differences, an interracial abolitionist movement developed and paved the way for women activists to mark their presence in the public arena and speak openly against slavery.

As we have noted, Black women in the US were much worse off than their White counterparts. Black women were held to impossible standards of virtue in order to 'prove' that they possessed the ideals of true womanhood, in particular purity. They had to constantly remain steadfast in their religious commitments, maintaining purity, undertaking domestic responsibility with utmost sincerity, and all the while remain submissive by adhering to patriarchal norms. Simultaneously, they were still treated as racially inferior and had to combat stereotypes that projected Black women as sex-obsessed and physically strong or impervious to pain. Such stereotypes continued to persist even after the Civil War.

Even Black abolitionist leaders, scholars, writers, and advocates largely maintained that women should follow the ideal of femininity laid down in White society, as their demand for racial equality did not extend to a critique of overlapping structures of patriarchy. Black men wanted women to enter the public space and get educated not for social change, but to become faithful companions for their husbands, good mothers for their children, and start private businesses instead of competing for the same jobs as men. In Black churches, women were often given only subordinate roles and responsibilities. However, churches still helped Black women by allowing them to become missionaries and enter public spaces. After the Civil War, the position of Black women changed, but they remained doubly marginalised. The burden on women increased, but they found little political support among Black men, since the latter saw that it was to their advantage to adopt the White patriarchal model of family.

The Suffrage Movement

The aftermath of the Civil War marked the beginning of a new struggle that aimed to remove racial and gender bias from the state constitutions. For this purpose, in 1866, the Eleventh National Women's Convention, a forum of abolitionist and women's rights activists, formed the **American Equal Rights Association (AERA)**. After the Civil War, the 15th Amendment, which removed the race bar on voting, was passed, allowing Black men to vote for the first time in US history. Some AERA members felt that an Act that only gave enfranchised Black men would only strengthen men's hold over the political establishment, since women of all races and ethnicities were excluded from voting. They opposed the 15th Amendment unless it was accompanied by a law granting women the right to vote. Other members supported the 15th Amendment as a partial victory on the road to universal suffrage; Frederick Douglass, for instance, believed that the Black male vote was more critical at that point, due to relentless racist violence and persecution. Such views were opposed by Sojourner Truth, who outlined the denial of human rights of American women and voiced concern that civil rights guarantee for men of colour only would mean failure of the fundamental cause for which the Civil War was fought. Susan B. Anthony and Elizabeth Cady Stanton both opposed the 15th Amendment. They threw their weight behind the women's suffrage movement, which they believed was a natural right essential to implement for gender equality and the right of women to participate in the country's public affairs.[45] However, both Anthony and Stanton were criticised for associating with Democrat George Frances Train, who was openly racist, and for using racist vocabulary in their articles. After many failures, both women leaders in 1869 established the **National Women Suffrage Association (NWSA)**, whose membership was limited to women and favoured implementing a constitutional amendment to overcome state voting restrictions. The **American Women Suffrage Association (AWSA)** was established in the same year by Lucy Stone, Henry Blackwell and Julia Ward Howe. Membership in this association was open to men. After two decades of antagonism, in 1890, both organisations were merged to become the **National American Woman Suffrage Association (NAWSA)**.

Wyoming and Utah were the first states where women's suffrage was incorporated into state constitutions in 1870 and 1896. From 1870 to 1910, approximately 500 campaigns were carried out in 33 states to secure women's suffrage, but many ultimately failed. This failure prompted some leaders of the suffrage movement to change tactics, and instead of seeking women's equality, they began to advocate that the right to vote would make women better mothers and help them in civic virtue. The Temperance Movement's advocates also started to demand women's suffrage as it would allow them to let women vote for prohibition. Educated women, especially those associated with the Progressive Movement, disliked this line of thought as they saw voting as the only path to fulfil the goal of women's reform, which would eventually assist in formulating woman-centred social policies. Some women felt that voting rights would prevent industrial conglomerates from exploiting the labour of women and children, and others thought that suffrage would give women the power to get involved in local bodies like school boards.[46]

There was massive opposition to women's suffrage as many believed it would devalue women's role as housewives and disturb the existing social order. The Roman Catholic Church opposed it. Among recent immigrants, women's suffrage was supported by the Russians, Jewish migrants, and Italians, but opposed by the Irish. Business corporations were opposed to women's suffrage. Among the political establishment, the question of women's suffrage was divisive. Southern politicians in particular wanted to prevent the equal right to vote as they wished to maintain their masculine privilege and control over women, and they also planned to continue the exploitation of women's and children's labour in the slave economy. This opposition formed the **National Association Opposed to Women's Suffrage**, which consisted of associations in 25 states. It came out with public campaigns, pamphlets, and journals to prevent the suffrage movement from gaining ground. There was another problem: NAWSA kept Black women leaders out of the organisation for fear of losing the support of elite White women from the South.

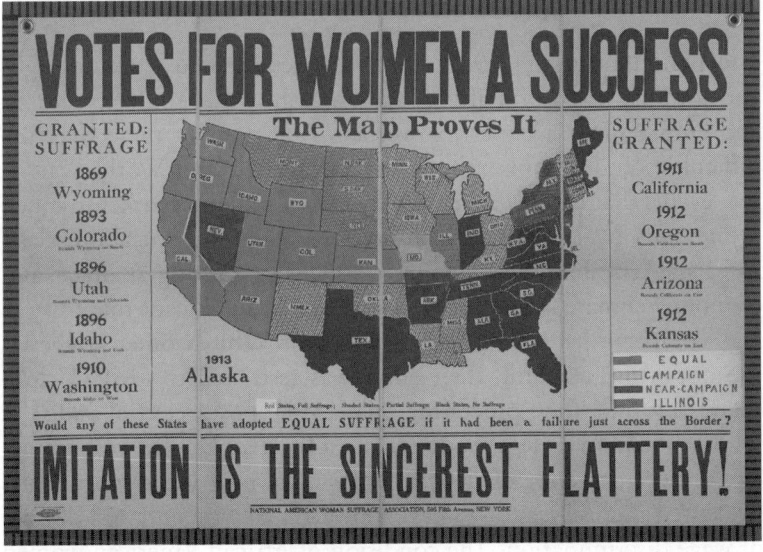

FIG. 9.2: Poster of the NAWSA showing states where suffrage had been granted (1912)

Source: Wikimedia Commons.

From 1900 to 1913, new leaders of NAWSA emerged who completely changed their strategy and sought public support. They began to organise parades and sought the help of labour unions, union reformers, and progressives. With women supporting World War I, more states ratified their constitutions to give women voting rights, forcing Congress in 1919 to amend the Constitution, and women finally secured voting rights in 1920. According to Sarah Eisenstein, in this period, working-class women began to gain an embryonic form of social consciousnesss that questioned the prevalent sexual ideology with the rise of female labour organisations and the beginning of radical feminist movements. Working women, in particular, presented three types of responses: conflictual, accommodationist, and negotiated.[47]

'Feminine Mystique'

The period from the 1920s to 1940s represented extreme highs and lows in terms of shifting economic growth, family structures, and employment avenues for women. Additionally, there were the difficulties endured over the Great Depression and World War II, two events that led to women's entry into the labour market in much greater numbers, albeit with limitations based on education, class, race, age, ethnicity and marital status. The shifting political and economic climate of the period also played a significant role.[48]

When compared with women of colour, White women got better job opportunities. Still, their entry was restricted to textiles, cloth manufacturing, food processing, managerial posts, clerical and sales jobs, school and college teaching, nursing, stenography, and typing. With the emergence of department stores, new job opportunities presented themselves to women. However, all women faced degrees of wage discrimination. The condition of African American women was much worse as they had even fewer job opportunities and generally could only secure employment in cigarette companies, as nurses or teachers, or in stores. During the Great Depression and the World Wars, they lost whatever little gains they had made.[49]

Labour unions continued to consider women labourers to be temporary workers. This mentality persisted even though the number of women in industrial jobs had increased considerably, and so had their work commitment. Another factor was that male workers regarded women as competitors for their jobs and used social pressure to keep them at the periphery. While the AFL encouraged women members, the fact remains that the executive council of AFL did not have single solitary female delegate, and the plight of women of colour continued to worsen. For this reason, the **Women's Trade Union League (WTUL)** continued to strive for better wages, a fair working environment, and active participation of women workers in union activities.

During the Great Depression, almost two-thirds of employed women lost their jobs or began to work for much lower wages due to job scarcity. Even domestic servants found themselves without jobs. Married women, despite financial hardships, were expected not to take up jobs; this pressure increased in 1932, when the **National Economy Act** was passed, promising a secure job only to one person in the family (with men being seen as the natural beneficiaries of the Act). When compared with married women, single women had better chances of employment, and this created a wedge between the two.[50]

During the period of the New Deal, historians observed that most of the federal employment, relief, and welfare programmes had excluded women, since it was assumed that by generating employment for men, the family's economic problems would be taken care of.[51] The National Recovery Administration (NIRA) and Civil Works Administration (CWA) ignored women's employment prospects. A similar situation was found with the Public Works Administration (PWA), which did not consider job creation in the fields dominated earlier by women workers. The Federal Emergency Relief Administration (FERA) only provided minuscule relief management to women. Even the Civilian Conservation Corps (CCC) secured jobs for rural men, and women who managed to secure employment were given lower wages. In its wage structure, the NRA completely overlooked domestic servants, farm labourers, and those engaged in repetitive light jobs. To further complicate the situation, the NRA banned work from home because it affected labour standards. All of this brought more woes to married women in particular.[52]

The **National Women's Party**, **National Federation of Business and Professional Women's Clubs**, and **League of Women Voters** pressured the government to overcome these hurdles and negligence, but they had little success.

The Works Progress Administration (WPA), developed in the second phase of the New Deal, reinforced the gender wage gap. The work undertaken by the WPA provided more employment opportunities for men. Whenever women's jobs were generated, they were paid lower wages or replaced when machines took over human labour. In all this, the situation was very different for African Americans, as both men and women were disadvantaged due to systemic racism and few found employment.

One of the best things to come out of New Deal's NRA programme was the legal recognition given to labour unions through the passage of the **National Labour Relations Act of 1935** was passed (see Chapter 6). It helped in the rise of the Congress of Industrial Organizations (CIO), which became the most prominent labour union in the industries involved in mass production. The partnership provided a platform for women workers to unite and form affiliated unions for workers in department stores, garment industry, and textiles; these unions included women of colour and men. However, these were minor gains. Even when the federal government attempted to change the law in favour of women, particularly women of colour, the southern Democrats opposed it.[53] During World War II, women joined the wartime effort. However, they continued to face systematic gender bias both in service and also from male colleagues. More women from the North joined the armed services compared to those from the South. Military service was not considered fit for women. Women joined wartime industries in large numbers, but after the war, they either left these jobs or were pushed out.

FIG. 9.3: 'War Mother', an example of propaganda pins given to women during the war (1916–1918)
Source: Wikimedia Commons.

At the end of World War II, there was a need to establish normalcy and a 'typical' environment for a society reeling from back-to-back crises and a return to traditional gender roles was part of this impulse: men wanted women to care for the home. The federal government supported this view, and instead of encouraging women who had taken up jobs, it wanted men to return to the workforce. A general perception developed that women cannot balance family and career demands. By 1944, the federal government was aided in their efforts for 'normalcy' by industrial heavyweights. Advertisements for home appliances urged women to return to the kitchen. Through the government's **Selective Service Act**, the state gave formal preference to men for jobs, and this meant more limited options of employment for women. Those who managed to secure a job received a much lower salary than men.

Added to this ideology was the issue of the Cold War, which placed more hurdles in the path of gender equality. Despite these impediments, the number of women in education increased. The Civil Rights Movement and anti-war protests led William Chafe to conclude that it was not suffrage but World War II that proved to be a 'turning point' in women's history.[54] On the other hand, S. J. Kleinberg opines that from the 1920s to the 1940s, there was a 'clash of gendered ideology and economic forces', with a revival of old social values due to the movement of the middle and upper classes towards suburbs.⁵⁵ Till the 1950s, affluent families had more children and women married early, and home responsibilities forced them into a position of passivity and dependence. During this time, US politics, academia, media, and television programming propagated the cult of true womanhood and sought to convince women to reject the 'masculine' sphere of work. Few women were in higher education, and the government gave more funds to sciences than to arts and humanities.⁵⁶ At the same time, a churning began among individual women, and these shifts could not completely push them away from the economic mainstream.

In the 1960s, women took advantage of the Civil Rights Act of 1964, which mandated all women and people of colour with the right to educate themselves in educational institutions. Nevertheless, there was hardly any representation of women in public office, and the main political parties sidelined women members and voters. The process of sidelining women became more apparent during the era of **McCarthyism**, when most women's voluntary organisations and antiracist organisations came under the scanner of federal government agencies. Among these was the **National Council of Negro Women**. Such monitoring and persecution forced women to leave these organisations and societies. Despite the aura of fear thus created, Black women continued to play a significant role in pushing for gender parity. They continued to raise their voices to secure civil rights, racial equality, the right to education, employment, and college education, and to end the segregation policy. According to S. J. Kleinberg, another reason for the resurgence of the women's movement in the 1960s was that the number of college-educated women increased. Educated women actively participated in the Civil Rights Movement and anti-war protests, and raised their voices for equal gender rights. Over time, more educated women began to understand the limits placed upon them by traditional gender norms. They continued to challenge these barriers, using collective action to demand political, social and economic solutions.

Notes

1. Barbara Welter, 'The Cult of True Womanhood: 1820–1860', *American Quarterly* 18, 1966, pp. 151–174.
2. Carroll Smith-Rosenberg, 'The Female World of Love and Ritual: Relations between Women in Nineteenth-Century America', *Signs*, 1975, pp. 1–29.
3. Thomas Dublin, *Women at Work: The Transformation of Work and Community in Lowell, Massachusetts, 1826-1860* (New York, 1979).
4. S. J. Kleinberg, *Women in the United States, 1830–1945* (New York, 1999).
5. Ibid.
6. Joan M. Jensen, *Loosening the Bonds: Mid-Atlantic Farm Women, 1750–1850* (New Haven, 1986).
7. Kleinberg, *Women in the United States*, p. 14.
8. Ibid., p. 14.
9. Ibid., pp. 15–16.
10. Ibid., p. 11.
11. Ibid., p. 19.
12. Elizabeth Fox-Genovese, *Within the Plantation Household: Black and White Women of the Old South* (Chapel Hill, 1988).
13. Ibid., pp. 20–21.
14. In multiple Indigenous cultures, the North American landmass is known as Turtle Island.
15. Fox-Genovese, *Within the Plantation Household*, p. 12.
16. Ibid.
17. Ibid., pp. 49–51.
18. See C. L. R. James, *The Black Jacobins: Toussaint L'Ouverture and the San Domingo Revolution*, 2nd revised ed. (New York, 1963). See also Eric Williams, *Capitalism and Slavery* (New York, 1967).
19. Walter Johnson, *River of Dark Dreams: Slavery and Empire in the Cotton Kingdom* (Cambridge, Massachusetts, 1967).
20. The concept of the Black Atlantic, first proposed by Paul Gilroy, centres the network of cultures that connected Black peoples, or African diaspora, around the Atlantic shores. This included not just the movement and cultures of enslaved people, but also the movements of free Black people across the USA, the Caribbean, South America, and so on. The notion of Black Atlantic also foregrounds the cultural contributions of the African diaspora to cultural sensibilities in the West.
21. Deborah Gray White, *Ar'n't I A Woman? Female Slaves in the Plantation South* (New York, 1999), p. 119.
22. Angela Davis, 'Reflections on Black Women's Role in the Community of Slaves' (1972). Silvia Frederici, *Caliban and the Witch: Women, the Body, and Primitive Accumulation* (New York, 2004). Maria Mies, *Patriarchy and*

Accumulation on a World Scale: Women in the International Division of Labour, reprint ed. (London, 1998). Selma James, *Sex, Race and Class: The Perspective of Winning, a Selection of Writings, 1952–1981* (Oakland, 2012).

23. White, *Ar'n't I a Woman?*, p. 120
24. Ibid., pp. 121–131.
25. Diana Paton, 'Gender History, Global History, and Atlantic Slavery: On Racial Capitalism and Social Reproduction', *American Historical Review* 127 (2), 2022, p. 22.
26. Ibid., pp. 23–26.
27. Ibid.
28. Ibid., pp. 43–46.
29. Ibid.
30. Linda Kerber, 'Separate spheres, female worlds, women's place: the rhetoric of women's history', *Journal of American History* 75, 1988, pp. 9–39
31. Ibid.
32. Ibid.
33. Kleinberg, *Women in the United States*, pp. 38–41.
34. There were others, too. Like *The Young Ladies' Reader*, *Godrey's Lady Book*, *Mother's Journal*, and *Mother's Assistant*.
35. Kleinberg, *Women in the United States*.
36. Ibid., p. 82.
37. Ibid., p. 83.
38. Ibid.
39. Ibid.
40. Ibid., p. 93.
41. Ibid., pp. 94–95.
42. Ibid., pp. 88–89.
43. Ibid.
44. Ibid.
45. Ibid., pp. 191–192.
46. Ibid., pp. 196–197.
47. Sarah Eisenstein, *Give Us Bread but Give Us Roses: Working Women's Consciousness in the United States: 1840 to First World War* (Boston, 1983).
48. Kleinberg, *Women in the United States*, p. 207.
49. Ibid., pp. 209–214.
50. Ibid., pp. 217–220.
51. Ibid.
52. Ibid., pp. 220–221.
53. Ibid., p. 226.
54. William H. Chafe, *The American Women: Her Changing Economic, Social and Political Role, 1920–1970* (New York, 1972).
55. Kleinberg, *Women in the United States*, p. 310.
56. Ibid., pp. 315–316.

Chapter 10

The Spanish-American War of 1898
The Onset of American Imperialism

Introduction

In the postbellum period, the US began to show more interest in the affairs of the Western hemisphere, establishing its spheres of influence and participating more extensively in world affairs. This indicated a shift away from the earlier policy of **isolationism**. The year 1890 was a watershed in US foreign policy, marking the emergence of a new imperialist vision that was in large part influenced by the business interests of large corporations that had evolved in the period from the 1860s to 1914.[1] American expansionism was based on a vision developed by US policymakers to control global affairs and make themselves impervious to economic downturns such as the economic depression of the 1890s. They felt the need to evolve a policy that would greatly strengthen the USA's standing as a world power, and this, according to Edward P. Crapol, marked the beginning of American imperialism.[2]

The Rise of US Imperialism

Multiple factors contributed to the USA's changing international strategies. *First*, according to Walter LaFeber, a radical departure from existing domestic policy within the US, with particular emphasis on the growth and development of business corporations, ushered in an economic revolution based on new scientific and ideological concepts that were already pushing the US towards the path of global engagement. The rapidly industrialised economy required markets to export manufactured goods.[3] *Second*, the USA's changing borders and wars in the neighbourhood influenced its policy. Events in the 1840s had set the stage for war with Mexico (1846–1848), which in turn sparked half a decade of conflict with Indigenous nations. The US was eventually victorious and opened up the trans-Mississippi region to White settlers, permitting the expansion of its borders and transnational transportation networks. This brought new regions and markets under US control, and allowed it to refine its military techniques. However, by the 1890s, frontier expansion ended, with the US now stretching from the Atlantic to the Pacific coast. Americans were forced to look beyond frontier avenues for further business development and profitable ventures.

Third, a severe economic depression in 1893 slowed down the American economy and forced the decision to expand and evolve the 'open door policy', which William Appleman Williams termed 'open door imperialism'. Americans entered the race for geopolitical control in the arena that Europeans dominated, but with some differences in approach. This policy of the open door was 'a classic strategy of non-colonial imperial expansion'. For Americans, openness became a pre-condition of freedom and liberal democracy. As noted earlier, it was also driven by a desire to reap greater profits than what was available at home.[4] Europe had already divided Asia and Africa among themselves in their imperialist pursuits; this, for the US, meant that it had to develop an approach to imperialism in Latin America and the Pacific region.

According to LaFeber, for a long time, many scholars misinterpreted the role of American policymakers, assuming that they had 'unknowingly' established an empire; in other words, greatness was thrust upon Americans, who were inherently exceptional. Questioning such assessments, LaFeber instead traces the ideology of imperialism to the **War of 1812**, which, he states, was not a 'great aberration' in American history, as Samuel Flagg Bemis's[5] influential scholarship suggested. The events of 1898–1900 were thus deeply embedded in the American experience and shifting domestic concerns.

Historians also highlight the role of William McKinley, US President from 1897 to 1901, who combined economic needs with military power and created effective governance mechanisms, overcoming any objections to American expansionism. LaFeber calls President McKinley a decisive, 'modern-day' chief executive who ushered in the modern era of US foreign policy. McKinley and his policymakers understood that the US would benefit economically, politically, and socially by evolving a new foreign policy based on complex linkages between geographical regions (the Caribbean, Hawaii, Cuba and the Philippines), which would become interconnected both economically and politically. He not only ensured that not only Spain, already a weakened power, was driven out of Cuba, but also intervened so that Cuban revolutionary forces would not win control of the country. Opposition to communist and revolutionary movements was seen as necessary for the expansion of American capitalism. Therefore, even much later, Americans sought to disallow revolutionaries in China, Mexico, Nicaragua, and Panama from capturing power through mass movements. This singular policy framework also ensured that within the USA, reactions to labour dissatisfaction, race riots, and episodes of economic depressions were controlled by an elite minority; it was not internal factors in themselves that pushed America towards imperialism, but rather the power elites' attempt to maintain their hold and control. According to Martin Sklar, the US was now more interested in inter-regional and intersectional approaches, along with national and international associations and identities.[6]

Expansionism in the Early Years

According to LaFeber, while US President Thomas Jefferson had already staked out the Western hemisphere as an arena under US control in the early 1800s and seriously considered the annexation of Cuba in 1808, Henry Clay, another prominent nineteenth-century leader, wanted Americans to dominate this region based on the

'Good Neighbourhood' policy. However, it was only in the aftermath of the War of 1812 and with the implementation of the Monroe Doctrine that the US was able to navigate possibilities of economic expansion in the Western hemisphere.[7] The annexation of Texas in 1845, followed by the war with Mexico in 1846–1848, which expanded US territories by almost one-fifth, were indicative factors for future American intervention. Historians also emphasise the role of Christian missionaries in propelling American expansionism within the parameters of Manifest Destiny. In the garb of a quest to spread the 'spirit of liberty' and 'virtuous' Anglo-Saxon institutions to uplift and civilise the 'inferior races', the federal government made concerted efforts to dispossess Indigenous nations and gain control over land and resources in North America. This logic of racial superiority was also used to justify intervention in Latin America.

By the early 1820s, Americans had turned their attention towards the Pacific, with a clear intention to take over the Hawaiian Islands. In 1784, the first American ship, the *Empress of China*, sailed to establish contact with China, and later, Japan opened its borders to the US, which marked their entry into Asian politics before the 1850s. A coherent American policy was evolving: it would protect its trade interests, traders, and missionaries.[8] The period also witnessed heightened nationalism that was supported by mass media, and which manifested in prominent identity markers or symbols such as the national anthem and the American flag. Exhibiting respect for the anthem, or prominently displaying the American flag, became the norm and reflected a nationalist cultural world.[9]

The Rise of Big Business Organisations

The American 'commercial empire', in LaFeber's words, had already begun to appear with the rise of big business organisations. The period from 1843 to 1857 was termed by Walt W. Rostow as the 'take off' stage; it marked a shift of political power, according to Charles Beard, from the planter class to emerging industrialists and financiers.[10] This was assisted by the development of robust federal banking systems, the imposition of high tariffs, and the **Homestead Act** that provided the impetus for the expansion of international markets, speculative capital, expansion of railroads, and which granted permission for the entry of foreign labour within the parameters of contract labour law.[11] The flow of capital from the Second Industrial Revolution was applied to new technologies and industrial units and also facilitated an increase in US exports (especially of cotton, tobacco, and wheat), purchase of foreign stocks and bonds, and the expansion of American construction and transport systems in the railways and industries outside the US.[12]

The Rise of New Frontiers

After the 1880s, Americans began to explore new commercial frontiers as the region west of the Mississippi frontiers was already suffering from overuse (by 1870, the American settlement process had outpaced 300 years of earlier settlement). This coincided with the development of four new trunk railway lines that connected with the Pacific coast; this network also aided in the rapid growth of the cattle industry and wheat farming. By the 1890s, climatic reasons and the end of railway expansion meant that Americans had to find new markets for jobs and products.[13] The period from the 1870s–1890s also saw increasingly frequent industrial strikes, race riots, class conflicts, and many social upheavals. The overproduction of industrial goods continued, increasing the demand for foreign markets and propelling policymakers to evolve a new expansionist foreign policy.

The Beginning of American Expansionism in Latin America

The Spanish-American War stemmed from the long history of US involvement in Latin America. The **Clayton-Bulwer Treaty of 1850** provided joint control of the US and Britain over any canal dug across the Isthmus by either of the two countries. Despite this treaty, the US aimed to expand its influence in the region and limit

European control. To fulfil this aim, the US in 1889 organised the first **Pan-American Conference** (also known as the **Confederation of American States**). The first region to come under the US radar was the island nation of Hawai'i, where, initially, Americans began to make inroads through missionaries and trade. In 1875, American sugar planters signed a treaty that opened a larger market for Hawaiian sugar in the US. In 1882, a new clause in the treaty gave the US a naval base at Pearl Harbor. With their foothold firmly established in the area, in 1893, Americans overthrew the Hawaiian monarchy and established the Republic of Hawai'i. President Cleveland gave the new government the US stamp of recognition, hoping to capitalise on the region for future expansionist forays into East Asia. According to LaFeber, the primary American interest in Hawai'i was to safeguard commercial passage for American goods in Central America.[14] The US also wanted control over the Samoan Islands in the South Pacific. Through an agreement in 1872, it acquired the harbour of Pago Pago. The problem, however, was that Germany and England also sought control over this island to establish their respective naval bases, which finally led to a tripartite agreement between all three nations to share it jointly. US blunders in handling Chile created problems in the later years. The US assisted Chilean revolutionaries but mishandled a dispute between American and Chilean sailors, which led to the death of one American sailor while another was wounded. The US threatened military action, and Chile was forced to pay the indemnity, creating animosity between the two countries.

In 1893, a fisheries or fur seal controversy, better known as the **Bering Sea Controversy**, arose between Britain and the US. Americans began to capture the Canadian ships in the region. The matter was ultimately settled by an international tribunal in 1911 that gave joint rights to the US, Japan, Britain, and Russia to hunt for seals in the region. Soon after this, another problem arose in Venezuela and British-controlled Guiana. The dispute was over the boundary claimed by the latter two, and when gold was discovered in the disputed territory, the desire for control intensified between the two nations. President Cleveland invoked the **Monroe Doctrine**, which prevented European interference in the Western hemisphere. The US and UK were frequently embroiled in conflict in these years.

The Spanish-American War of 1898 257

However, with the sudden outbreak of the **Boer War** in South Africa, Britain was forced to recognise that it needed a solid international ally in world affairs as all the major European nations were already its enemies. This historic turnaround by Britain marked a new era in international diplomacy that later defined a stable alliance between the US and Britain during World War I.

FIG. 10.1: 'The Great Rapprochement', poster used to promote the United States and Great Britain Industrial Exposition (1898)
Source: Wikimedia Commons.

The Spanish-American War needs to be understood in the context of growing internal consensus in the US that control over Latin America was necessary to fulfil its economic and military objectives. Despite being only a brief war, it marked a turning point in US foreign policy and established its status as a world power. For the US, the strategic location of Cuba (which would allow it to easily spread a wide net over Latin America), its sugar industry, and its markets made it an attractive site to control. The conflict was precipitated by the USA's emergence as a new imperialist power and its desire to showcase its new naval force. It also wanted to establish a naval base in Cuba and take over all the Spanish 'possessions' in the Pacific. Wealthy Americans also had substantial investments in Cuba and wanted to expand their economic base.

Some historians also blame 'yellow journalism', a term used for sensationalism and exaggeration in journalism, as an important factor that generated public sentiment in favour of US involvement in the war (see also Chapter 5). Rival papers *New York Journal* (run by William Hearst) and *New York World* (run by Joseph Pulitzer) wrote explosive headlines about Spanish atrocities in Cuba to gain readers' attention and increase circulation. Accounts of Spanish generals forcing Cuban guerilla fighters and civilians into concentration camps stirred the sympathy of the American public, who began to demand US action in the region. Another factor was the publication of a letter by Spanish minister de Lome stating that President McKinley was a 'spineless politician'. This letter fanned the flames of public anger and spurred public antipathy against Spain. This was followed by the explosion of the battleship USS *Maine* in Havana harbour, which Americans assumed was Spain's doing. The words 'Remember Maine' became a war cry, even though later investigation attributed the explosion to an accident, and this became the immediate cause of the conflict.

The Spanish-American War commenced on 11 April 1898. Congress accepted President McKinley's proposal to declare war with the singular purpose of assisting Cuban nationalists in their long struggle for 'liberty and freedom'. By this time, the USA had built a decisive naval force, ranked third among the world's naval fleets. The high tariffs imposed to protect American industries had been used to construct the maritime workforce. Two books also influenced Americans: *The Influence of Sea Power upon History, 1660–1783* by Alfred Thayer Mahan, and *The Naval War of 1812* by Theodore Roosevelt. War propagandists used these books to encourage the clamour for war. Roosevelt, as Assistant Secretary of the Navy, ordered Commodore George Dewey of the American Far East Fleet stationed at Hong Kong to capture the Spanish Philippines, which was accomplished on 13 April 1898, with the assistance of Filipino insurgent Emilio Aguinaldo. According to LaFeber, the aim was to develop American interests in Asia. However, the Germans sent five warships that were more robust than those operated by the US. Britain stepped in to broker peace between the two countries at this crucial juncture. This ushered in a new era of diplomatic friendship between Britain and the USA.

The American Navy made some apparent blunders in the beginning of the war. However, it recovered quickly and was able to capture strategic posts. In the meantime, Roosevelt was permitted to organise his three regiments of volunteer cavalry known as 'Rough Riders' to capture San Juan Hill outside Santiago in Cuba—this was a debacle and led to the death of 5,000 US soldiers due to inefficiency. Lessons from this war were later used to strengthen the American infantry and improve its combat readiness, particularly in the context of World War I.

The 'splendid little war' (a term used by Secretary of State John Hay) ended with the **Treaty of Paris on 12 August 1898**. Under the provisions of this treaty, Cuba was granted independence. However, to retain America's hold, McKinley forced Cuba to assent to the **Platt Agreement**, which granted the US the right of military intervention and additionally paved the way for the acquisition of naval bases in Cuba. Spain was forced to retain the heavy Cuban debt. Puerto Rico and Guam were ceded to the US, and the US agreed to pay US $20,000,000 to Spain for sovereignty over the Philippines. With this, the United States placed its imprint on the world map as a new imperialist power. In Philippines, it ostensibly set out to 'civilise' the Filipino people 'until they learnt the art of self-governance', reflecting a White supremacist ideology. From this period onwards, US trade and control over Puerto Rico and Cuba expanded, and it found an easy outlet to enter Latin America and establish military bases to control the Western hemisphere. The acquisition of the Philippines, Guam, and Hawai'i opened shipping routes to Japan and China, culminating in the 'open door policy'. This policy provided both reason and ease of accessibility for economic penetration into East and Southeast Asia, or the 'Far East'.

The fundamental ethos of American foreign policy was now shifting towards a 'new imperialism', evident in the policies articulated by McKinley. He contended that the US should assume the responsibility of Christianising and civilising the native population of the Philippines. America now wished to enlarge its national prestige by creating an empire. Business classes hoped to find new opportunities for investments, markets, and loans, and cheap sources for raw materials to power their growing industries. The Philippines would also provide an ideal military naval base for the US to expand its influence in Asia and prevent the territorial expansion of other imperial powers like Japan or Germany that also had imperialist ambitions in Asia.

The Importance of the War

The 'splendid little war' marked the decline of the great Spanish empire in the Americas that had begun with the arrival of Christopher Columbus. US involvement in Asia heralded the arrival of a new player in the race to acquire colonies, and was the most visible impact of the policy shift from isolationism to imperialism. There was a gradual recognition of the rise of the US as a new world power, and this war was supported by both the northern and the southern states, thereby ending the bitterness caused during the Civil War. However, once the people of the Philippines became aware of the USA's imperialist ambition, they began an independence movement, resulting in war from 1899 to 1903. The US succeeded in retaining control only after orchestrating brutal killings and massive destruction in the name of liberty and the civilisational process. This marked the emergence of American imperialism, which drew from the ideology of racial superiority that had already marked its establishment as a settler colonial state, and which recast non-White peoples as the 'White man's burden'. The growing prominence of such ideologies only compounded the problem of racism within the US. There were sane voices within the US who opposed this form of imperialism, arguing that it went against the notion of freedom that the US supposedly championed.

Historians have understood this war in various ways. According to the **Realist School** of the 1950s, by the end of the nineteenth century, Americans were more concerned with the 'legalism and moralism' of the world, based on an understanding of the realities of power and the fact that the US was not all that different from other nations. It was just one more player in a global diplomatic game whose rules were set by a balance of power politics. George F. Kennan carried forward this line of interpretation in *American Diplomacy, 1900 to 1950*.[15] Kennan believed that the US became a great world power not because Americans understood Asian affairs, but because British officials manoeuvred them into supporting China's open door policy. The realist approach was further refined by Norman Graebner,[16] who emphasises the 'means–ends' question. Did the US have the means to achieve its diplomatic ends at that specific point? In his view, Americans were guided not by a realistic understanding of their power, but by unrealistic beliefs in the power of morality and legality.

The **Revisionist School** of historians is best represented by William Appleman Williams, who wrote *The Tragedy of American Diplomacy*. In this book, links were formed for the first time between economic changes inside the US and their consequent impact on foreign affairs. For Williams, American policy was not engineered by British officials but by US leaders who clearly understood its implications and wanted to expand the nation's economic interests. Williams presented this argument in *The Contours of American History*, which presents the era after the 1890s as the 'age of corporation'.[17] He expanded this idea in *The Roots of the Modern American Empire*, emphasising that the rise of American individualism and the desire for continental expansionism led to the overproduction of agricultural and industrial surplus.[18] The solution to this growing problem was to conquer world markets and use government help, if necessary, in the process. In other words, Williams brought together domestic and foreign policies to reach a new theoretical model. This argument was further extended by Thomas J. McCormick, who said three groups—government, businesses, and labour organisations—worked closely to shape America's national policy to optimise production goods and create markets where they could sell products or buy cheap raw materials.

In the book *Gray Steel and Blue Water Navy*, B. Franklin Cooling successfully proved that domestic economic interests and foreign policy needs both contributed to the impulse to build modern naval ships. These were meant to protect America's expanding overseas interests. The move brought Andrew Carnegie's United States Steel Corporation into the picture, establishing a military-industrial alliance that allowed the state to rapidly develop its 'Great White Fleet'. This was instrumental in winning the Spanish-American War and expanding American imperialism in the Pacific region.[19]

Conclusion

The 1890s was a decade of great foreign policy successes for the US, perhaps best reflected in Britain's recognition of the US as the supreme power in the Western hemisphere. New players within America, such as giant corporations and banking groups, began to play a significant role as they began scouting for buyers of industrial goods and bank capital. In a departure from earlier patterns, the land America acquired in the 1890s was now utilised to develop naval stations, for example in Hawai'i, the Caribbean, and the Philippines, to secure complete protection for overseas American commerce. All this became possible as the federal government's organisational structure, under President McKinley, had become more effective in terms of defining and executing foreign policy imperatives. McKinley's administration dominated over Congress and used US military power overseas without securing a congressional mandate.

Notes

1. William Appleman Williams, *The Tragedy of American Diplomacy* (New York, 2012).
2. Edward P. Crapol, 'Coming to Terms with Empire: The Historiography of Late-19th Century American Foreign Relations', *Diplomatic History* 16 (4), 1992, pp. 573–597.
3. Walter LaFeber, *The New Empire: An Interpretation of American Expansion, 1868–1898* (New York, 1998), p. 2.
4. Eric Foner, *Give Me Liberty! An American History*, third ed. (New York, 2011).
5. Samuel Flagg Bemis, *John Quincy Adams and the Foundation of American Foreign Policy* (New York, 1981).
6. Martin Sklar, *The United States as a Developing Country* (New York, 1992), p. 30.
7. LaFeber, *The New Empire*, pp. 3–4.
8. Ibid., p. 5.
9. Foner, *Give Me Liberty!*, p. 658.
10. See Charles A. Beard and Mary R. Beard, *The Rise of American Civilization*, vol. 2, (New York, 1927), p. 199.
11. LaFeber, *The New Empire*, p. 7.
12. Ibid., pp. 9–10.
13. Ibid., pp. 12–13.
14. Ibid., p. xxxii.
15. George F. Kennan, *American Diplomacy, 1900 to 1950* (Chicago, 1951).
16. Norman Graebner, *Foundations of American Foreign Policy: A Realist Appraisal from Franklin to McKinley* (Wilmington, 1985).
17. William Appleman Williams, *The Contours of American History* (Cleveland, 1961).
18. William Appleman Williams, *The Roots of the Modern American Empire* (New York, 1969).
19. B. Franklin Cooling, *Gray Steel and Blue Water Navy: The Formative Years of America's Military-Industrial Complex, 1881–1917* (New York, 1979).

CHAPTER 11

A History of US Intervention in World Wars I and II

Introduction: The Emergence of American Exceptionalism

The Spanish-American War propelled the United States as an imperialist power with hegemony over the Philippines, Puerto Rico, Cuba, Hawai'i, the Virgin Islands, and a stretch of land adjacent to the Panama Canal. Still, instead of simply magnifying its power as a territorial imperialist nation, the US was extending its hold over global affairs in a twofold manner, *first*, by projecting its varied ethnic communities as representatives who were now engaged in international politics, and *second*, by influencing the world through the power of '**American exceptionalism**'. Taken together, these two strategies awarded the US its economic, cultural, and intellectual capacity to dominate the world economy and geopolitics, and it was already a formidable industrial power that was beginning to threaten Britain, France, and Germany. It is also at this juncture that the USA began to pursue the 'open door' foreign policy, driven by the realisation that the rapid expansion of an industrial and consumer economy required tapping into new sources of raw material as well as new markets to absorb surplus production. It therefore launched a paradigm of unrestricted international trade and investment, while promoting the American brand of liberalism and democracy. Corporations exerted pressure for a new foreign policy that differed from that of Europe. To justify and normalise its dominance in the global economy and geopolitics, the US projected itself as the force behind the 'maintenance of world peace', and this quickly became its new foreign policy motto. On the surface, the US never openly stated a shift in its foreign policy as this process was still developing, during which the country emphasized internal matters rather than external affairs.

A close examination of domestic politics reveals the rise of a new class of politicians who may be termed 'imperialists' due to the emphasis they placed on US intervention to establish 'world peace' and enable the USA's continued economic growth. This led to a push for the application of the **Monroe Doctrine** and the **Isthmian policy**, as well as the policy of '**peace by arbitration**'. Foreign immigration saw new restrictions, even as the US pursued an 'open-door policy' and demanded unprecedented access to markets and resources in different parts of the world. With war clouds looming over the horizon, it was clear that Europe would need to import American food, manufactured products, and arms. European nations were ready to pay in gold and borrow from American banks. This initiated a massive American capital investment process, completing the transformation of its economy into a capitalist-imperialist system, which was evident during the presidency of Woodrow Wilson.

LIBERAL INTERNATIONALISM AND AMERICAN MILITARISM

The presidency of Woodrow Wilson, therefore, marked a new chapter in America's foreign policy with the formulation of what has been termed '**liberal internationalism**', a policy of American intervention in colonised regions to 'make the world safe for democracy'.[1] According to Lloyd E. Ambrosius, the most significant aspect of Wilson's legacy was the glorification of the 'liberal tradition' in US foreign policy, which led to the rise of the principles of **Wilsonianism** that projected America as an exemplar of democracy, capitalism, freedom, and human rights.[2]

FIG. 11.1: A cartoon praising Theodore Roosevelt's move to build the Panama Canal (1904)

Source: Wikimedia Commons.

Wilson's predecessors had laid the groundwork for such a policy. During his term in office, Theodore Roosevelt partitioned the world into two diametrically opposed zones: the 'civilised' and 'uncivilised', drawing from prevailing ideas that Western civilisation represented the 'pinnacle' of human society. This became the ideology undergirding his foreign policy. The consequences of such an ideology first became visible in Central America, where Roosevelt separated Panama from Colombia and acquired control over the newly independent state of Panama, with the larger goal of successfully building Panama

Canal. These events made the US 'an international police power' in the Western hemisphere. American intervention in the Dominican Republic, Cuba, Honduras, and Costa Rica reflected the country's growing ambitions in international politics, both militarily and economically.³ During William Howard Taft's presidency, foreign policy saw a shift towards '**Dollar Diplomacy**' that emphasised economic influence over Latin America and Africa. Under Woodrow Wilson, another aspect was added to US foreign policy—a missionary zeal to propagate American economic domination through democratic idealism that came to be known as '**moral imperialism**'. This projection of benign dominance notwithstanding, the reality was that during Wilson's tenure, America was more frequently militarily engaged than ever before in its history.

Woodrow Wilson's New World Order

Britain had dominated geopolitics in Europe and internationally since the defeat of French emperor Napoleon. The **unification of Germany** under the policies of Bismarck led to the rise of a new European imperial power that began to challenge Britain's dominance in international politics and commerce. By 1900, this polarisation began to divide Europe between the **Triple Alliance**, represented by Germany and Austria-Hungary, and the **Triple Entente**, which included Britain, France, and Russia. When World War I began in 1914, America declared neutrality, that is, it sought to uphold its free trade rights at sea with the two warring power blocs. Amid this intense conflict in Europe, President Wilson in 1914 announced a set of **Fourteen Points** to the US Congress, reflecting his vision of a new world order. This vision laid the foundation for Wilsonianism and liberal internationalism. He also defined the USA's wartime aims, which termed the struggle as one being waged not against the German people but against their autocratic government. This liberal tradition was governed by the principles of:

   (i) national self-determination, based on national sovereignty and democratic self-government;

(ii) open-door economic globalisation based on competitive markets across the globe for trade and financial investments;
(iii) collective security (which would later manifest in the postwar organisation called the **League of Nations**); and
(iv) a progressive view of the history of humanity, based on the Wilsonian vision of a better world in the future.[4]

Wilson's vision is today seen as problematic: While it was alert to the essential principle of global interdependence, it failed to adequately understand diversity in needs and aspirations across the world. His liberalism lacked realism.[5]

The USA also wanted all nations to accept the **Declaration of London (1909)**, which granted concessions to countries not participating in World War I. Britain refused to accept this as international law and initiated its own set of rules to destroy Germany's foreign trade. To do this, it set out to prevent any neutral ships from entering German ports or neighbouring countries and attempted to stop any goods from being shipped to Germany, thus limiting the USA's commerce with Germany and its allies. Britain also invoked the clause of a continuous voyage to stop US goods from being shipped to neutral countries that shared a border with Germany. President Wilson's protest did not sway Britain. In the meantime, the clouds of war intensified over Europe when Germany began to deploy a new naval weapon, the submarine, to break the British blockade. In 1915, Germany sent these submarines to the British Isles and declared that all enemy ships entering the area would be sunk. Germany also warned the citizens of neutral countries not to travel on Allied ships.

In this tense atmosphere, the British ship *Lusitania* was sunk by Germany near Ireland in 1915, in which many US citizens lost their lives. In response, Wilson pressured Germany to stop submarine warfare. However, in August 1915, when another British ship, the *Arabic*, was sunk, it became clear that the US was being pushed to enter the **Great War** (another term used for World War I). In March 1916, the French ship *Sussex* was sunk, killing two Americans. Wilson issued an ultimatum to Germany that led to the **Sussex**

Pledge, where Germany agreed not to sink ships without regard for the lives of ordinary passengers.

The majority of Americans, based on their ethnic identity, were opposed to participation in the War. Women's groups also opposed such a move. Regardless, it was became clear that the US would join the war when, in 1916, Wilson began to formulate the policy of 'preparedness' and asked Congress to pass several defense measures. This included the **National Defense Act**, which increased the size of the army and brought state militia under the federal government. Congress sanctioned funds for the construction of battleships and other essential naval vessels, the **US Shipping Board** was constituted to purchase, operationalise, and manage merchant ships, and the **Council of National Defense** was set up to chalk out plans to mobilise and utilise resources in the event of the War. In the meantime, the US sent a delegation to negotiate peace, but the warring nations showed little interest in such an endeavour. In the presidential elections of 1916, Wilson was re-nominated as a candidate of the Democratic Party with the famous slogan, 'He kept us out of war'. After the elections, Wilson made another attempt at peace and stated that his peace efforts were aimed at 'peace without victory', but the result remained the same.

By January 1917, two factors had emerged that pushed the US into the War. Germany announced the resumption of the sink-on-sight submarine campaign against all ships around the British Isles. Further, British intelligence orchestrated a well-crafted leak of a letter penned by German foreign minister Zimmermann, where Zimmerman promised Mexico the return of Texas, New Mexico, and Arizona if it joined forces with Germany against the USA; Japan, too, was offered an alliance with Germany. Congress passed the resolution to join the fight on 6 April 1917. Historians believe public knowledge of the letter, along with British propaganda, swayed the American public in favour of War. The US was also concerned that its economic interests and institutions would be adversely impacted in the case of a German victory. According to historian Arthur Link, who ascribes nobler aspirations to the USA, Wilson entered World War I not only to ensure the defeat of Germany but to produce a peace that would genuinely make the world 'safe for democracy'. This would automatically guarantee the protection of other American interests.⁶

FIG. 11.2: President Woodrow Wilson asking Congress to declare war on Germany (2 April 1917)
Source: Wikimedia Commons.

Before going into war, Congress passed the **Selective Service Act** that required all eligible men to register for military service. The **War Industries Board** was created to manufacture war supplies and the **War Shipping Board** to make ships needed to transport men and supplies (and to replace losses from submarine assaults). Railroads were brought under federal control to help efficiently transport war goods, materials, and armaments. The **Fuel Administration** was enacted to conserve coal and oil and increase production. The **Food Administration** encouraged farmers to produce more for wartime needs. Higher taxes were imposed, and government bonds were floated to secure a continuous money supply.

In October 1918, the German government appealed to Wilson to negotiate peace based on the Fourteen Points. After a month of secret negotiations, an armistice was concluded on 11 November 1918. Wilson had hoped for a balanced treaty, but the USA's European allies made stringent demands, and the President soon realised that to fulfil his dream of the League of Nations, he would have to compromise on the issues of self-determination, open diplomacy, and several other aspects. At the end of negotiations for the **Treaty of Versailles**, out of the Fourteen Points only the League of Nations was carried forward, which he made an integral part of the treaty. The problem was that Wilson had failed to involve the leading Republicans in this treaty process, and they, therefore, stalled the treaty in the Senate Committee. To overcome this problem, he began a nationwide tour. On 25 September, 1919, Wilson suffered a severe stroke from which he never fully recovered. Taking advantage of his ill health, the Senate rejected the Versailles Treaty and the League of Nations.

According to William Appleman Williams, Wilson took the USA into World War I as a crusade based on 'the imperialism of idealism'.[7] It was an effort to impose American values on the world and defeat the growing ambitions of Lenin and the Soviet Union. On the other hand, according to George F. Kennan, the President was driven entirely by his faith in legal and moral concerns, based on the imperative to make the world safe for democracy, and did not understand the realities of world power. His policy of helping the Allies destroy Germany also destroyed any chance of a long-term balance of power in Europe, since that would have required having Germany at its centre. Kennan argued that the Fourteen Points made the US the more 'righteous' party in the conflict, but also created a power vacuum that would gradually be occupied by Nazi militarism (in central Europe) and Soviet expansionism (in eastern Europe).[8] The same line of thinking is evident in Norman Graebner's analysis. Woodrow Wilson was guided, according to Graebner, not by a realistic understanding of power but by unrealistic belief in the power of Western morality and legality. The President therefore established a foreign policy direction that was unlikely to be accepted. Instead of looking within, he was guided by the might of American power and by anti-communist anxieties.⁹

In *Political Origins of the New Diplomacy*, Arno Mayer has emphasised the close association between domestic political realities and their impact on US foreign policy.¹⁰ Western Europe and the USA feared the growing influence of **Bolshevism**, and they joined hands to contain Bolshevism rather than build a healthy Europe. Taking this line of understanding further, in Lloyd Gardner's view, one needs to analyse how Wilson viewed American interests vis-à-vis the rest of the world. The President knew that creating an orderly and open world system was necessary to protect US interests. However, wherever he applied this, it resulted in a revolution, such as in Mexico, Russia, and Haiti. The situation forced Woodrow Wilson to use military power to establish his dream of an orderly system, leading to repeated military interventions.¹¹

Over time, a scholarly consensus has emerged that Wilson failed to create the kind of democratic Europe he aspired to because he was trapped between conservative western European leaders and the eastern European revolutionaries. The President also realised that if he insisted on self-determination, eastern Europe would become entirely communist. Therefore, the President decided to contain the threat of communism by sacrificing his ideal of self-determination.

In the 1950s, most historians believed that the main reason for President Wilson's decision, despite reservations, was the German declaration in January 1917 of all-out submarine warfare. This explanation is no longer considered sufficient. Arthur Link, who wrote a biography on Wilson, has argued that the President was convinced that the USA needed to be a full participant in the formulation of the postwar world to secure agreement to principles that Wilson thought were critical to America's domestic interests, in particular, freedom of seas and liberal international trade. The goal was to defeat Germany and bring peace to make the world 'safe for democracy' and secure all US interests.¹²

At the end of World War I, Europe was devastated, and this opened a period in global history that the geographer Isiah Bowman has termed 'a new world'. The old broken world was rife with global disturbance and economic disorder. According to Lloyd

E. Ambrosius, this new world international order was shaped by two forces: integration and fragmentation. Despite the ominous emergence of global problems, the fact remains that at the end of World War I, the USA became a 'creditor nation' that was exporting goods and capital on an unprecedented scale, giving it phenomenal power over the global economy. The upward movement of the US dollar was now closely linked to the maintenance of political stability in Latin America, Asia, and postwar Europe. The maintenance of world order thus became the core of US foreign policy, and it was projected as the pursuit of democracy and liberalism across the globe.

World War II and the United States

American participation in World War I showcased the resilience of the American people and enlarged the role of the federal government in wartime mobilisation and economic development. This, in turn, assisted in economic growth and development, generating jobs and creating avenues for entry of women into the workforce. The interwar period challenged patriarchal gender relations and brought about significant shifts in social geography as people migrated from rural to urban areas.

By the time of World War II, the US had begun to assume a more significant international role, along the foreign policy noted earlier that placed a priority on military preparedness and security as a necessary means of protecting the American values of freedom, democracy, and capitalism. In the words of President Dwight D. Eisenhower, the war pushed the country towards building a 'military-industrial complex' that became the hallmark of the federal government. In the period from 1941 to 1945, the US cemented its status as a global superpower. Assuming the role of 'the leader of the free world' while also making its foreign policy more 'interventionist', the US developed an anti-communist ideology in response to the expansion of communism in East Europe and East Asia. World War II also marked the end of the Great Depression and the nation leapt forward in economic terms, providing greater impetus to the creation of a new social ideology based on US imperialism and 'free' enterprise that was touted as a means to end all social conflict. On **Victory Day (1 September 1945)**, President Harry S. Truman declared on radio that America had 'the greatest strength and the greatest power which man has ever created'.[13]

The Pre-World War II Context

By 1933, facing the consequences of the Great Depression and with his focus on the New Deal, President F. D. Roosevelt implemented the '**Good Neighbour Policy**' that focused on non-interventionist US Policy in Latin America. This marked a significant shift from the earlier American policy of establishing Latin America as its sphere of influence. US forces were withdrawn from Haiti, and treaties were signed with Cuba and Panama that ended their status as American protectorates. Germany, in the meantime, wanted to prevent Latin American countries from aligning with the Allied powers and attempted to expand its trade relations, using propaganda and espionage to spread its influence on the continent. These efforts were nullified due to the USA's policy, along with assistance provided by the Allied powers.

In Asia, Japan's imperial ambitions had become problematic for the US by 1931. Japan was beginning to show its aggressive expansionist plans as it invaded Manchuria and later moved into the interior of China by taking over the city of Nanjing. After a brief interlude due to an economic depression, it resumed this process in 1937, resulting in the **Sino-Japanese War**. Japan aimed to reduce its financial dependence on imported commodities through its policy of establishing the 'Greater East Asian Co-Prosperity Sphere'.

In Europe, the rise of Adolf Hitler and **Nazism** in Germany was marked by a military campaign to take control over the entire continent. The same line of thought was pursued in Italy by Benito Mussolini through the ideology of **Fascism**, and Italy invaded Ethiopia. Hitler supported and armed General Francisco Franco of Spain who, in 1936, engineered a military coup to overthrow a democratically elected government. Hitler also unleashed a genocidal campaign against Jewish people. The Nazi Party systematically deprived them of all citizenship rights within Germany and eventually condemned millions to imprisonment and death in infamous concentration camps. At this juncture, the USA, along with Britain and France, continued to pursue a policy of 'appeasement' to maintain peace in Europe by acceding to all of Hitler's demands, making the dictator bolder and more aggressive. The US Congress continued to pursue twin policies of neutrality and an open door policy by enacting a series of **Neutrality Acts in 1935** to prevent the US from getting entangled in European wars. Simultaneously, the Acts were meant to protect American trade and commerce, even with Germany and Japan. In 1938, Hitler conquered Austria and Sudetenland (in Czechoslovakia), a strategic move that would later lead to the conquest of Czechoslovakia. With the **Munich Agreement of 1938**, Britain and France, both of whom were anxious to limit the influence of communism in Europe, continued to accept Germany's demands. In a surprise move, Joseph Stalin of the Soviet Union signed a nonaggression pact with Germany, which allowed Hitler to invade and conquer Poland on 1 September 1939, using its lightning war-fighting strategy known as **blitzkrieg**.

Europe had now entered World War II, but the USA continued to maintain neutrality. By 1940, following a fresh wave of German invasions, the region of Scandinavia came under German control, as did Belgium and the Netherlands. On 14 June 1940, Germany took over Paris. In September 1940, a new politico-military axis was formed, comprising Germany, Italy, and Japan. With the fall of France, Britain was now alone in fighting forces of Nazism and Fascism, and after the **Battle of Britain in 1940–1941**, when London faced the brunt of direct German air assault, Britain requested US assistance. The American Congress implemented the National Defense Act. The purpose was to prevent the supply of war material to Germany and instead give the same to Britain and to increase the manufacture of US naval ships in preparation for entry into the war. The situation had become so grim in Europe that Britain was forced to send delegates from the Ministry of War to open negotiations with the US. Both countries agreed they would jointly tackle and defeat

Germany and then turn their attention towards Japan. The US also agreed to station a substantial naval force, the US Pacific Fleet, at Pearl Harbor.

In the meantime, Japan and the Soviet Union were engaged in intensive warfare over control of the Soviet-Manchurian border. When Japan invaded Mongolia, it began to make overtures to Germany in a bid to weaken the Soviet Union. However, the **Nazi-Soviet Nonaggression Pact of August 1939** was a hurdle in this plan, and Japan was forced to abandon its expansionist plans.

Congress agreed in 1940 to sell armaments to Britain on a '**cash and carry' policy** that meant that arms had to be bought by Britain by paying in cash and taken to Britain in their ships. However, when it became clear that Britain was no longer in a position to pay, Congress passed the **Lend-Lease Act**, which provided military aid to Britain, China, and the Soviet Union. Hitler abrogated the Nonaggression Agreement with Russia, and Germany invaded Russia in June 1941. To stifle and squeeze the Japanese economy, America froze all Japanese assets in the US and ended all trade and commerce between the two nations. With the fast-changing world scenario, the US witnessed the emergence of an 'interventionist' group who wanted the country to step in. This group included Jewish refugees as well as others who had fled Germany and the European countries run over by Hitler. They exerted pressure on the US to declare war against Germany. The establishment of the **Freedom House** that declared war in Europe as a struggle between dictatorship and the 'free world' caught the attention of the American public.

Before the country moved into the war, significant changes were brought about in the role and functioning of the national government that eventually led to the establishment of the **War Production Board**, the **War Manpower Commission**, and the **Office of Price Administration**, which was essential to establish structured control over the shipping and manufacturing industries, including regulations for the working classes, fixing of salaries, prices of basic commodities, and rentals. Wartime requirements pushed demand and led to a massive increase in employment, the creation of new jobs, and the issuance of **war bonds** and application income tax directly from weekly paychecks. To boost business corporations further, they were given incentives like low-interest loans, significant tax concessions, and government contracts that ensured profits. These changes, in turn, led to the rise of military-industrial production bolstered by scientific research, and the USA began to produce new types of naval vessels, fighter aircrafts, and weapons. The phenomenal rise of military corporations generated more urban-industrial employment, relegating the rural economy to the background. The South again began to lag behind other parts of the US. The motto of the war was 'Four Freedoms'—freedom from wants, freedom of speech, freedom of religion, and freedom from fear—and it served to unify the nation. The **Office of War Information**, established in 1942, used advertisement and media to generate support for the war. Women, too, began to get employment in great numbers, leading to demands for equality in pay and better job opportunities.

Japanese Aggression

Germany's successes in Europe pushed Japan to become an equally aggressive partner in Southeast Asia. To tackle the growing Japanese aggression, Roosevelt had the Pacific Fleet conduct a naval exercise at the Hawaiian Islands. In the meantime, Japan demanded the handover of French Indochina and extended its demand to the British government to stop supplying aid to China during the Sino-Japanese War. To strengthen its position in Asia, Japan also signed the **Tripartite Pact** with Germany and Italy, which clearly aimed to place hurdles before the US and thereby prevent its entry into the war.

As Japan's intentions became clear, the USA moved to initiate steps to place an economic embargo on Japan. It stopped the sale of scrap material to Japan using the provisions of the National Defense Act. The matter was serious enough for Japan to dispatch its ambassador, Admiral Kichisaburo Nomura, to the US for negotiations. Behind the scenes, however, Japan in 1941 signed a **Nonaggression Treaty** with the Soviet Union. Despite the treaty, when Germany invaded Russia, Japan too began to concentrate its energies on the expansionist conquest of Southeast Asia. The US responded to these developments by imposing sanctions against Japan, including an oil embargo. The federal government also froze all German assets in the US, and ordered the closure of German consulates in the country.

THE AMERICAN ENTRY INTO THE SECOND WORLD WAR

Japan sent a proposal to the US stating that if the latter agreed to stop assisting China and stopped building military bases in China, Thailand, and the Dutch East Indies, and also restored all trade with Japan, then Japan would stop all its military activities in the region of Southeast Asia, including the French Indochina (which would guarantee Philippine's neutrality). The US rejected these offers on 6 December 1941. The next day, on 7 December 1941, Japan bombarded Pearl Harbor, an act termed by Americans as an unlawful 'sneak attack'. On 8 December 1941, Congress declared war on Japan. Responding to these rapid shifts, Germany on 11 December 1941 declared war on the US., This marked the American entry into World War II. The foray into war, albeit late, was forced by the confrontational aggression of Germany, Japan, and Italy. American policymakers were convinced that Germany and Japan could threaten American interests and security in Europe and the Pacific region. At the beginning of the war, Americans were more interested in defeating the Japanese.[14]

The attack on Pearl Harbor, an American naval base in Hawai'i, was a Japanese intelligence failure as US Navy aircraft carriers were not stationed at Pearl Harbor. However, the attack pushed Roosevelt to openly pursue the policy of 'intervention'. Internally and externally, the administration moved to attack Nazi sympathizers, supporters of isolationist policy and anti-Semites in the US. Although the US had allied with the Soviet Union during the war, the federal administration internally began to use its intelligence agencies to limit the communist influence within the country. Roosevelt emphasised that the USA needed to eradicate 'the sources of international brutality completely'. It was important to stop

A History of US Intervention in World Wars I and II 279

FIG. 11.3: The USS *Shaw* explodes as Japan attacks Pearl Harbour (1 December 1941)
Source: Wikimedia Commons.

Japan, which had brought French Indochina, Burma (present-day Myanmar), Siam (present-day Thailand), and the Dutch East Indies, all essential regions of influence, under its control.

Japan took over Guam, the Philippines, and the Pacific Islands and received military assistance from Germany, bringing its submarines to sink Allied merchant and naval ships in the famous **Battle of the Atlantic**. However, the tide began to turn when, in May 1942, in the **Battle of the Coral Sea**, the US Navy forced the Japanese to retreat and stop its invasion of Australia. The Japanese also suffered another defeat in the **Battle of Midway Island**, which helped the US army capture the Guadalcanal islands and the Solomons in the western Pacific region. Americans were more involved in the Pacific than Europe at this stage. The US used its aircraft carriers in 1942 to destroy four Japanese aircraft carriers within this policy framework.

It began to develop better and more powerful warships and aircraft, but despite these technological strides, Japan offered stiff resistance against surrender. From 1943 to 1944, Japan engaged in man-to-man combat on every island that stretched from China and Burma to India, which resulted in enormous losses for the Allied forces. This war in the Pacific region completely changed the nature of naval warfare.

America in Africa and Europe

The combined British and American forces attacked North Africa, defeating the famous German commander Erwin Rommel. Both countries again joined forces to destroy a sizeable fleet of German submarines, and then turned their attention towards Italy, which Germany had overtaken. On 6 June 1944, the combined American, British, and Canadian forces landed at Normandy; they liberated Paris by August of the same year. On the eastern front, Germany had stationed 3 million troops in 1941 and the battle began to take over Stalingrad. However, this ended in a humiliating defeat for Germany in January 1943. This defeat was a turning point in World War II, as Russians defeated the Germans in the **Battle of Kursk**, also known as the greatest tank battle in the military history of the world. The German army lost about ten million soldiers on the Russian front, and this forced Hitler to initiate his final assault, also known as the 'final solution', a campaign of mass slaughter of Jews, Slavs, Romani people, and sexual minorities in the Nazi concentration camps. This came to be known as the **Holocaust**.

In the meantime, with the death of President Roosevelt in March 1945, Harry S. Truman became the President right at the time when the US was approaching a breakthrough in the secret **Manhattan Project**, which aimed to develop nuclear bomb technology. According to some sources, President Truman was told that US forces had two options: either to continue a protracted battle or to invade Japan by dropping a nuclear bomb. Truman accepted the second option, and the first bomb was dropped on Hiroshima on 6 August 1945, followed by another atom bomb on Nagasaki on 9 August 1945. The bombs killed an estimated 150,000–146,000 people, most of whom were civilians, and triggered serious health effects in those who were exposed to radiation as well as their descendents. The bombings led to Emperor Hirohito's declaration of surrender.

Shift in US Foreign Policy

Before and after World War I, US foreign policy was influenced by 'corporatism' or 'associationism', with bankers and exporters who functioned together to take control of overseas markets, backed by the federal government in its quest to compete with European giants and cartels. This policy was the antithesis of 'free enterprise'. However, the federal government still encouraged the acquisition and control of foreign markets and the capture of raw materials, for example oil reserves in West Asia and North Africa that were monopolised by British and French companies. Scholar Joan Hoff Wilson terms this as freedom-of-manoeuvre 'independent internationalism' that assisted in expanding US interests without impacting domestic politics. However, the Great Depression of 1929 led to the collapse of associationism and independent internationalism.

Richard Steele,[15] William E. Leuchtenberg,[16] Robert Dallek,[17] and others believed that till 1940, Roosevelt was more involved with domestic concerns and pursued an isolationist policy. However, when the war broke out in Europe, it became clear that the US would have to enter the war, and the only question was 'when'. When Roosevelt was in his third term, he pushed the USA into war. Scholarly opinion later began to change—Britain released archival records of talks held between Roosevelt and British Prime Minister Winston Churchill in August 1941, three months before the Pearl Harbor incident. In these discussions, Roosevelt declared that the US would support Britain in its war efforts and increase its military supply. Roosevelt also ensured that if this supply were going to be stopped by Germany, it would provide a good pretext for the US to enter the war against Germany.

Historians then began to analyse the reasons for this sudden shift in the US position. They now believe that after World War I, hyper-patriotism in the US led to an increase in supporters of the

Ku Klux Klan (KKK) and the doctrine of the supremacy of the White race. America implemented new immigration laws to keep out the 'outsiders' like Catholics, Jewish people, and people from East and Southeast Asia. Racism had crystallised along the lines of a clear social divide between European Americans on the one hand, and Black, Indigenous, and East Asian people on the other, with the latter being branded as 'savages'. In the US, as in Europe, people from Asia and Africa were cast as 'exotic', 'uncivilised' peoples of the Orient. These racist attitudes influenced foreign policy. Japan, for Roosevelt, represented the worst form of 'human slavery' or 'pagan brutality', and Japanese military generals were described as 'virtually mad dogs', barbarians who wanted to push the world back into the Dark Ages. In American eyes, Japan's expansionist policy was a complete 'violation of fundamental principles of world peace and order' in which the only acceptable imperialism was one driven by Christian idealism. Roosevelt termed the Japanese 'Prussians of the East' and Japan a 'predatory nation' that wanted to dominate the world.

This new foreign policy transformed the global posture of the US, projected itself as a necessary force to stabilise and reform the postwar political and economic order and counter the growing 'threat' of the Soviet Union. By the end of 1950, this attitude had set the pattern for the Cold War. The end of World War II led to a feverish arms race, aid programmes to developing countries as a form of soft power, and the formation of political and military alliances that began to divide the world into two poles.

Conclusion

American popular culture has often referred to World War II as the 'Good War'. For a long time historians only looked at it from the perspective of the Allied victory, which in turn reflected the victory of liberal democracy and free enterprise against authoritarianism and militarism.[18] William Appleman Williams believed that World War II expanded the American frontier, extending the vision of Manifest Destiny, and the atomic bomb became a 'self-starting magic lamp' to herald the beginning of the American century. The war was considered a positive factor for the US economy and military, introducing new war machines and fighting power. Due to mass conscription of men, women took over jobs in multiple sectors. It represented the time of prosperity, morality, and the rise of American power.[19] At the end of the war, international politics revolved around four factors: (*i*) the atomic bomb that the US had developed by bringing together scientists, engineers, and managers to invent a weapon with unlimited destructive capabilities; (*ii*) the rise of communism under Stalin and the growing power of the Soviet Union; (*iii*) the rising and expanding power of the US; and (*iv*) the decline of both Europe and Japan.

The world was now confronted with two ideologically opposed, expansionist superpowers. Having learnt its lesson from the Great Depression, the US now firmly believed that the world's economies were interdependent; therefore, a postwar economic collapse in Europe would be catastrophic for the US as well, and provide an opportunity for the spread of communism. This thinking guided a new military policy known as the **Truman Doctrine**, and political and economic policies were termed the **Marshall Plan**. The Truman Doctrine extended economic and military aid to nearly a hundred countries worldwide.[20]

The war also altered American society and economy. The western states began to play a significant role in war production with the rise of aircraft manufacturing companies, which also became major employers after 1940, supplying the Allied war efforts. One such company was Lockheed, which later expanded its manufacturing centre in Georgia. The Californian shipyards began to develop Liberty Ships, and San Francisco, Los Angeles, San Diego, and Seattle were designated as embarkation points for the Pacific War. General Dynamics was registered with its headquarters in Missouri, and most aerospace industries came up in Texas. The movement towards the West led to a massive increase in the population of these states, fueling urbanisation and the emergence of new industries like tourism and leisure activities. Thus, the wartime period saw economic growth in California, Arizona, and Florida, along with the spectacular development of Miami and Las Vegas. The federal bureaucracy expanded unprecedentedly, more Americans were brought under the income tax net, and massive structural deficits were undertaken during the war. This was the first time after the American Revolution that Americans consented to be taxed to raise funds for war efforts to preserve Britain.[21] The upsurge in urban population sparked tensions, however, with incidents of racial and ethnic violence. The war also led to a rise in incidence of psychological illnesses.

On the home front, with adult men being drafted in the war, factories and offices had to open their doors to women. While this shift had its positive effects in terms of bolstering women's movements, it also placed immense pressure on women, who now had a dual burden of labouring in the formal workforce as well as in the home. The stress of wartime and the fact that children were unattended at home may have contributed to increasing juvenile delinquency. This period also saw a rise in the rate of divorce.[22] In 1940, the federal government introduced conscription and built up a large standing army. The War Board controlled necessary resources and produced war-related material, which had a greater impact on the US economy than the National Recovery Administration (NRA). The government became more involved with prices and wage controls, rationing, consumer protection and labour arbitration. The war also granted the American President **The Second War Powers Act of 1942**, which assisted in declaring a state of emergency.

Propaganda became an important arena of warfare. According to Fletcher Pratt, the **Office of Censorship** controlled public and private communication in the US. The **Office of War Information** produced propaganda that resulted in war being reported as a rightful social imperative. The radio broadcast and its commercials dominated the public imagination. The *Reader's Digest*, which carried stories of optimism, courage, and hope, saw increased circulation. Hollywood movies like *Up in Arms* and *This is the Army* presented to the American audience both escape into a musical world of superheroes, and a means to boost patriotism. What the US public did not see was the violence of the US armed forces, nor was it privy to the worst tendencies of the army, including rampant racism.

'War is inherently destructive—wasteful of human and natural resources, disruptive of normal social development.'[23] War pushed the government to politicise everyday life and assisted in the creation of a leviathan state structure. The government, through its propaganda machine, created a haunting image of Europe surrounded on one side by German National Socialism, and on the other side by Imperial Japan in Asia. The war propelled the rise of a 'warfare state' that tied corporate and New Deal liberalism with nationalism. The role of President Roosevelt's feat of winning four terms in office reflected his ability to stay and legitimise the process of expansion of the powers of the federal government with full consent of the American public.[24]

At the same time, the fact remains that this was an extremely gruesome war. The struggles endured by the nations in the World War II were unprecedented in scale. A new era of postwar modernisation was introduced after this through the application of new technologies (particularly the use of the jet aircraft, which revolutionised warfare and reduced geographical distances, along with the use of the radar, which also changed the manner of fighting wars). World War II and its aftermath indicated the rapidly changing face of war. Modern medicine, for instance, had a transformative effect. Earlier, hunger and illnesses had been responsible for wiping out entire armies. However, the application of the new insecticide DDT now increased agricultural yield, and the invention of the antibiotic penicillin greatly reduced the mortality rate of combatants.[25]

Notes

1. Eric Foner, *Give Me Liberty! An American History*, third ed. (New York, 2011), pp. 715–717.
2. Lloyd E. Ambrosius, *Wilsonianism: Woodrow Wilson and His Legacy in American Foreign Relations* (New York, 2002).
3. Foner, *Give Me Liberty!*, p. 719.
4. Ambrosius, *Wilsonianism*, p. 2.
5. Ibid., p. 5.
6. Arthur S. Link, ed., *Woodrow Wilson and a Revolutionary World. 1931–1921* (Chapel Hill, 1982).
7. William Appleman Williams, *The Contours of American History* (Cleveland, 1961).
8. George F. Kennan, *American Diplomacy, 1900 to 1950*.

9. Norman A. Graebner, *The Versailles Treaty and its Legacy: The Failure of the Wilsonian Vision*, reprinted (New York, 2014).

10. Arno Mayer, *Political Origins of the New Diplomacy, 1917–1918* (Chicago, 1951).

11. Lloyd C. Gardner, *Safe for Democracy: The Anglo-American Response to Revolution, 1913–1923* (New York, 1984).

12. Link, *Woodrow Wilson and a Revolutionary World*.

13. Harry S. Truman, Radio Address to the American People after the Signing of the Terms of Unconditional Surrender by Japan, 1 September 1945. *The American Presidency Project*, available at https://www.presidency.ucsb.edu/documents/radio-address-the-american-people-after-the-signing-the-terms-unconditional-surrender (accessed October 2025).

14. Michael C. C. Adams, *The Best War Ever: America and World War II* (Baltimore, 1994), p. 7.

15. Richard W. Steele, 'The Great Debate: Roosevelt, the Media, and the Coming of the War, 1940–1941', *Journal of American History* 71 (1), 1984, pp. 69–92.

16. William E. Leuchtenberg, *The FDR Years: On Roosevelt and His Legacy* (New York, 1995).

17. Robert Dallek, *Franklin D. Roosevelt and American Foreign Policy, 1932–1945: With a New Afterword* (New York, 1995).

18. Ibid.

19. Ibid., p. 11.

20. Godfrey Hodgson, *An America in Our Time: From World War II to Nixon, What Happened and Why* (New York, 2005).

21. James R. Sparrow, *Warfare State: World War II and the Age of Big Government* (New York, 2011).

22. See Adams, *The Best War Ever*. It is important to note that a rising rate of divorce may be due to a range of factors, from changing religious and cultural attitudes, to incompatibility and postwar trauma, or even increasing financial independence for women (which meant that women could find modes of sustenance outside the framework of marriage).

23. Adams, *The Best War Ever*, p. 12.

24. Sparrow, *Warfare State*, pp. 6–11.

25. David Reynolds, *One World Divisible: A Global History since 1945* (New York, 2000), pp. 9–11.

References

Adams, Michael C. C. 1994. *The Best War Ever: America & World War II*. Baltimore: John Hopkins University Press.
Allen, Richard L. 2001. *The Concept of Self: A Study of Black Identity and Self-Esteem*. Detroit: Wayne State University Press.
Ambrosius, Lloyd E. 2002. *Wilsonianism: Woodrow Wilson and His Legacy in American Foreign Relations*. New York: Palgrave Macmillan.
Argersinger, Peter H. 1995. *The Limits of Agrarian Radicalism: Western Populism and American Politics*. Lawrence, Kansas: University Press of Kansas.
Baptist, Edward. 2014. *The Half Has Never Been Told: Slavery and the Making of American Capitalism*. New York: Basic Books.
Beard, Charles A., and Mary R. Beard. 1927. *The Rise of American Civilization*, vol. 2. New York: Macmillan.
———. 1930. *The Rise of American Civilization: The Industrial Era*. New York: Macmillan.
Beckert, Sven. 2014. *Empire of Cotton: A New History of Global Capitalism*. New York: Knopf.
Beckert, Sven and Christine Desan, ed. 2018. *American Capitalism: New Histories*. New York: Cambridge University Press.
Bemis, Samuel Flagg. 1981. *John Quincy Adams and the Foundations of American Foreign Policy*. New York: Greenwood Heinemann.

Bernstein, Barton J. 1968. 'The New Deal: The Conservative Achievements of Liberal Reform'. In *Towards a New Past: Dissenting Essays in American History*, pp. 263–288. New York: Knopf.

Blight, David W. and Gooding-Williams, Robert. 1997. 'The Strange Meaning of Being Black: Du Bois's American Tragedy'. In *The Souls of Black Folk*, W. E. B. Du Bois, ed. David Blight and Robert Gooding-Williams. Boston: Bedford Books.

Bone, Robert A. 1965. 'The Background of the Negro Renaissance'. In *The Negro Novel in America*, pp. 51–108. New Haven: Yale University Press.

Boyer, Paul S., Clark, Clifford E., Halttunen, Karen, Hawley, Sandra, Kett, and Joseph F. 2001. *Enduring Vision: A History of American People*, vol 2. Boston and New York: Houghton Mifflin Harcourt.

Brinkly, Alan. 1982. 'The New Deal and Southern Politics'. In *The New Deal and the South*, ed. James C. Cobb and Michael V. Namarato, pp. 97–116. Minneapolis: University of Mississippi Press.

Broderick, Francis L. 1959. *W.E.B. Du Bois: Negro Leader in a Time of Crisis*. Stanford: Stanford University Press.

Brody, David. 1980. *Workers in Industrial America: Essays on Twentieth-Century Struggle*. New York: Oxford University Press.

Burns, James MacGregor. 1956. *Roosevelt: The Lion and the Fox*. New York: Harcourt, Brace and Co.

C. Peter Ripley. *Slaves and Freedmen in Civil War Louisiana*. Baton Rouge: Louisiana State University Press. 1976.

Carter, Dan T. 1985. *When the War was Over: The Failure of Self-Reconstruction in the South, 1865–1867*. Baton Rouge: Louisiana State University Press.

Chafe, William H. 1972. *The American Women: Her Changing Economic, Social and Political Role, 1920–1970*. New York: Oxford University Press.

Chandler, Alfred D. 1962. *Strategy and Structure: Chapters in the History of the Industrial Enterprise*. Cambridge, Massachusetts: MIT Press.

———. 1977. *The Visible Hand: The Managerial Revolution in American Business*. Cambridge, Massachusetts: The Belknap Press.

Chip, Berlet, and Matthew N. Lyons. 2000. *Right-Wing Populism in America: Too Close for Comfort*. New York: The Guilford Press.

Clarence L. Mohr. 1986. *On the Threshold of Freedom: Masters and Slaves in Civil War Georgia*. Athens, Georgia: University of Georgia Press.

Cohen, Michael David. 2012. *Reconstructing the Campus: Higher Education and the American Civil War*. Charlottesville: University of Virginia Press.

Combs, Barbara Harris, and Obie Clayton. 2018. 'An Introductory Essay to the Special Volume of *Phylon*'. *Phylon* 55 (1 and 2): 3–8.

Commons, John R. 1921. *History of Labour in the United States*, vol. 1. New York: Macmillan.

Conkin, Paul K. 1967. *The New Deal*. Arlington Heights: AHM.

Conrad, Sebastian. 2016. *What is Global History?* New Jersey: Princeton University Press.

Cooling, B. Franklin. 1979. *Gray Steel and Blue Water Navy: The Formative Years of America's Military-Industrial Complex, 1881–1917*. Hamden, Conn.: Archon Books.

Corey, Lewis. 2012. *The Decline of American Civilization*. Delhi: Cosimo Classics.

Crapol, Edward P. 1992. 'Coming to Terms with Empire: The Historiography of Late-19th Century American Foreign Relations'. *Diplomatic History* 16 (4): 573–597.

Cripps, Thomas. 1993. *Slow Fade to Black: The Negro in American Film, 1900–1942*. New York: Oxford University Press.

Dallek, Robert. 1995. *Franklin D. Roosevelt and American Foreign Policy, 1932–1945: With a New Afterword*. New York: Oxford University Press.

Davis, Angela. 1972. 'Reflections on Black Women's Role in the Community of Slaves'. *The Massachusetts Review* 13 (1/2), pp. 81–100. Available at https://palmm.digital.flvc.org/islandora/object/ucf%3A4865 (accessed October 2025).

Davis, Ronald L. F. 1982. *Good and Faithful Labour: From Slavery to Sharecropping in the Natchez District, 1860–1890*. New York: Greenwood Press.

Dawley, Alan. 1976. *Class and Community: The Industrial Revolution in Lynn*. Cambridge, Massachusetts: Harvard University Press.

———. 1985. 'Paths to Power after the Civil War'. In *Working for Democracy: American Workers from the Revolution to the Present*, ed. Paul Buhle and Alan Dawley. Madison: University of Illinois Press, pp. 41–51.

Diana Paton. 2022. 'Gender History, Global History, and Atlantic Slavery: On Racial Capitalism and Social Reproduction'. *The American Historical Review* 127 (2): 726–754.

Du Bois, W. E. B. 1926. 'The Shape of Fear'. *The North Atlantic Review* 223 (831): 291–304.

———. 1933. 'Marxism and the Negro Problem'. *Crisis* 40 (5): 103–104, 118.

———. 1935. *Black Reconstruction in America: An Essay Towards a History of the Part Which Black Folk Played in the Attempt to Reconstruct Democracy in America, 1860–1880*. New York: Harcourt, Brace and Co.

———. 1940. *Dusk of Dawn: An Essay Toward an Autobiography of a Race Concept*. New York: Harcourt, Brace and Co.

Dublin, Thomas. 1979. *Women at Work: The Transformation of Work and Community in Lowell, Massachusetts, 1826–1860*. New York: Columbia University Press.

Dubofsky, Melvyn. 1994. *The State and Labor in Modern America*. Chapel Hill: University of North Carolina.

———. 1996. *Industrialism and the American Worker, 1865–1920*, 3rd ed. Wheeling, Illinois: Herlan Davidson, Inc.

Dunning, William A. 1904. *Essays on the Civil War and Reconstruction and Related Topics*, 2nd ed. University of Michigan Press.

Eisenstein, Sarah. 1983. *Give us Bread but Give us Roses: Working Women's Consciousness in the United States: 1840 to First World War*. New York: Routledge.

Essien-Udom, E. U. 1962. *Black Nationalism*. Chicago: University of Chicago Press.

Eulau, Heinz. 1959–1960. 'Neither Ideology nor Utopia: The New Deal in Retrospect'. *Antioch Review* 19 (Winter): 523–537.

Faulkner, Harold Underwood. 1960. *American Economic History*. 8th ed. New York: Harper & Row.

Ferguson, Thomas. 1984. 'From Normalcy to New Deal: Industrial Structure, Party Competition, and American Public Policy in the Great Depression'. *International Organization* 38 (1): 41–94.

Flynn, John T. 1956. *The Roosevelt Myth*, revised ed. New York: The Devin-Adair Company.

Foner, Eric, ed. 1997. *The New American History*, revised and expanded edition, Philadelphia: Temple University Press.

Foner, Eric. 1988. *Reconstruction: America's Unfinished Revolution, 1863–1877*. New York: Harper and Row.

———. 2005. *Forever Free: The Story of Emancipation and Reconstruction*. New York: Vintage Books.

———. 2011. *Give Me Liberty! An American History*, 3rd ed. New York: W. W. Norton & Co.

Fox-Genovese, Elizabeth. 1988. *Within the Plantation Household: Black and White Women of the Old South*. Chapel Hill, NC: University of North Carolina Press.

Frederici, Silvia. 2004. *Caliban and the Witch: Women, the Body, and Primitive Accumulation*. New York: Penguin.

Freedman, Estelle B. 1997. 'The History of Family and the History of Sexuality'. From *The New American History*, ed. Eric Foner, revised and expanded edition, pp. 285–305. Philadelphia: Temple University Press.

Friedel, Frank. 1952–1973. *Franklin D. Roosevelt*, 4 vols. Boston: Little Brown.

Gardner, Charles M. 1950. *The Grange, Friend of the Farmer: A Concise Reference History of America's Oldest Farm Organization, and the Only Rural Fraternity in the World, 1867–1947*. Washington, DC: Washington National Grange.

Gardner, Lloyd C. 1984. *Safe for Democracy: The Anglo-American Response to Revolution, 1913–1923*. New York: Oxford University Press.

Gerber, D. A. 1980–1981. 'A Politics of Limited Options: Northern Black Politics and the Problem of Change and Continuity in Race Relations Historiography', *Journal of Social History* 14: 235–255.

———. 1980–1981. 'A Politics of Limited Options: Northern Black Politics and the Problem of Change and Continuity in Race

Relations Historiography'. *Journal of Social History* 14 (2): 235–255.

Gerd, Horten. 2002. *Radio Goes to War: The Cultural Politics of Propaganda during World War II*. Berkeley: University of California Press.

Goldfield, Michael. 1993. 'Race and the CIO: The Possibilities for Racial Egalitarianism during the 1930s and 1940s'. *International Labor and Working-Class History* 44: 1–32.

Goodwyn, Lawrence. 1978. *The Populist Moment: A Short History of the Agrarian Revolt in America*. New York: Oxford University Press.

Gordon, Colin. 1994. *New Deals: Business, Labour, and Politics in America, 1920–1935*. New York: Cambridge University Press.

Gordon, Linda. 1990. *Woman's Body, Woman's Right: A Social History of Birth Control in America*, 2nd ed. New York: Penguin.

———. 1994. *Pitied But Not Entitled: Single Mothers and the History of Welfare*. New York: Free Press.

Graebner, Norman A. 2014. *The Versailles Treaty and its Legacy: The Failure of the Wilsonian Vision*, reprint ed. New York: Cambridge University Press.

———. 1985. *Foundations of American Foreign Policy: A Realist Appraisal from Franklin to McKinley*. Wilmington: Scholarly Resources Inc.

Gutman, Herbert G. 1976. *The Black Family in Slavery and Freedom, 1750-1925*. New York: Pantheon.

———. 1977. *Work, Culture, and Society in Industrialising America: Essays in American Working-Class History*. New York: Vintage.

Hacker, Louis M. 1947. *The Shaping of the American Tradition*. New York: Columbia University Press.

Harding, Vincent. 1981. *There is a River: The Black Struggle for Freedom in America*. New York: Harcourt.

Hardy, Sheila and Hardy, P. Stephen. 2007. *Extraordinary People of the Civil Rights Movement*. Washington, DC: Library of Congress.

Harold Underwood Faulkner. 1960. *American Economic History*, eighth edition. New York: Harper and Row.

Harrison, Alferdteen. 1991. *Black Exodus: The Great Migration from the American South*. Minneapolis: Mississippi University Press.

Hawkins, Hugh. 1962, *Booker T. Washington and His Critics: The Problem of Negro Leadership*. Boston: D.C. Heath.

Hawley, Ellis. 1996. *The New Deal and the Problem of Monopoly: A Study in Economic Ambivalence*. Princeton: Princeton University Press.

Hays, Samuel P. 1957. *The Response to Industrialism, 1885–1914*. Chicago: University of Chicago Press.

Healey, Joseph F. 2007. *Diversity and Society: Race, Ethnicity, and Gender*. California: Pine Forge Press.

Henry Demarest Lloyd. 1894. *Wealth Against Commonwealth*. New York: Harper and Co.

Hicks, John Donald. 1931. *The Populist Revolt: A History of the Farmer's Alliance and the People's Party*. Minneapolis: University of Minnesota Press.

Hodgson, Godfrey. 2005. *An America in Our Time: From World War II to Nixon, What Happened and Why*. New Jersey: Princeton University Press.

Hofstadter, Richard. 1955. *The Age of Reform: From Byran to FDR*. New York: Knopf.

Holt, Thomas C. 1990. 'The Political Uses of Alienation: W. E. B. Du Bois on Politics, Race, and Culture, 1903–1940'. *American Quarterly* 42 (2): 301–323.

Horten, Gerd. 2002. *Radio Goes to War: The Cultural Politics of Propaganda during World War II*. Berkeley: University of California Press.

Hummel, Jeffery R. 1996. *Emancipating Slaves, Enslaving Free Men: A History of the American Civil War*. Chicago: Open Court.

James, C. L. R. 1963. *The Black Jacobins: Toussaint L'Ouverture and the San Domingo Revolution*, 2nd revised ed. New York: Vintage Books.

James, Selma. 2012. *Sex, Race and Class: The Perspective of Winning, a Selection of Writings, 1952–1981*. Oakland: PM Press.

Jayne, Gerald. 1986. *Branches without Roots: Genesis of the Black Working Class in the American South, 1862–1882*. New York: Oxford University Press.

Jeffrey O. G. 2019. *Black Power: Radical Politics and African American Identity*, revised ed. Baltimore: John Hopkins University Press.

Jensen, Joan M. 1986. *Loosening the Bonds: Mid-Atlantic Farm Women, 1750–1850*. New Haven: Yale University Press.

Johnson, Walter. 1967. *River of Dark Dreams: Slavery and Empire in the Cotton Kingdom*. Cambridge, Massachusetts: Belknap Press.

Josephson, Matthew. 1934. *The Robber Barons: The Great American Capitalists, 1861–1901*. New York: Harcourt, Brace and Co.

Karl, Barry D. 1963. *Executive Reorganization and Reform in the New Deal: The Genesis of Administrative Management, 1900–1939*. Chicago: University of Chicago Press.

Kaysen, Carl, and Donald F. Turner. 1959. *Antitrust Policy*. Boston: Harvard University Press.

Kennan, George F. 1951. *American Diplomacy, 1900 to 1950*. Chicago: University of Chicago Press.

Kerber, Linda. 1988. 'Separate Spheres, Female Worlds, Women's Place: The Rhetoric of Women's History. *Journal of American History* 75 (1): 9–39.

Kersten, Andrew E., and Clarence Lang. 2015. *Reframing Randolph: Labor, Black Freedom, and the Legacies of A. Philip Randolph*, vol. 12. New York: NYU Press.

Kessler-Harris, Alice. 2003. *Out to Work: A History of Wage-Earning Women in the United States*. New York: Oxford University Press.

Keyssar, Alexander. 1986. *Out of Work: The First Century of Unemployment in Massachusetts*. New York: Cambridge University Press.

Kirby, John B. 1980. *Black Americans in the Roosevelt Era: Liberalism and Race*. Knoxville: University of Tennessee Press.

Klare, Karl E. 1978. 'Judicial Deradicalization of the Wagner Act and the Origins of Modern Legal Consciousness, 1937–1941'. *Minnesota Law Review* 65: 265–239.

Kleinberg, S. J. 1999. *Women in the United States, 1830–1945*. New York: Macmillian.

Klepp, Susan, et al. 1992. *The Unfortunate: The Voyage and Adventures of William Moraley, an Indentured Servant*. Philadelphia: Pennsylvania State University Press.

Kolko, Gabriel. 1963. *The Triumph of Conservatism: A Reinterpretation of American History, 1900–1916*. Chicago: Quadrangle Books.

Kraditor, Aileen S. 1981. *The Ideas of the Women Suffrage Movement, 1890–1920*. New York: W. W. Norton & Co.

LaFeber, Walter. 1998. *The New Empire: An Interpretation of American Expansion, 1868–1898*. New York: Cornell University Press.

Leff, Mark. 1994. *The Limits of Symbolic Reform: The New Deal and Taxation, 1933–1939*. New York: Basic Books.

Lester, Connie L. 2006. *Up from the Mudsills of Hell: The Farmers' Alliance, Populism and Progressive Agriculture in Tennessee, 1870–1915*. Athens: University of Georgia Press.

Leuchtenberg, William E. 1995. *The FDR Years: On Roosevelt and His Legacy*. New York: Columbia University Press.

———. 1963. *Franklin D. Roosevelt and the New Deal, 1932–1940*. New York: Harper & Row.

Levine, Bruce. 2013. *The Fall of the House of Dixie: The Civil War and the Social Revolution That Transformed the South*. New York: Random House.

Levine, Daniel. 1962. 'The Social Philosophy of Albert J. Beveridge'. *Indiana Magazine of History* 58 (2): 101–116. Available at https://www.jstor.org/stable/27788983 (accessed October 2025).

Lincoln, Charles Eric. 1960. 'The Black Muslims in the United States', dissertation submitted to the Boston University.

Link, Arthur S., and Richard L. McCormick. 1983. *Progressivism*. Arlington Heights, Illinois: Harlan Davidson.

Link, Arthur S., ed. 1982. *Woodrow Wilson and a Revolutionary World, 1931–1921*. Chapel Hill: University of North Carolina Press.

Locke, Alain. 1925. *The New Negro: An Interpretation*. New York: Albert and Charles Boni.

Maggor, Noam. 2017. 'To Coddle and Caress These Great Capitalists: Eastern Money, Frontier Populism, and the Politics of Market Making in the American West'. *American Historical Review* 122 (1): 55–84.

Marable, Manning, Charles Lemert, and Cheryl Townsend Gilkes. 2016. *The Souls of Black Folk: W.E.B Du Bois*, 100th anniversary ed. New York: Routledge.

Mayer, Arno J. 1951. *American Diplomacy, 1900–1950*. Chicago and London: University of Chicago Press.

McGerr, Michael E. 1986. *The Decline of Popular Politics: The American North, 1865–1928*. New York: Oxford University Press

———. 2005. *A Fierce Discontent: The Rise and Fall of the Progressive Movement in America*. New York: Oxford University Press.

Meier, August. 1980. *Negro Thought in America, 1880–1915*. Ann Arbor: University of Michigan Press.

Menand, Louis. 2001. *The Metaphysical Club*, 1st ed. New York: Farrar, Straus and Giroux.

Mies, Maria. 1998. *Patriarchy and Accumulation on a World Scale: Women in the International Division of Labour*, reprint ed. London: Zed Books.

Misa, Thomas J. 1995. *A Nation of Steel: The Making of Modern America, 1865–1925*. Baltimore: The John Hopkins University Press.

Montgomery, David. 1993. *Citizen Worker: The Experience of Workers in the United States with Democracy and the Free Market during the Nineteenth Century*. New York: Cambridge University Press.

Moore, Albert. 1943. 'One Hundred Years of Reconstruction of the South'. *Journal of Southern History* 9: 153–165.

Morris, Thomas. 1996. *Southern Slavery and the Law, 1619–1860*. Chapel Hill: University of North Carolina Press.

Mowry, George E. 1958. *The Era of Theodore Roosevelt*. New York: Hamish Hamilton.

Myers, Gustavus. 1910. *History of the Great American Fortunes*, vols 1 and 2. Chicago: Charles H. Kerr & Company.

Myrdal, Gunnar. 1962. *An America Dilemma: The Negro Problem and Modern Democracy*. New York: Harper and Row.

Neimi Jr., Albert W. 1980. *U.S. Economic History*. Chicago: Rand McNally Publishing Company.

Nevins, Allen. 1940. *John D. Rockefeller, The Heroic Age of American Enterprise*, 2 vols. New York.

———. 1953. *Study in Power: John D. Rockefeller, Industrialist and Philanthropist*, 2 vols. New York.

Noble, David F. 1977. *America by Design: Science, Technology, and the Rise of Corporate Capitalism*. New York.

Nye, David E. 1991. *Electrifying America: Social Meanings of a New Technology, 1880–1940*. Cambridge, Massachusetts: MIT Press.

Oghar, Jeffrey O. G. 2019. *Black Power: Radical Politics and African American Identity*, revised ed. Baltimore: John Hopkins University Press.

Ojha, Archana. 2025. *History of the United States of America: From Independence to the Civil War*. New Delhi: Orient BlackSwan.

Parrington, Vernon L. 1927. *Main Currents in American Thought: An Interpretation of American Literature from the Beginning to 1920*, vol. 3, 1860–1920: The Beginnings of Critical Realism in America. New York: Harcourt, Brace and Co.

Patterson, James T. 1967. *Congressional Conservatism and the New Deal: The Growth of the Conservative Coalition in Congress, 1933–1939*. Lexington: University Press of Kentucky.

Polakoff, Keith I. 1973. *The Politics of Inertia: The Election of 1876 and the End of Reconstruction*. Baton Rouge: Louisiana State University Press.

Postel, Charles. 2007. *The Populist Vision*. New York: Oxford University Press.

Powell, Lawrence N. 1999. *New Masters: Northern Planters during the Civil War and Reconstruction*. Fordham University Press.

Purcell, Jr., Edward A. 1967. 'Ideas and Interests: Businessmen & the Interstate Commerce Act'. *Journal of American History* 54 (3): 561–578.

Quadagno, Jill S. 1988. *The Transformation of Old Age Security: Class and Politics in the American Welfare State*. Chicago: University of Chicago Press.

Radosh, Ronald. 1972. 'The Myth of the New Deal'. In *A New History of the Leviathan*, ed. Ronald Radosh and Murray Rothbard, pp. 146–187. New York: Dutton.

Ransome, Roger L., and Richard Sutch. 2001. *One Kind of Freedom: The Economic Consequences of Emancipation*, reprint ed. New York: Cambridge University Press.

Rayford W. Logan. 1967. *The Betrayal of the Negro: From Rutherford B. Hayes to Woodrow Wilson*. 2nd edition. New York: Collier Books.

Reynolds, David. 2000. *One World Divisible: A Global History Since 1945*. New York: Norton.

Rhode, Paul W. and Richard Sutch. 2006. Table CA192–207, 'Gross national product: 1869–1909 [Gallman]', in *Historical Statistics of the United States, Earliest Times to the Present: Millenial Edition*, edited by Susan B. Carter, et al. New York:

Roark, James L. 1973. *Masters without Slaves: Southern Planters in the Civil War and Reconstruction*. Stanford University.

Roediger, David R. 1994. *Towards the Abolition of Whiteness: Essays on Race, Politics and Working Class History*. London and New York: Verso.

———. 2014. *Seizing Freedom: Slave Emancipation and Liberty For All*. New York: Verso.

Rogin, Michael. 1962. 'Voluntarism: The Political Functionals of an Antipolitical Doctrine', *ILR Review* 15 (4): 521–535.

Rose, William Lee. 1976. *Rehearsal for Reconstruction: The Port Royal Experiment*. New York: Oxford University Press.

Ross, Edward Alsworth. 1907. *Sin and Society: An Analysis of Latter-Day Iniquity*. Boston and New York: Houghton Mifflin Company.

Rothbard, Murray N. 2002. *A History of Money and Banking in the United States: The Colonial Era to World War II*. Auburn, Alabama: Ludwig Von Mises Institute.

———. 2009. *Man, Economy and the State*, 2nd ed. Auburn: Ludwig von Mises Institute.

Schatz, Ronald W. 1983. *The Electrical Workers: A History of Labor at General Electric and Westinghouse, 1923–1960*. Urbana: University of Illinois Press.

Schlesinger, Arthur M., Jr. 1957–1960. *The Age of Roosevelt*, 3 vols. Boston: Houghton Mifflin.

———. 1986. *The Cycles of American History*. Boston: Houghton Mifflin.

Schulman, Bruce. 1991. *From Cotton Belt to Sunbelt: Federal Policy, Economic Development, and the Transformation of the South, 1938–1980*. New York: Oxford University Press.

Simkins, Francis B. 1932. *South Carolina during Reconstruction*. Chapel Hill: University of North Carolina Press.

Simons, Algie Martin. 1929. *Production Management: Control of Men, Material and Machines*. Chicago: American Technical Society.
Sitkoff, Harvard. 1985. *Fifty Years Later: The New Deal Evaluated*. New York: Knopf.
Sklar, Martin. 1992. *The United States as a Developing Country*. New York: Cambridge University Press.
Skocpol, Theda. 1992. *Protecting Soldiers and Mothers: The Political Origins of Social Policy in the United States*. Cambridge, Massachusetts: Harvard University Press.
Slez, Adam. 2020. *The Making of the Populist Movement: State, Market and Party on Western Frontier*. New York: Oxford University Press.
Smith-Rosenberg, Carroll. 1975. 'The Female World of Love and Ritual: Relations between Women in Nineteenth-Century America'. *Signs* 1 (1): 1–29.
Sparrow, James T. 2011. *Warfare State: World War II & The Age of Big Government*. New York: Oxford University Press.
Stampp, Kenneth M. 1965. *The Era of Reconstruction: 1865–1977*. New York: Vintage.
Staughton, Lynd, ed. 1967. *Reconstruction*. New York: Harper and Row.
Steele, Richard W. 1984. 'The Great Debate: Roosevelt, the Media, and the Coming of the War, 1940–1941'. *The Journal of American History* 71 (1): 69–92.
Summers, Mark W. 1984. *Railroads, Reconstruction, and the Gospel of the Radical Republicans 1865–1877*. New Jersey: Princeton University Press.
Terrill, Robert. 2010. *The Cambridge Companion to Malcolm X*, 3rd reprint. New York: Cambridge University Press.
Thorstein Veblen. 1902. *The Theory of Leisure Class: An Economic Study of Institutions*. New York: Macmillan.
———. 1932. *The Theory of Business Enterprise*. New York: Charles Scribner's Sons.
Tipple, John. 1959. 'The Anatomy of Prejudice: Origins of the Robber Baron Legend'. *Business History Review* 33 (4): 510–523.

Tomlins, Christopher. 2010. *Freedom Bound: Law, Labor, and Civic Identity in Colonizing English America, 1580–1865*. New York: Cambridge University Press.

Tucker, Barbara M. 1984. *Samuel Slater and the Origins of the American Textile Industry, 1790–1860*. New York: Cornell University Press.

Tugwell, Rexford G. 1992. *The Diary of Rexford G. Tugwell: The New Deal, 1932–1935*. New York: Greenwood.

Vincent, Theodore G. 1976. *Black Power and the Garvey Movement*. San Francisco: Ramparts.

Vogel, Todd, ed. 2001. *The Black Press: New Literary and Historical Essays*. New Brunswick, New Jersey and London: Rutgers University Press.

Walter, Licht. 1995. *Industrializing America: The Nineteenth Century*. Baltimore and London: John Hopkins University Press.

Watkins, Marilyn P. 1996. *Rural Democracy: Family Farmers and Politics Western Washington, 1890–1925*. New York: Cornell University.

Weiss, Nancy J. 1983. *Farewell to the Party of Lincoln: Black Politics in the Age of FDR*. Princeton, N.J.: Princeton University Press.

Welter, Barbara. 1966. 'The Cult of True Womanhood: 1820–1860'. *American Quarterly* 18 (2): 151–174.

White, Deborah Gray. 1999. *Ar'n't I A Woman? Female Slaves in the Plantation South*. New York: W.W. Norton & Co.

White, John. 1985. *Black Leadership in America 1895–1968*. New York: Longman.

Whitfield, Stephen J., ed. 2004. *A Companion to 20th-Century America*. New York: Blackwell Publishing.

Wiebe, Robert H. 1967. *The Search for Order, 1877–1920*. New York: Hill & Wang.

William R. Leach. 1993. *Land of Desire: Merchants, Power and the Rise of a New American Culture*. New York: Vintage Books.

Williams, Eric. 1967. *Capitalism and Slavery*. New York: Capricorn Books.

Williams, William Appleman. 1961. *The Contours of American History*. Cleveland: W. W. Norton and Co.

———. 1969. *The Roots of the Modern American Empire*. New York: W. W. Norton and Co.

———. *The Tragedy of American Diplomacy*. W.W. Norton & Company. 2012.

Williamson, Joel. 1965. *After Slavery: The Negro in South Carolina During Reconstruction, 1861–1877*. Chapel Hill: The University of North Carolina Press.

Wilson, Joan Hoff. 1971. *American Business and Foreign Policy, 1920–1933*. Kentucky: University of Kentucky Press.

Woloch, Nancy. 1984. *Women and the American Experience*. New York: McGraw-Hill.

Woodward, C. Van. 1960. *The Burden of Southern History*. Baton Rouge: Louisiana State University Press, 1960.

———. 1974. *The Strange Career of Jim Crow*, 3rd revised ed. New York: Oxford University Press.

X, Malcolm and Alex Haley. 2001. 'From The Autobiography of Malcolm X'. In *Writing New England: An Anthology from the Puritans to the Present*, ed. Andrew Delbanco. Cambridge, MA and London, England: Harvard University Press, pp. 402–415.

Zinn, Howard, ed. 1966. *New Deal Thought*. Indianapolis: Bobbs-Merrill.

Index

381-day boycott of the Montgomery Bus company 205
1934 Securities and Exchange Commission 143

abolitionism 162–63, 236, 239
abolitionist movement 163, 173, 238, 240
Act of Secession 23
Adamson Act 134
African American movement 9, 37, 161, 169, 183, 186, 190, 197, 212
African American Vernacular English (AAVE) 171
African Communities League 193
African Methodist Episcopal Church (AME) 162, 164
age of industrialisation 89
agricultural
　economy 115, 122, 139, 144, 225–27
　labour/labourers 34, 47, 119
　practices 115, 121
　produce 34, 117, 140
　production 5, 36, 74, 144
Agricultural Adjustment Act (AAA), 1933 142, 144, 148, 156
agriculture 36, 65, 101–03, 114, 135, 144, 177, 225–28
Alabama Christian Movement 209

America. *See also* United States of America (USA)
　as a naval power 13
　corporate power in 125
　industrial progress in 54
　nineteenth-century 104
　political upheaval in 123
　transformation of 123
American Civil War (1861–1865) 1
American Colonization Society (ACS) 162–63
American Communist Party 201
American Federation of Labour (AFL) 7, 91–97, 134, 151, 202, 245
American Negro Academy 186
American(s)
　capitalism 8, 54, 152, 228, 253
　economy 66, 70, 74, 104, 151, 157, 225, 252
　exceptionalism 264
　expansionism 251, 253–54
　history 4, 21, 43, 75, 84, 111, 113, 221, 252
　imperialism 13, 55, 251, 260, 262
　labour/labourer 76, 80, 89, 95–96, 99, 122
　middle class/middle-class 98, 122, 135
　politics 14, 112, 131, 136

revolution 78, 122, 153, 228, 233, 284
society 2, 9, 11, 50, 56, 60, 67, 70, 109, 112, 183, 213, 221, 283
woman/women 11, 110, 152, 223, 226, 235, 238–39, 241, 244
Ancient Order of Hibernians (AOH) 86
anti-Black
   bias 37, 132
   mobilisation 184
   riots 184
anti-communist movement 10
Anti-Saloon League 123, 128
anti-slavery movement 165
anti-strike associations 93
Arkansas 3, 23, 30
Atlanta 37, 54, 178–79, 186, 196, 204, 207
Atlanta Compromise 178–79
atom bomb/atomic bomb 280, 282–83

'Back to Africa' 171, 190
balance of power 261, 271
bank/banking 8, 29, 56, 60–61, 65, 68, 112, 114, 119–20, 131–32, 139–42, 147, 165, 254, 262, 265
Banking Act of 1935 151
bankruptcy 44, 120, 139
Battle of Britain in 1940–1941 275
Battle of Kursk 280
Battle of Midway Island 279
Battle of the Coral Sea 279
Beef Trust 130
Bering Sea Controversy 256
Big business(es) 4, 53–54, 56–58, 60, 63, 71, 74, 87–89, 93–95, 112–13, 124, 131–32, 135, 181, 254
   corporations 4, 53, 56, 89, 113, 124, 132, 135, 181
   organisations 54, 63, 74, 131, 254

Bituminous Coal Labour Board 149
Black
   citizens 2–4, 9, 27, 38, 174, 203
   community(ies) 9, 11, 31, 36–37, 39, 127, 152, 161, 166–67, 169, 171, 177, 183–87, 191, 193, 195–96, 214, 218, 220–21
   economy 166, 172, 185, 190
   education 49, 177
   identity 9, 163, 171
   movement 182, 188
   nationalism 171, 195–97, 219
   organisations 202, 204, 216
   political rights 172, 175
   politics 48, 187
   power 10–11, 163, 192, 197, 201, 213–14, 216
   prisoners 9, 38, 66
   separatism 164, 197, 218
   soldiers 165, 203, 218
Black America 170, 192
Black churches 31, 36, 47, 166, 206, 209, 241
Black Codes 3, 19, 24–26, 47, 165, 175
Black community(ies) 9, 11, 31, 36–37, 39, 127, 152, 161, 166–67, 169, 171, 177, 183–87, 191, 193, 195–96, 214, 218, 220–21
Black labour/labourer 17, 24–25, 31, 35, 47–48, 176, 193, 229
Black leader/leadership 9, 48, 163, 168–69, 179–82, 184, 186, 197, 211, 220
Black Muslim movement/community 11, 217
Black Nationalist Organisation 218
Black Panther Party 216
Black Party 201
Black rights 10, 31, 163, 164, 167–68, 175, 202–03, 212–13, 221
   movement 167, 213, 222
Black voters 20, 26, 32, 123, 173, 202, 207–08
   disenfranchisement of 20, 123, 173

304 Index

Black-White relations 187
Black women 11–12, 34, 39, 47, 126, 164, 180, 228–34, 239–41, 243, 248
   enslavement of 228
   entry in the public space 39
Black workers 15, 25, 34, 37, 41, 47, 88, 90–93, 97, 169, 175, 178, 202
Black youth 183, 213, 221
blitzkrieg 275
Bloody Sunday (7 March 1965) 212
Boer War 257
boycott(s) 10–11, 134, 172, 204–06, 214
Britain 6, 13, 54, 130, 232, 255–57, 259, 262, 264, 267–68, 275–76, 281, 284. *See also* United Kingdom (UK)
Brotherhood of Sleeping Car Porters (BSCP) 202, 205
Bureau of Corporations 130
Bureau of Refugees, Freedmen and Abandoned Lands 25
Burma (Myanmar) 279, 280
business(es)
   development 179, 191, 252
   interests 153, 251
   practices 67, 68, 112, 129, 133, 146
   retail 61, 165

capitalism 8, 15, 44, 54, 60–61, 67, 69–71, 78, 90–91, 97, 99, 103, 121, 124, 141, 152, 155, 157, 191, 196–97, 225, 228, 253, 265, 273
   American 8, 54, 152, 228, 253
   Black 191, 197
   consumer 60, 67
   corporate 8, 71
   industrial 44, 54, 69, 78, 121
   mercantile 225
   slavery 228
   welfare 99
capitalistic system 87, 93
care work 101, 234

carpetbagger(s) 3, 27–29, 31, 41–42, 44, 46
cases
   Brown v. Board of Education 204
   Plessy v. Ferguson 9, 39, 175
central America 194, 256, 266
central Europe 271
chattel slavery 5, 30
Chautauqua Movement 127
China 253–54, 260–61, 274, 276–78, 280
Chinese Exclusion Act, 1882 81
Christianity 204, 207, 210
Churchill, Winston, British Prime minister 281
citizenship 3, 20, 26, 50–51, 61, 183, 238, 275
   rights 3, 20, 51, 183, 275
civil disobedience movement 11, 206
Civilian Conservation Corps (CCC) 142, 146, 245
civil rights 2, 4, 12, 21, 31, 39–40, 45, 49–50, 163–64, 172–73, 188, 192, 197, 201–03, 205–09, 211, 219, 241, 248
   violations 4, 49
Civil Rights Act(s) 4, 9, 19, 21, 25–27, 29, 37, 49, 54, 165, 211–12, 215, 248, 275
   Act of 1866 4, 19, 25
   Act of 1875 9, 27, 37
   Act of 1964 211, 248
Civil Rights Movement 10–11, 36, 44, 152, 169, 186, 213–14, 247–48
Civil War 1–4, 12, 17–22, 24, 27–28, 30, 34–36, 38, 42–43, 48–50, 53–54, 64, 67, 70, 78–79, 83–84, 103, 114, 116–17, 120, 128, 161–65, 175, 189, 232–35, 239–42, 260
   aftermath of the 53, 241
   consequences of the 3
   end of the 1, 17, 21
Civil Works Administration (CWA) 146, 245

Index 305

class(es)
  business 136, 146, 181
  capitalist 76, 84, 87
  conflicts 255
  consumer 74, 141, 145
  labouring 6, 10, 79, 87–88, 95
  middle 61, 86, 98, 122, 124, 126, 128, 135–36, 155, 179, 182, 187, 191, 201, 204, 233
  planter 2–3, 30–31, 254
  professional 61–62
  upper/upper- 91, 205, 233–34, 248
Clayton Act 67, 133–34
Clayton Antitrust Act of 1914 133
Clayton-Bulwer Treaty of 1850 133, 255
clergy 128, 135, 207, 239
Cleveland, Grover, US President 54, 113, 130, 239, 256
Cold War 247, 282
collectivisation 7, 79, 116
colonial era/period 5, 11, 50, 77
colonialism 75, 228
colonisation 76, 163, 180, 227
Colored Convention Movement 165
Colored Farmers' National Alliance and Cooperative Union 116
commercialisation 102, 109, 135
Commodity Credit Corporation 142
commodity(ies) 57, 61–62, 76, 88, 94, 121, 145, 149, 232, 274, 276
  agricultural 145, 149
  essential 88, 94
  production 145
communism 79, 272–73, 275, 283
Communist Party of America 190
companies 54, 56–61, 63–64, 66, 75, 99, 103, 112, 116–17, 119, 130, 146–47, 151, 165, 180, 195, 225, 244, 281, 283
  buying and selling of 151
  holding 56, 58, 64
  monopolistic 56, 63, 146
  railroad 54, 56, 63, 66, 112, 116, 119, 130

Compensated Emancipation Act of 1862 21
Compromise of 1877 20
concentration camps 13, 258, 275, 280
Confederacy 1, 18, 23–24
Confederates 22, 26, 38
Confederate States of America 22
Confederation of American States 256
Congress of Industrial Organization (CIO) 148, 151, 202, 246
Congress of Racial Equality (CORE) 11, 203–04, 209, 211, 213–14, 216, 221
consciousness 6, 78, 82, 92, 94, 98, 101, 103, 106, 108–09, 110, 156, 170, 188, 191, 194, 197, 203, 222, 225
  class 6, 94, 98, 103, 156
  labour 78, 101, 108, 110, 225
  political 194, 203, 222
conservatism 44, 151–53, 214, 221
conservatives 10, 124, 154
constitutional rights 129, 175, 236
consumer(s) 57–62, 67, 74, 89, 106, 125, 129, 141–42, 145, 148, 234, 264, 284
  capitalism 60, 67
  economy 148, 264
  protection 125, 129, 284
Continental Congress of the American Working Class 96
convict lease system 164
Coolidge, Calvin, US President 153, 196
cooperative movement 118, 122, 190
Corporate Patent Agreement 59
corruption 4, 27, 29, 40, 42, 44, 48, 67, 112–13, 124–25, 128
Cotton Trust 64
Council of National Defense 269
credit 5–6, 34, 48, 56, 60, 62, 114, 117–18, 125, 134, 225
  availability of 5

crop-lien system 34, 65
Cuba 13–14, 253, 258–59, 264, 267, 274
Cullen-Harrison Act of 1933 141
culture 14, 53, 60–62, 80, 93, 101, 103, 121–22, 157, 166, 169, 171–72, 185, 191, 220, 223, 227, 233, 235, 282
  African American 169, 185
  American 169, 185, 191
  Black 171–72
  folk 171
  patriarchal 101, 223

Declaration of London 268
Declaration of the Rights of the Negro Peoples of the World 196
Deep South 18, 228
democracy 29, 45, 61, 71, 113, 121, 125, 141, 148, 153, 156, 252, 264–65, 270–73, 282
  industrial 148, 156
  liberal 125, 252, 282
  safe for 265, 270–72
democratic
  governments 43, 44
  movement 90
  tradition 41, 46
Democratic Party 20, 30–31, 41, 92, 94, 96, 131, 141, 216, 269
Democrat(s) 20, 24, 27, 30–32, 43–44, 118, 121–23, 242, 246
Detroit 10, 172, 215, 217, 219
Detroit Red 217
dictatorship 148, 276
direct action 79, 98, 204, 209, 214
disenfranchisement 20, 26, 38, 162, 174, 181
disparity(ies) 33, 74, 88, 113, 213
doctrine of 'separate but equal' 204
domestic
  service 103, 226
  work 47, 224, 226. *See also* care work

domesticity 81, 109, 224, 233, 235
Dominican Republic, the 14, 267
Douglass, Frederick 164–65, 167, 191, 239–41
  role of 164
drought 117, 139, 145
  drought of the 1930s 139
Du Bois and Washington 191
Du Bois, W. E. B. 10, 21, 31, 40, 50, 81, 164, 166–67, 170–73, 179, 181–82, 184–92, 196–97, 201, 214, 228
  as a civil rights leader 192
  ideological thought 190
Dutch East Indies 278–79

East Asia 256, 273
economic
  activity(ies) 5, 83, 110, 147, 182
  conditions 75, 82, 115, 117
  crisis 30, 35, 139
  expansion 8, 45, 254
  exploitation 115, 124
  growth 1, 28, 44, 53, 55, 70, 113, 120, 152, 154, 244, 265, 273, 283
  hardship 8, 112, 152
  recovery 141, 146–47
economic depressions 27, 41, 63, 82, 86, 89, 94, 106, 110, 113, 120, 122, 128, 251, 252–53, 274
  depression of 1873 27, 41, 86, 89, 106, 110
  depression of 1890s 122, 251
  depression of 1893 120, 252
  depression of 1929 2, 201, 281
  depression of 1930s 70
Economy Act of 1933 141
economy(ies)
  agricultural 54, 115, 122, 139, 144, 225–27
  global 54, 83, 265, 273
  industrial 44, 54, 228
  rural 114–15, 119, 226, 277
  southern 1, 4, 36

education 12, 22, 29–30, 37, 39, 49, 105–06, 110, 114, 124, 126–27, 134, 148, 162, 164–65, 167–69, 173–74, 176–78, 181–83, 186–92, 196–97, 204, 215–16, 218, 221, 233–34, 236, 238, 244, 247–48
educational institutions 4, 37, 62, 65, 188, 192, 194, 248
egalitarianism 6, 49, 216
Eisenhower, Dwight D., US President 273
elections 20, 23, 27, 39, 50, 94–95, 112, 117, 119, 125, 129–32, 134, 148, 208, 218, 269
electricity 5, 57, 59–60, 144, 147
electrification 58, 152
Emancipation 17–18, 20–21, 33, 36, 46, 163, 165–66, 168, 232
Emancipation Proclamation 17–18, 21, 46, 165, 168
Emergency Banking Act 141
emigration 163, 175
Emperor Hirohito's declaration of surrender 281
Enforcement Act 20
Enforcement Acts of 1870–1871 49
England 91, 108, 256
enslaved people 2–3, 18, 21–22, 24, 30, 48, 162–63, 186, 226, 230, 232
enslavement 1, 3, 12, 17, 34, 50, 66, 77, 161, 164, 168, 171, 179, 189, 227–28, 229–31
enslavers 1–2, 17–18, 22, 24, 30, 42, 46–48, 161, 163, 228, 230–32
entrepreneurs 29, 69–70, 191
equality
　before the law 4, 26, 50
　economic 44, 148, 153
　political 39, 127, 153, 187
　social 78, 153, 190, 194, 196, 207
　struggles for 21
espionage 98, 274
ethnicity(ies) 5, 79, 81, 95, 99, 156, 171, 241, 244

Europe 2, 53–54, 76–77, 80, 95, 113, 116, 120, 127, 152–53, 184–85, 225, 252, 265, 267–68, 271–83, 285
European
　affairs 14
　powers 13
　wars 275
European Americans 17, 80, 151, 282
exceptionalism 264
Executive Order 8802 202
expansionism 251, 253–54, 261, 271

Factory Girls' Association 107
factory(ies) 5–6, 28, 41, 53, 78–79, 101–04, 107, 114, 126, 194, 284
fair-trade practices 146
Farm Credit Administration (FCA) 142
farmer(s) 2–3, 6–8, 30, 34, 46–48, 66, 102, 112, 114–22, 124, 128, 134–35, 141–42, 144–45, 149, 179, 201, 225, 270
　association(s) 115
　cooperative movement 122
　small 30, 115, 119–20, 122
　tenant 2, 34, 116, 201
farming 33, 115, 145, 182, 226, 255
Farm Security Administration (FSA) 144, 149
Father Divine 172, 202
Father Divine's Peace Movement 202
Federal Civil Rights Commission 203
Federal Communications Commission (FCC) 143
Federal Crop Insurance Corporation (FCIC) 144
Federal Deposit Insurance Corporation (FDIC) 142, 147
Federal Emergency Relief Act 146
Federal Emergency Relief Administration (FERA) 143, 146, 245
Federal Farm Loan Act 134

308 Index

federal government 2, 10–11, 14, 18, 21, 41, 48–50, 54, 65, 67, 71, 84, 87, 95, 113–14, 117–18, 124, 129–30, 139, 141, 147–50, 152, 164, 203, 207–08, 246–48, 254, 262, 269, 273, 278, 281, 284–85
   control over US industries 130
   powers of the 129, 285
Federal Highway Act of 1916 134
Federal Housing Administration (FHA) 143, 146
Federal Reserve Act of 1913 132
Federal Reserve Banks 132
Federal Reserve Board 132, 151
Federal Society of Journeymen Cordwainers (shoemakers), Philadelphia 78
Federal Trade Commission 67, 132, 147
Federal Trade Commission Act of 1914 67, 132
Federal Warehouse Act of 1916 134
Federation of Organized Trades and Labour Unions 91
Fellowship of Reconciliation (FOR) 203–04, 206
Female Labour Reform Association (FLRA) 107–08, 110
financial
   crisis of 1873 115
   panic of 1837 116
First International Convention of Negro Peoples of the World 195
First Pan-American Conference 256
Florida 9, 66, 283
Food Administration 270
food riots 94
France 54, 264, 267, 275
Franco-Persian War 116
freedmen 3, 19, 25, 33–35, 42–43, 45, 49, 136, 161, 163, 186
Freedmen's Bureau 19, 25, 28, 37, 47, 164, 176
   creation of the 176
   tenure of the 25
Freedmen's Bureau Act of 1865 37

freedom 2–3, 7, 10, 15, 17–19, 21, 25, 29, 33–36, 47, 63, 67–68, 78, 86, 102, 106, 108, 148, 152, 154, 161–64, 168, 176, 179, 189, 191, 208, 216, 225, 230, 252, 258, 261, 265, 272–73, 277, 281
   economic 34, 68, 148
   movement 168
   personal 7, 152, 154, 225

Gandhian civil disobedience movement 11
Gandhian concept of satyagraha 207
Gandhi, Mahatma 207, 214
Garveyism 219
Garvey, Marcus 10, 164, 166–67, 171, 180, 190, 192–97, 202, 214, 216
   arrival in the USA 194
   deportation to Jamaica 196
   economic and political views 197
   religious views 196
   role as a Black leader 196
gender 61, 79, 90, 93, 99, 101–02, 108–09, 126, 136, 152, 167, 223, 227–32, 234, 241–42, 246–48, 273
   equality 101, 108, 242, 247
   relations 136, 227, 229, 273
   roles 102, 223, 232, 247
Georgia 18, 30, 37, 66, 196, 204, 207–09, 283
German colonisation of Africa 180
Germany 54, 233, 256, 260, 264, 267–72, 274–81
   unification of 267
Ghana 190, 207
ghettos 80, 169–70, 217, 222
Gilded age 4, 6, 66–67, 87
Glass-Steagall Banking Act 147
Good Neighbour Policy 274
Good War 282
Grand Cyclopes 30
Grand Dragons 30
Grand Eight-Hour League of Massachusetts 88

Index

grandfather clause/grandfather's clause 38, 173
Grand Wizards 30
Granger farm protests 120
Granger movement 115–16
Great Depression of 1929 2, 8, 33, 139–41, 143, 146, 149, 151, 154, 156, 158, 172, 201, 244–45, 273–74, 281, 283
Great Destiny 189
Greater East Asian Co-Prosperity Sphere 274
Great Famine (1845–1852) 226
Great Migration 10, 36, 39, 48, 80, 170, 183
Great Northward Migration or the Black Migration 36
Great Plains 121, 139, 145
Great War 268
Greenback Party 95, 116
Guam 13, 259–60, 279
guerrilla warfare 216
Guffey-Snyder Coal Act of 1935 149

Haiti 14, 165, 180, 272, 274
Hampton Institute, Hampton, Virginia 37, 176–77
Harlem (neighbourhood in New York City) 41, 169–72, 180, 183–84, 191, 194–95, 197, 215, 219
Harlem Renaissance 41, 169–72, 180, 184, 191
Harper's Ferry, Virginia 17, 165
Harvard University 10, 127, 185
Havana Harbour 13, 258
Hawai'i 256, 260, 262, 264, 278
Haymarket Affair 84
Headright System 75
Hepburn Act of 1906 130
Hiroshima 280
Hispanics 81
historiography 42, 67, 152
Hitler, Adolf 274–76, 280
holding companies 56, 58, 64
Hollywood 284

Home Owners Loan Corporation 143, 146
Homestead Act, 1862 1, 21, 37, 254
Honduras 193, 267
Hoover, Herbert, US President 61, 139, 141, 153
House of Representatives 20, 27, 107
hydropower projects 130, 142

idealism 29, 267, 271, 282
identity(ies) 6, 9, 12, 41, 75, 83, 106, 109–11, 163, 168–71, 176, 183–84, 186, 189, 192, 197, 214, 219–20, 222, 230, 254, 269
   African 186, 220
   African American 41, 171
   American 41, 171, 184
   cultural 83, 189
Illinois 57, 115, 166
immigrant(s) 3, 6, 11, 54, 75–77, 79–81, 83, 85, 91, 93–95, 97–98, 104, 110, 119, 124, 127, 136, 152, 193, 223, 226, 233, 243
immigration 2, 5, 96, 103, 113, 119–20, 127–28, 225, 235, 265, 282
Immigration Act of 1917 127
Immigration Act of 1924 127
imperialism 12–13, 55, 196, 213, 251–53, 260–62, 267, 271, 273, 282
independence 6–7, 18, 25, 33, 42, 48–49, 101, 103–04, 106, 110, 161, 170, 175, 179, 182, 189, 192, 196, 219, 220, 231, 238, 259–60
   declaration of 7, 219, 238
   economic 7, 18, 25, 33, 42, 48–49, 101, 103–04, 106, 110, 175, 179, 182, 189, 196
Indian Reorganization Act 152
Indigenous peoples 14, 54, 136, 152, 226–27
industrial
   accident(s) 75, 82, 85
   expansion 1, 41
   production 4, 139, 142, 277

progress 54, 68, 80
revolution 53, 58, 62, 67, 174, 255
industrialisation 4, 8, 42, 66, 80, 89, 104, 109, 113, 131, 135–36, 167, 174–75, 182, 225, 235, 238
Industrial Workers of the World (IWW) 7, 96–98
industry(ies)
   defence 172, 202
   domestic 139
   heavy 67, 79
   textile 79–80, 102–03, 106
inflation 79, 117, 122, 129, 145, 154
information revolution 182
internationalism 265, 267, 281
International Socialist Conference 84
International Typographical Union 78, 93
International Workers' Day 84
International Workingmen's Association 88
Interstate Commerce Commission Act of 1887 116
Interstate Commerce Commission (ICC) 116, 130, 209
Ireland 86, 233, 268
Irish
   labour/labourers 7, 86
   lobby 13
iron and steel/iron and steel business 59, 132
Iron Molders' International Union 78
Islamic brotherhood 220
isolationism 12, 251, 260
Italy 274–75, 277–78, 280

Jackson, Andrew, US President 128
Jacksonian era/period 89, 122
Jamaica 192–93, 195–96
Japan 13, 254, 256, 260, 269, 274–80, 282–83, 285
   imperial ambitions 274
Japanese aggression 277
Jefferson, Thomas, US President 253

Jim Crow laws 9, 20, 28, 30, 38, 127, 168–69, 183, 188, 205
   implementation of 20, 28
   legal action against 183
'Jobs and Freedom' March 211
John Hopkins Institute for Research 127
Johnson, Andrew, US President 2, 19, 24, 45
   era and policies of 45
   political career 24
   reconstruction plans 2, 19
Johnson, Lyndon, US President 20, 25–26, 38, 42–43, 47, 212–13
   impeachment motion against 20
   plan 24, 38
   process of impeachment against 25
   radical plan to impeach 26
   vagrancy laws 25, 47
Joint Committee on National Recovery to Fight Discriminatory Practices 202
Journey of Reconciliation 204

Keating-Owen Act 134
Kennan, George F., US President 261, 271
Kennedy, John F., US President 208, 210, 219
King, Jr, Martin Luther 10, 167, 192, 201, 204–05, 214–15, 219
   arrest and imprisonment 207
   awarded the Nobel Peace Prize 211
   direct-action protest programme 209
Knights of St. Crispin (shoemakers) 78
Knights' Rail Workers 90
Korean War 190
Ku Klux Klan 3, 9, 19–20, 27, 29–30, 173, 184, 203, 282
   establishment of the 19
   first terror group in the US 27
   resurgence of the 184

Index 311

revival of the 9
terror acts of the 29–30

labouring classes 6, 10, 79, 87–88, 95
labour/labourer
  contract 77, 255
  hard 34, 82, 176, 230
  movement 5, 74–75, 122, 131, 190
  relations 36, 48, 75, 80, 83, 101, 143, 148, 246
  skilled 78, 82, 87, 182
  union 5, 7, 55, 62, 68, 78, 81–82, 84, 87–89, 91–95, 121–22, 129, 133, 143, 146, 169, 172, 225, 244, 246
  unskilled 79, 88
  women 75, 104, 107, 245
Labour Representation Committee 94
Labour's Bill of Grievances 93
land 3–4, 6, 10, 18, 21–22, 28, 33–34, 37–39, 45, 47–48, 50, 54, 61–62, 66, 74–76, 88, 114, 119, 130, 134, 145, 177, 179, 207, 216, 218, 226–27, 230, 232, 254, 262, 264
  ownership 33, 119, 179
  redistribution process 38
  sacred 54, 227
Land Grant College Act 114
landlords/landowner(s) 2, 33–34, 37, 42
Latin America 194, 252, 254–55, 258, 260, 267, 273–74
laws
  segregation 173, 175, 216
  ten-hour workday 89
Lead Trust 64
League of Nations 268, 271
Lend-Lease Act 276
liberalism 152, 155, 264, 268, 273, 285
liberty(ies) 6, 26, 28–29, 88, 93, 98, 131, 141, 254, 258, 260

Lincoln, Abraham, US President 2–3, 18–24, 42, 126, 211
  assassination of 19, 24
  presidential Reconstruction Plans 2, 22
  pressure on 21
  Ten Percent Plan 19, 22–23
  victory in the 1864 presidential elections 23
Lincoln's America, end of 3, 42
literacy tests 9, 38, 175, 182
Long Strike (1875) 86
Louisiana 3, 9, 18, 23, 32, 39, 208, 226, 232
Louisiana Purchase 226
Louisville Ordinance 173
Lowell Female Labour Reform Association 107
Lowell Textile Mill, Massachusetts 7, 101, 103, 105–08, 111
low-tariff agreement 147
lynching 31, 39, 127, 173, 183
Lynch law 9

Madam C. J. Walker Hair Culturist Union of America 180
Malcolm X 10–11, 164, 167, 201, 213–16, 219–22
Manhattan Project 280
marketing 5, 56–58, 60, 70, 115, 117, 145, 225–26
market(s) 4, 6–7, 36, 53–67, 70–71, 74, 76–78, 83, 86, 114, 116, 120, 122, 132, 139, 143, 147, 151, 157, 169, 225–26, 233, 244, 252, 255–56, 258, 260–62, 264–65, 268, 281
  free 53, 71, 151
  internal 54, 56, 62, 83
  international 65, 120, 255
Marshall Plan 283
Maryland 37, 164, 232, 238
Massachusetts 7, 88–89, 97, 102, 107–08, 164, 185, 217, 240
mass movement 171, 192
mass production 5, 59–62, 234, 246

McKinley, William, US President 129–30, 253, 258–60, 262
  assassination of 129
Meat Inspection Act 130
Mechanic's Union of Trade Association, Philadelphia 78
mechanisation 83, 113, 227
merger movement/mergers 56–57, 59, 63, 64, 71, 133
Mexican Americans 81, 94
Mexico 14, 252–54, 269, 272
middle class/middle-class 61, 86, 98, 122, 126, 135–36, 179, 182, 187, 191, 201, 204, 233
migrants 120, 131, 169, 193, 243
migration 10, 15, 39, 41, 54, 86, 168, 172
militarism 12, 213, 271, 282
military 1, 4, 9, 13–14, 18, 20–22, 25–27, 30–31, 40, 43, 54, 84, 113, 161–62, 216, 218, 252–53, 256, 258–60, 262, 270, 272–83
  action 27, 256
  aid 276, 283
  rule 30, 43
  service 161, 216, 270
Military Reconstruction Acts of 1867 19
mines/mining 18, 59, 75, 80–82, 85, 97
minority(ies) 66, 98, 167, 253, 280
Mississippi 3, 25, 32, 39, 59, 203, 209, 232, 252, 255
mixed-race ancestry 161, 185
mobilisation 55, 163, 167, 175, 184, 202, 234, 273
modernisation 30, 115, 131, 169, 175, 186, 285
Molders' Union 88
monopolistic companies 56, 146
monopoly(ies) 34, 54, 56–57, 63–64, 67–69, 89, 114, 125, 130, 133, 151, 153, 157
  struggle against 153
Monroe Doctrine 13, 254, 256, 265

Montgomery Bus Boycott 206, 214
Montgomery, David 10, 88–89, 156, 205–06, 212, 214
Montgomery Improvement Association (MIA) 205
Moorish-American Science Temple 202, 217
morality 125, 165, 214, 224, 230, 234, 261, 271, 283
Morrill Land-Grant Act of 1862 21, 114
Munich Agreement of 1938 275
Muslim Mosque Incorporated 219
Mutual Aid Society 110

National Association for the Advancement of Colored People (NAACP) 10–11, 127, 163, 170, 172–73, 182, 186, 189–92, 201–03, 205–06, 213–14
  aim of the 192
  efforts of 203
  establishment of the 163, 186
National Association of Funeral Directors 180
National Association of Manufacturers and Citizens' Alliances 93
National Association of Negro Insurance Companies 180
National Association of Real Estate Dealers 180
National Banker's Association 180
National Banking Acts 54
National Banking System 21
National Bar Association 180
National Butchers' Protective Association 57
National Colored Convention 162
National Defense Act 269, 275, 277
national economy 67, 71, 83
National Grange of the Order of Patrons of Husbandry 114
National Housing Act, 1934 146
National Industrial Recovery Act (NIRA) 145–46, 148, 245

nationalisation 117
nationalism 14, 129, 131, 171–72, 190, 195–97, 202, 219, 254, 285
  new 129, 131
National Labour Board 146
National Labour Reform Party 88
National Labour Relations Act of 1935 148, 246
National Labour Relations Board (Wagner Act) 143, 148
National Labour Union (NLU) 7, 88–89
National Negro Business League, Boston 179, 183
National Press Association 180
National Reclamation Act of 1902 130
National Recovery Administration (NRA) 142, 145–46, 156–57, 245–46, 284
National Urban League (NUL) 163, 170, 183–84, 201, 213–14
National Youth Administration (NYA) 143, 150
Nation of Islam (NOI) 11, 216–19
Nazi
  concentration camps 280
  militarism 271
Nazi Party 275
Nazism 141, 274–75
Nazi-Soviet Nonaggression Pact of August 1939 276
Neutrality Acts 275
new Black identity, rise of 171
New Deal 2, 8, 139, 141–44, 146–58, 172, 201–02, 245–46, 274, 285
  First 141, 144, 147, 151
  policies 158, 201
  programmes of the 141–44, 149, 151–52, 154–55, 202
  Second 141, 146, 148–49, 151–52, 246
New England Workingmen Association (NEWA) 108
new freedom 131–32

New Jersey 98, 150, 166, 202, 215
  lumber camps 98
New Negro 41, 170–72, 184
New Negro Movement 170
Niagara Movement of 1905 170, 173, 182, 189, 191
Nicaragua 14, 193, 253
Noble and Holy Order of the Knights of Labour, Philadelphia 7, 89
non-violence 11, 206, 214
non-White women, enslavement and exploitation of 227
North America 1, 13, 53, 75, 218, 221, 254
nuclear bomb 280

oath of allegiance 24
Oath of Loyalty to the Union 22–23, 26
Office of Censorship 284
Office of Price Administration 276
Office of War Information 277, 284
Oil Trust 64
open door policy 252, 260–61, 265, 275
Order of the Pale Faces 30
Organization of AfroAmerican Unity (OAAU) 220

Pacific Railroad Act 1
Pacific War 283
Pan-African Conference 186
Pan-Africanism 185, 190, 197, 220
Pan-Africanist movement 186
Pan-African movement 192–93
Panama 13–14, 193, 253, 264, 266, 274
Panama Canal 13, 193, 264, 266
patriarchal 12, 81, 101, 103–04, 106, 108, 223–24, 229, 232–35, 240–41, 273
  logic 103, 235
patriarchy 103, 241
patriotism 12, 281, 284. *See also* nationalism

314 Index

Pawtucket Canal 102
Pearl Harbour incident 279
Pennsylvania 59, 85, 98, 130, 186, 204
People's March 213
People's Party 112
period of Reconstruction 48, 161, 165
Philadelphia 6, 10, 54, 78, 86, 89, 162, 183, 186–87, 203, 219, 235
Philippines, the 13–14, 253, 259–60, 262, 264, 279
  neutrality 278
plantation(s) 5, 24, 36, 47, 81, 182, 193, 226, 228–29, 231
planters 30–31, 34–36, 47–48, 256
plutocracy 119, 128–29
policy(ies)
  foreign 12, 251, 253, 255, 258, 260, 262, 264–67, 271–73, 281–82
  protectionist 54
  racial 161, 165, 204, 211
  social 127, 152, 242
political
  action 45, 89, 92, 110, 184
  activism 90, 96, 129, 163, 170, 216
  establishment 10, 241, 243
  participation 5, 37, 39, 93, 121, 123, 165, 170, 182
  party(ies) 38, 44–45, 94–95, 98, 216, 248
  support 50, 94, 241
pools (business) 58, 63, 116, 118
populism 121–22
Populist movement 7–8, 34, 62, 112–14, 121–23
Populist Party 112, 119–21, 131
Posse Comitatus Act of 1878 9
postbellum period 112, 166, 168, 251
post-Civil War period 42, 79, 120, 128
power(s) 2, 4, 6, 13–14, 18, 21–22, 27, 45–46, 49, 84, 86, 124, 129–30, 136, 147, 154, 157, 169, 224, 236, 253–54, 260, 262, 272, 274, 285
  military 4, 253, 262, 272
  political 22, 46, 84, 136, 157, 169, 224, 236, 254
presidential pardon 22
presidential pocket veto 23
Presidential Reconstruction Acts 29
Presidential Reconstruction Plan 2
Printer's Union 193
Progressive era/period 112, 124–25, 127–28, 136, 167, 184, 201
Progressive movement 8, 113, 123, 129, 135–36, 141, 153, 242
progressivism 124, 131, 136
Prohibition Party 128
Public Contracts Act 148
Public Utilities Holding Company Act 151
Public Works Administration (PWA) 142, 145–46, 245
Pullman Railroad Boycott 84
Pure Food and Drug Act 130

race riots 41, 127, 129, 172–73, 214–15, 253, 255
racial
  discrimination 12, 33, 131, 169, 172, 183–84, 202, 204, 207, 212, 216, 221
  equality 1, 3–4, 18, 21, 27, 42, 44, 50, 155, 162–65, 167–69, 171, 178, 182, 190–91, 203–04, 211, 241, 248
  integration 37, 43, 172, 191, 213
  pride 172, 194–96, 220
  segregation 9–10, 24, 28, 30, 37–38, 127, 151, 179, 186–87, 207, 209, 213
  violence 4, 10, 12, 19, 25, 27–28, 49, 127, 136
racialisation 193
radicalism 121, 125, 167, 214
Railroad and Warehouse Commission 115

Reconstruction 2–4, 9, 17, 19–21, 24–31, 33–37, 39–51, 136, 161, 165–66, 168, 173–76, 179, 183, 186, 189, 232
  failure of 33, 41, 165, 232
  first phase 19
  policies 28, 43, 165, 176
  process 20, 37, 45
  programme 2, 46
  radical/radical phase 2, 19–20, 27, 30, 176
  second phase of the 24, 246
  'splendid failure' of the 189
Reconstruction Act of 1867 26
Reconstruction Acts, provisions of the 3, 19, 26, 29, 39, 49
Reconstruction era/period 3, 9, 17, 25, 36, 43–44, 46–47, 50–51, 173
Red Scare 129
Red Shirts 30, 32
reform(s)
  economic 8, 30, 121, 123
  movement 90, 123–24, 136, 236, 239
  political 8, 112–13
  progressive 50, 123–24
  public/public demand for 152–53
  tariff 130, 132
Republican Party 1, 4, 17, 19–20, 22, 24, 28–31, 35, 39, 48, 53, 93, 95, 130, 165, 183
Republicans 1–4, 9, 17, 19–20, 22, 24–32, 35, 37, 39–40, 42–45, 48, 50, 53, 93, 95, 118, 122–23, 130–31, 165, 183, 233, 271
reunification 2, 19, 22, 43, 49
Revenue Act 151
revolutionary
  goals 97–98
  movement 110, 253
Revolutionary War 161
Rifle Clubs 32. *See also* Red Shirts
rights
  civic/civil 2, 4, 12, 21, 31, 39–40, 45, 49–50, 163–64, 172–73, 188, 192, 197, 201–03, 205–09, 211, 219, 241, 248
  equal 179, 186, 202, 237–39
  political 45, 47, 49, 102, 131, 172–73, 175, 178, 184, 188, 190–91, 211, 234
  to vote 2–3, 38, 49, 125–26, 134, 162, 170, 180, 238–39, 241–43
Roosevelt, Franklin D., US President 8, 13, 93, 113, 123–25, 129–32, 141, 146, 148–50, 152–55, 157, 172, 180, 201–02, 259, 266, 274, 277–78, 280–82, 285
  administration 148
  conflict with Congress 130
  death of 280
  electoral victory in 1932 201
  government 149
  measures 154
  policies 157
rural America 116–17, 132
Rural Electrification Administration (REA) 144
Rural Electrification Agency (REA) 149
Russia 12, 256, 267, 272, 276–77
Russo-Japanese War of 1905 13

saloons 83, 171, 235
San Francisco 6, 283
Scalawags 29–30, 46
scientific management 55, 80, 93, 99, 135
secession 21–22, 24
Second Industrial Revolution 53, 58, 62, 67, 174, 255
Second War Powers Act of 1942 284
Securities and Exchange Commission 143, 147
Security Act of 1933 147
segregation 9–11, 17, 24, 27–28, 30, 37–38, 41, 80, 127, 151, 162, 165–66, 168, 170, 172–75, 178–80, 183, 186–87, 190, 192, 204–05, 207–10, 212–13, 215–16, 248. *See also* racial: segregation

316 Index

Selective Service Act 247, 270
self-respect 110, 187, 220
Selma–Montgomery March 212
Selma Voting Rights Campaign in Selma 211
Senate Committee 271
'Separate but equal' provisions 9, 39, 175, 204
sharecropper(s) 2, 33–34, 42, 48, 116, 144–45, 175, 201
sharecropping 3, 33, 35–36, 47, 65, 174, 191, 233
   system 3, 33, 35, 191
Sherman Antitrust Act of 1890 129, 133
sink-on-sight submarine campaign 269
Sino-Japanese War 274, 277
Slave Rebellion at Harper's Ferry, Virginia 165
slavery 2, 5, 9, 17, 19–21, 23, 29–30, 33–34, 44–47, 49–50, 66, 162–63, 165, 168, 176, 179, 228–30, 232–33, 237–40, 282
   abolition of 17, 23, 163
slave(s) 17–18, 22, 24, 50, 161–62, 165, 171, 226, 228–32, 243
   codes 24
   economy 17, 243
   labour 50, 161–62, 226
social
   change 11, 79, 125, 241
   justice 15, 29, 124, 131, 190, 192
   movement 121, 128, 238
   order 24, 90, 243
   problems 14, 113, 124, 136
socialism 79, 81, 90, 95, 141, 185, 190–93, 196, 220
Socialist Labour Party 7, 95–96
socialist movements/revolution 11, 96, 216
Socialist Party of America (SPA) 7, 95–96, 123
Social Security Act of 1935 150
Social Security Board (SSB) 144
South America xiv, 163

South Carolina 3, 9, 24, 32, 35, 39, 48
Southeast Asia 260, 277–78, 282
southern
   politics 29, 123, 155, 174
   states 2, 19–22, 24–27, 29, 38–39, 42, 44, 47, 64, 151, 168, 174–75, 180, 204, 212, 232, 260
Southern Christian Leadership Conference (SCLC) 11, 207, 209
Southern Homestead Act 37
sovereignty 122, 259, 267
Soviet Union 190, 271, 275–78, 282–83
   expansionism 271
   threat of the 282
Spain 253, 258–59, 274
Spanish-American War of 1898 12, 251
Springfield race riot of 1908 173.
   See also race riots
squad system 35
square deal 129
Standard Oil Company 58–59, 64, 68–69, 125
St Luke's Penny Savings Bank 180
stock exchange 147
stock market 139
strike(s) 7, 21, 74, 79, 84, 86–87, 90–94, 96–98, 106–07, 111, 113, 129–30, 133–34, 148, 154, 193, 225, 235, 239, 255
Student Non-Violent Coordinating Committee (SNCC) 11, 207, 211, 213–14, 216, 221
suffrage 23, 40, 50, 96, 136, 164, 241–43, 247
   movement 242–43
Sugar Trust 64
superpower 1–2, 12, 15, 273, 283
suppression 86, 169
supremacist organisations 3, 49
Supreme Court 9, 38–39, 64, 130, 145, 148, 151, 174–75, 204
Sussex Pledge 268

Taft, William Howard, US President 129–30, 180, 267
Talented Tenth 171, 186, 191–92, 214
tariff(s) 4, 20, 30, 54, 65, 119, 130–32, 139, 147, 226, 254, 258
tax/taxation 4, 6, 9, 27, 38, 40–41, 48, 66, 71, 112, 117, 119, 124–25, 130, 132, 134, 139, 144, 148, 150, 156, 175, 270, 276–77, 284
technological advancements/advances 12, 79
Technological Revolution 53
technology(ies) 50, 53–54, 56–57, 62, 66, 71, 87, 104, 122, 182, 234, 255, 280, 285
telegraph/telegraphy 57, 59, 83, 119, 143
Temperance Movement 12, 125, 164, 235–36, 242
tenancy 33, 174
tenant farmers 2, 33, 116, 201
Ten-Hour Movement/Strike 101, 107–10
Tennessee Valley Authority (TVA) 142, 147
terror 27, 29–31, 41–42, 184
organisations 42
'Teutonic germ' theory 14
Texas 3, 66, 81, 117, 232, 254, 269, 283
textile mills 18, 53, 75, 103–04, 107, 110, 225
Thailand 278–79
The Negro Factories Corporations 194
trade 5–6, 76–79, 83–84, 89–90, 96, 105, 116, 130, 133–34, 139, 142, 146–47, 176, 188, 229, 232, 238, 254, 256, 259, 264, 267–68, 272, 274–76, 278
agreement acts 147
foreign 147, 268
free 130, 267
international 264, 272
relations 274

unfair practices 142
unions 5–6, 78, 83–84, 89, 96.
See also union(s)
unrestricted international 264
Treaty of Paris of 1898 13, 259
Treaty of Versailles 271
Tripartite Pact 277
Triple Alliance 267
Truman Doctrine 283
Truman, Harry S., US President 172, 203, 274, 280, 283
trusts (business) 56, 58, 63, 129, 131
Tuskegee Institute, Alabama 177, 191
two-party system 155

Underwood-Simmons Tariff Act of 1913 132
unionisation 75, 79, 148
unionism 90, 99, 238
Union League 28, 245
union(s) 5–7, 55, 62, 68, 78–79, 81–84, 86–98, 101, 111, 121–22, 129, 133, 143, 146, 148, 169, 172, 202, 213, 225, 244–46
craft 90–92
labour 5, 7, 55, 62, 68, 78, 81–82, 84, 87–89, 91–95, 121–22, 129, 133, 143, 146, 169, 172, 225, 244, 246
trade 5–6, 78, 83–84, 89, 96
United Auto Workers 206
United Kingdom (UK) 256
United Mine Workers of America 130
United Nations (UN) 205, 220
United Nations (UN) Human Rights Commission 220
United States Housing Authority 144
United States of America (US/USA)
armed forces 14, 172, 202, 284
as a 'reluctant power' 14
as a technocratic nation 2
citizens 20, 26, 181, 268

citizenship 3, 20, 26, 50, 61, 183
economy 89, 112, 151–52, 154, 283–84
emerged as a global superpower 1, 273
emergence of an industrial nation 74
entry into World War I 95
foreign policy 12, 251, 253, 258, 260, 262, 264–65, 267, 272, 273, 281–82
interventions in the two World Wars 2
labour relations in the 48, 80
participation in the two World Wars 1
race relations in the 77
wartime aims 267
world's 'first modern nation' 15
United States Steel Corporation 59, 64, 262
Universal Negro Improvement Association (UNIA) 193–96, 217
  eight-point aim of 194
  motto of 193
untouchability 207
urbanisation 42, 64, 113, 128, 131, 136, 157, 182–83, 225, 235, 283
US Army 14, 94, 184, 279
  entry of Black people into the 38, 184
  voluntary enlistment in the 94
US Congress 2, 11, 19, 21–23, 25–26, 37, 40, 45, 80, 96, 112, 114, 130, 134, 141, 144, 148–49, 154–55, 202–03, 210, 212, 226, 244, 246, 258, 262, 267, 269–70, 275–76, 278
  Fourteen Points to the 267, 271
US Constitutional Amendments 3, 17, 20, 22, 24–26, 28–29, 45, 49–50, 132, 134, 164–65, 167, 173–74, 203
  13th Amendment 17, 22, 24–25, 45, 164–65, 174

14th Amendment 3, 20, 26, 28–29, 45, 49–50, 165, 173, 203
15th Amendment 3, 20, 26, 28–29, 45, 49–50, 165, 173, 203, 241–42
16th Amendment 132, 134
17th Amendment 134
18th Amendment 134, 141
19th Amendment 134
21st Amendment 141
US Department of Labour 41
US imperialism 251, 273
US Presidential election(s) 20, 23, 27, 50, 94–95, 130–31, 208, 269
  1864 election(s) 23
  1876 elections 20, 27, 50
  1912 elections 131
  1916 elections 94, 269
  1960 elections 208

vagrancy laws 25, 47
Venezuela 13, 193, 256
veto power 25
Vietnam War 211
Voting Rights Act 215

Wade-Davis Bill 22
Wagner Act 143, 148
Waltham-Lowell system of production 102
War Industries Board 270
War Manpower Commission 276
War of 1812 12, 53, 252, 254, 259
War Production Board 276
War Shipping Board 270
Washington, Booker T., US President 9–10, 93, 95, 132, 165–67, 175–84, 186–88, 190–91, 193–96, 204, 206, 211–15
  accommodationism 188
  conciliatory and moderate approach 179
  'father of Black capitalism' 191
  goals of self-help 194
  ideals of self-reliance 195

Western Europe 272
Western Federation of Miners 96
westward expansion 1, 102, 161, 226, 233
Whigs 22, 29, 46
Whiskey Trust 64
White
  America 170
  Americans 33, 81
  community(ies) 176, 178, 191, 231
  population 19, 21, 34, 42, 49, 162, 169, 179, 188, 196
  settlers 77, 169, 226, 252
  society 46, 178, 189, 214, 217, 230, 232, 241
  supremacist organisations 3, 49
  supremacy 14, 31, 38, 127, 162, 175
  voters 32, 48
  workers 39, 41, 90, 169, 175, 190
White Brotherhood League 30
Wilsonianism 265, 267
Wilson, Woodrow, US President 8, 94, 113, 123, 129, 131, 133–34, 141, 265, 267–68, 270–72
Womanhood 109–10, 223–24, 227, 230, 232–34, 236, 240, 248
women
  educated 126, 248
  enslaved 228–32, 237
  Indigenous 11, 227–28
  worker(s) 7, 81, 101–02, 104, 106–11, 225, 245–46
Women's Christian Temperance Union 128
women's rights 109–10, 113, 224, 238–39, 241
workday 78, 84, 88–89, 93, 106–08, 134
workers 6–7, 10, 15, 25, 34–35, 37, 39, 41, 47, 56, 66, 71, 75, 78–84, 86–98, 101–02, 104–11, 114, 122, 124, 127–28, 130, 134, 141, 146, 148–50, 169, 173, 175–76, 178, 190, 193, 202, 206, 217, 225, 235, 245–46
Workingmen's Benevolent Association (WBA) 86–87
Workmen's Compensation Act 134
Works Progress Administration (WPA) 143, 149–50, 246
World War I 10, 41, 53, 64, 94–96, 98, 125, 129, 149, 170–71, 183–84, 190, 197, 244, 257, 259, 267–69, 271–73, 281
World War II 12, 61, 172, 203, 205, 244, 246–47, 273–75, 278, 280, 282, 285

yeoman/yeomen farmers 2–3, 30, 48, 121